For: Leigh

With

[handwritten signature]

B^{THE}ROKEN H_{EART}
^{OF} GOD

A life of wandering in the spiritual jungle

1- 250-642-2441

MARK BATTERBURY

Order this book online at www.trafford.com/06-2960
or email orders@trafford.com

Most Trafford titles are also available at major online book retailers.

Note for Librarians: A cataloguing record for this book is available from Library
and Archives Canada at www.collectionscanada.ca/amicus/index-e.html

Printed in Victoria, BC, Canada. on 100% Recycled Paper.

ISBN: 978-1-4251-1201-1

*We at Trafford believe that it is the responsibility of us all, as both individuals
and corporations, to make choices that are environmentally and socially sound.
You, in turn, are supporting this responsible conduct each time you purchase a
Trafford book, or make use of our publishing services. To find out how you are
helping, please visit www.trafford.com/responsiblepublishing.html*

*Our mission is to efficiently provide the world's finest, most comprehensive
book publishing service, enabling every author to experience success.
To find out how to publish your book, your way, and have it available
worldwide, visit us online at www.trafford.com/10510*

www.trafford.com

North America & international
toll-free: 1 888 232 4444 (USA & Canada)
phone: 250 383 6864 ◆ fax: 250 383 6804
email: info@trafford.com

The United Kingdom & Europe
phone: +44 (0)1865 722 113 ◆ local rate: 0845 230 9601
facsimile: +44 (0)1865 722 868 ◆ email: info.uk@trafford.com

10 9 8 7 6 5 4 3

This book is dedicated to
Jeffrey Wolf Green

With special thanks to

Carolyn Bateman and Priska Stabel
For editing and encouragement

TABLE OF CONTENTS

THE BROKEN HEART OF GOD

"being human means
blind, nameless desires sleep on your face
unknown love shines through your eyes."

Mary Field, Nepal, 1974

INTRODUCTION

The warm, fragrant air of the Indian night blew on my face as I rode the roof of a Tata truck from Bodh Gaya to Varanasi. After many rough and dusty hours I heard the booming sound of tires on metal as we crossed the bridge over the Ganges. To the left I saw the long crescent of faint lights that is the waterfront of this holy city. I thumped on the cab and the driver stopped to let me down. His teeth and eyes shone for a moment as he lit a beedie before driving on, leaving me in silence and darkness.

I found a path down to the river bank, and began walking. The air was filled with the scent of flowers that grew in fields to my right. To my left the reflection of a full moon rippled on the water. It was dark beside the river and the sand was soft under my feet. Then I saw the fires of the main burning ghat. The night was vibrating with the power and mystery of the world's oldest city.

When I reached the burning ghats I sat on the steps of a temple to rest. Seven funeral pyres sent spirals of sparks into the night and cast shadows onto the stone walls behind me. The air was heavy with the sweet smell of burning human flesh. Sleeping dogs were curled up near the fires and someone was snoring gently under a blanket.

I kept walking along the empty riverbank until reaching Harischandra ghat, where the legendary king Harischandra did his penance by tending the funeral pyres. A few piles of embers still glowed in the dark near the water. By starlight I found a place to sit on a stone balcony overlooking the river. It was where the Brahmin priests sat by day to conduct rituals for pilgrims. I folded my blanket and sat in the half lotus posture to meditate until dawn. It was beautiful to be a part of that ancient mystery and feel the power of the goddess hold me through the night.

An Indian guru had given me the name Harischandra, and I had felt honored to have the name of a man who had been willing to give up a kingdom and do such humble work in his search for truth. Feeling alienated from western culture, I had left home to search for the meaning and purpose of my life. I sat on the ancient stones, in the heart of the mystery that is India, and waited.

Chapter 1: *Childhood*

My parents made the difficult choice to leave England after the Second World War to begin a new life in Canada. My mother left a home where a servant ironed her father's newspaper in a "morning room" that was reserved for that purpose alone. My father left a public school in Wimbledon, where his father had been co-owner and principal.

We arrived in Halifax harbor in 1949 on the last voyage of a Cunnard ocean-liner, the *Aquatania*. She had four funnels, but only two of her engines were working on that final journey. My earliest memory is of a long, white wake reaching towards the horizon behind us. Perhaps it is imagined: I was only two at the time. In Halifax, my parents spent their last savings on an old Ford and a small trailer. My father drove us across the continent to Vancouver, and then we took the ferry to Victoria on Vancouver Island, and drove the few remaining miles to Brentwood Bay and an English style private school, where my father had a teaching position waiting for him.

Two weeks after our arrival, the school burned down. My mother was pregnant with my brother, Edward. I had an elder brother, Adrian, and an elder sister, Susan. We had no work, no money, no relatives, and no friends. It was my mother who asked that we be allowed to continue to use the cottage that the school provided for our accommodation. My father got temporary work doing farm labor. Later, we all worked on Logana farms, picking berries that were made into sickly-sweet wines that we never thought of drinking.

Two years later my father was teaching again, this time at St. Michael's University School, and we were able to buy our first home. I can clearly remember the excitement of the day we moved in. We had a green 1942 GMC wagon. My parents sat in front, my mother held Edward on her lap, and I was in the back between my elder brother and sister. I stood on the seat, and peered ahead between my parents' shoulders. It was a country lane with a green center patch of grass stretching ahead of us until we turned into our driveway. It was 1950, and for 9,400 dollars we had a four-bedroom house on half an acre of oceanfront land. The house was heated by a wood and coal furnace, and had outside plumbing, so nobody wanted it: but for a family from England who had just been through a war, this was no hardship at all. In the kitchen was a wood burning cook-stove. 5345 Parker Avenue will always be home, for that was where my childhood was, and in all my searching I have not found anything more sacred than childhood.

There were very few houses along the beach in those days. The lots were wide and the beauty of oceanfront, country living was not yet appreciated: it was considered remote and inconvenient. But we loved it, and my soul was nourished by the spirit of nature. Years later, when all the dreams of childhood had been shattered, this green and golden landscape still formed a deep place in my consciousness, and that vision supported me through years of darkness when no other comfort could be found.

Every day the milkman left two glass bottles of milk standing on the front porch. In cold weather when I went to fetch them I would find the paper cap of the bottle lifted up on an inch of frozen cream. Each Monday the iceman would deliver a block of ice for the icebox. On weekdays the mailman would drive by, putting the mail into the metal box that stood beside the road in front of our house. Every summer we would order a truckload of mill-ends for the cook-stove. The driver would always have a beard and a turban, and my parents explained that they came from India. The truck would back onto the property and dump the pile of wood, and it was one of our summer chores to get it stacked in the basement. Then, in the fall, the coal-man would come and deliver a ton of coal in sacks that were poured down a chute into a bin in the basement. At the back of the house there was a small platform and a clothesline stretched out over the wooded ravine that led down to the beach. The washing machine had a wringer, and our clothes were hung out to dry. In winter, they had to be dried in the basement.

My mother worked all the time in the house. My father left for work every day while we were having breakfast. On Saturdays, he would get off work at noon, and come home in time for lunch. He would always bring a long loaf of French bread with him. On weekends, and in the long summer evenings, my father would work around the house and on the land. Using a shovel, he dug all the road allowance land in front of our house: a strip 150' by 20', and planted potatoes.

Everything was magical: strawberries ripening in the spring, corn ripening in the summer, plums and pears ripening in the fall. The seasons turned slowly and were measured by changes in nature that we could see, smell, taste and hear. In summer, the tide was low in the morning, and wide bars of sand were exposed to the heat of the sun. All afternoon the water was warmed as it came slowly in over the hot sand. Above the tide line, there was a line of seaweed and kelp, then an area of small stones, and finally deep, white sand that was full of tiny sparkling jewels. Above all this, the forests and fields seemed to go on forever.

After lunch one Christmas day, I noticed something for the first time: a small patch of gray time. In a day that had always been magic from beginning to end, this short time of boredom had no place. I made the mistake of thinking that this was due to growing up, and that a kind of tiredness and loss of interest in life was what growing up was about. It certainly looked that way. My parents were different: I just did not see them as I saw other adults that came into my life at the age of ten. Most were gray. Occasionally one would appear who had a sparkle in their eyes, but this was rare. I was determined this would never happen to me.

I lived in two worlds. There was home and family, and the glorious presence of nature, and then there was school, which was unmitigated disaster. At five, my parents took me to kindergarten in a well-intentioned effort to give me some social experience prior to starting grade one. Kindergarten was a room full of kids where a supervisor put a box of toys on the floor and invited us to take our pick. A scramble followed, as the children competed for whatever toy was considered most prestigious. The more aggressive children naturally fared best, but the object of the struggle was clearly to establish dominance, not to play. The girls were just as aggressive as the boys, although their tactics were different. I did not have many toys and preferred the playground of nature, and so had no interest in this great initiation. I felt alienation for the first time. It was total, and I made no effort to overcome it: there was simply no incentive. The pattern for the next forty years was set in that moment.

Seeing my misery, my parents did not take me there again, and slowly the dreaded day came for my first day of school. My mother left me in the care of the principal and his secretary. The principal was a gray man, and his secretary a gray woman. One by one we were invited into her office, where she prepared us for our meeting with this awesome man, our principal. My preparation consisted of being told to undo my belt and zipper. Then, when I went in to meet the principal, his hand could slip easily into my pants. I thought it was some kind of inspection to see if I was ready for grade one. I must have passed.

It went downhill from there. The cruelty of the teachers was nothing compared to the shaming and torment meted out by my peers. Gym was the worst. Any team that got stuck with me would emit a chorus of loud groans:

"We got Batterbury! Now we've had it! We will never win!" Every time I fumbled the ball my team mates would glare at me with loathing and contempt. The team leader, who felt responsible for the success of his team, always seemed like a far older boy than me: almost a god, in fact, so much was the respect given to athletes. A typical team sport in winter: four teams would line up facing four basketball hoops. Each boy would dribble the ball up, and return to the team after scoring a basket. The game would usually end with three teams having finished, leaving me alone at a hoop, trying in vain to sink the ball while the rest of my team hurled threats and insults at my miserable back.

Failure followed failure. If I closed my eyes to avoid seeing the desolation of the playground, someone would notice, and a cry of "blind! blind! Batterbury is blind!" would go up. I once joined in a snowball fight, desperate to be part of something, but within seconds the two teams had forgotten their war, and a circle of fifty children surrounded me, their common target.

The road I walked to and from school was a mile of danger, a gauntlet, where every turn might conceal some clever ambush. My only wish was to pass unnoticed and return to the security of home. This seldom happened.

I never spoke of my suffering. My parents suspected something was wrong, but the world they came from was vastly different: a world where children were raised by paid nannies before being sent to boarding school. Enough of this difference had been passed along to add strangeness to my obvious lack of ability and aggression, and this attracted relentless persecution from the other children.

At the end of grade six the graduating students were traditionally presented with a bible to take with them in memory of their elementary school years. I refused this bible: it was clear to me that something was wrong, something was missing, and I could not accept this symbol of a culture I did not want.

With sports and any other social activity so obviously out of the question, I soon learned to focus on work. The farmers in the area came to know me, and every summer I would have more than one position waiting. I worked with ponies, taking kids from the city for a short ride in return for a dime: five cents for management, five cents for me. I picked berries on Mr. Wellman's loganberry farm. I mowed lawns. Always hardworking, never late, I was in demand in a rural economy that had no minimum wage. As soon as my younger brother was old enough, I took him with me. He was hardworking, too, and content to follow me until growing into fierce independence. Fortunately for me, the concept of "child-labor", with the implication of exploitation, had not yet arisen, and I was left with something to take pride in.

Still, I remember the fifties as a glorious decade: it was my childhood, after all, and although we were so poor that if my mother lost a quarter it upset the week's budget, for the most part, we were a happy family. That was also the golden age of my father. From the beginning, he had no doubts about my mother, and no doubts about wanting a family. His MA from Cambridge had been a guarantee of employment in England, but was hardly recognized in western Canada. He found the Canadian school system impossible, and eventually landed a job with the Department of Education, as a writer of correspondence courses for those people who lived in remote areas and had no access to schools. From the age of forty until sixty-five, he hardly missed a day of work. Upon retirement he received a huge check for all that unclaimed sick leave. He was the rock upon which our family life was built, and my mother was the tireless energy that made it possible. In all the years I lived at home, I never once heard him complain.

The first real shadow fell when my elder sister and brother reached puberty, and went wild. Suddenly, there was something powerful and dark in the house. They were fourteen and sixteen when I was only eleven, and had no idea about sexuality. Terrible things were happening. My sister ran away from home, was returned by the police, and then she disappeared for a whole summer. My brother was always in trouble at school or with the police, and my parents were always worried. I desperately needed home to be a safe and happy place, and was willing to make any sacrifice. I made the decision never to have any problems, never to be any trouble, and in this way unconsciously sacrificed myself in an attempt to save my family.

It is said that therapists are made in the family, and perhaps this is also true of seekers. I understood very little of what was happening, but I knew something was wrong. My early experiences made me determined to find some other path, a way to live that was more in harmony with my soul.

Chapter 2: *Teenage Years*

At sixteen the first miracle happened. I was suppressing everything, so that the storms of adolescence appeared to pass me by. I continued to take refuge in nature, and one day went on an overnight journey to the top of Mt. Arrowsmith. This was an old volcano where the remains of a crater at the summit held a small lake set like an emerald in ragged stone cliffs. On the way down from the highest point, I decided to take a shortcut across the top of an icepack that leaned against the shady side of the crater. Somehow I felt invincible that day, and believed that even gravity could not touch me. Next moment I fell and slid down the ice on my heels and elbows towards either death or serious injury on the rocks below. With no time for thought, I just let go: there was nothing else to do. The expected disaster did not happen: some angelic hand seemed to steer me among the rocks onto a long tail of gravel that was not visible from above. I skidded to a stop, and my momentum left me in a standing position, gazing with wonder at the sparkling beauty of the lake.

The mountain and the sky, the vultures that circled above – we were all held in the same clarity of consciousness, and I was filled with the joy of being alive. The scrapes and cuts on my hands, elbows and back were a small price to pay for this experience.

This unexpected jolt had shifted my attention entirely into the here and now, and given me a welcome break from my mind. It also awakened me to a singular purpose in life. On the way down the mountain, as my normal worried state of mind returned, all I wanted was to find some way, any way, to regain and keep that clarity and freedom.

But with the growing pressure of sexuality only adding to my sense of alienation, my secret depression soon became worse. I plodded through the routines of school, did fairly well on the academic level, and continued to endure endless shaming and humiliation. For some reason my growth was delayed, and I did not mature sexually as fast as the others. I still had the genitals of a boy, after the rest of my gym class had matured into young men. This fact, of course, could not be concealed in the locker-room:

"Hey Batterbury! What does a plane have that you don't? …a cock-pit! Haw haw haw."

Adding to my insecurity as sexual feelings began to grow was the fact that some overworked English doctor had botched my circumcision, and left about half my foreskin intact. This pulled the head of my penis to one side whenever I had an erection. I was acutely vulnerable about this, and was convinced that no girl would give such a deformity a second glance. I made several futile attempts to correct this condition myself, using a razor blade. The pain and the blood would stop me, until obsessive misery forced me to another attempt. All this I kept within.

I remember a school counselor calling me to his office to express his concern. I was amazed at this kindly act, but insisted that everything was fine: opening up and trusting a teacher was not yet a possibility.

During elementary school, I suffered from asthma, and during high school, from eczema. I would get rashes on my face, hands, and genitals that itched and occasionally bled. I was often sick from respiratory infections, and finally, at the age of sixteen, had my tonsils removed. All my life I had been smaller than other boys my age, and now I suddenly grew six inches in two years, until at six feet I was slightly taller than average.

One day I read an article in the paper about a holy man from India called Maharishi Mahesh Yogi who would be visiting the area to teach meditation. The article described how a mantra slowly carried the mind back to its source, the origin of consciousness itself. This was very exciting, and seemed to offer the key to regaining the freedom I had known on the mountain. I went to hear the Maharishi talk at a high-school gymnasium, and his words and presence inspired me to learn to meditate. After the talk I met some Hare Krishna devotees outside the gymnasium who invited me to attend a Sunday feast, and I went and heard devotional music, and tasted delicious vegetarian food. These were the choices.

I decided to receive initiation from the Maharishi: the idea of solitary meditation appealed to me. I made an offering of fifteen dollars and a small piece of white cloth, and was taught a mantra by an assistant to the yogi from India. It all seemed very new and wonderful, and I believed that I would compensate for my worldly failure by cultivating some secret inner glory.

In this way I first became aware of the concept of "enlightenment" or self-realization. As it seemed to offer a cure to my intense suffering, as well as to glorify the isolation from this world that I was already accustomed to, I seized upon any teachings about our spiritual nature with great enthusiasm. Here, at last, was something that did not involve competition, aggression, or social grace. In fact, my very failings seemed in some strange way to be an advantage. I had plenty of time to meditate: after all, I had no social interactions to distract me. I was very consistent in my two times of mediation a day, but of course kept the whole thing a secret, as meditation had not yet gained any social acceptance and would no doubt have attracted more ridicule.

Throughout school, I had always been above average in my ability to learn, and had entered university at eighteen with a second-class scholarship, confident of becoming a marine biologist. I intended to study the river systems of the Pacific North West and the lives of the fish that lived in them. I knew the local rivers and streams well, and could predict when each species of salmon and trout would appear on their annual spawning run. But at the university level, even though I attended every class, and did hours of homework daily, I barely managed to get C's and D's. With this my last hope for any kind of social integration vanished, and my sense of personal failure became complete. With a sinking heart, I enrolled in the second year of the Bachelor of Science program, knowing that it was futile.

Then the second miracle occurred.

It was one of those rare occasions when, one evening, I found myself in the same place as my elder brother, Adrian. Throughout my life, I had from time to time encountered people who took an interest in me simply because of the enormous popularity that Adrian enjoyed. He was a hero: always irreverent, always in trouble with authority, and fearless in the defense of what he saw as right. He was the life of any party he attended. Hated by the clean-cut and athletic, he was adored by the growing number of revolutionaries and artists. When I first entered junior high school, I had been surprised to find myself instantly surrounded by a group of boys my own age that, having no hope of basking in the presence of my elder brother, seized upon me as a substitute. I had not known how great his reputation and popularity where until that moment. I looked around me, bewildered and in no way prepared to be such a hero. They quickly perceived my weakness and vulnerability, and I was abandoned in disgust and later tormented by these disappointed, leaderless boys.

On this particular evening I had been invited to a small house where one of Adrian's friends lived. It was very exciting to be included in such an adventure: these elders had a whole, secret life that I could only imagine. They were drinking beer: pot was not quite available yet. I sat in the darkened room and listened to the music. There was a sense of excitement there, and a few young women showed up. Everyone seemed to know each other, and no one questioned my presence there.

At one point the conversation faded and for the first time I really heard the blues that had been playing in the background. The deep, rough voice and simple blues guitar were talking to me. It was Leadbelly, singing: "Keep your hands of her! Keep your hands off her! Keep your hands off her, you hear what I say, you know she don't belong to you." He got to the line: "Her name is Rosy, and she ain't so nosey.... but boy, she sure is cozy!" My mind just stopped again, and for the first time I heard the music with my heart. I had been trying to follow the meaning of the words, but there really wasn't any: it was the feeling, the emotion of the song that touched me in a place I did not know I had. It was so powerful that I did not mind when Adrian, with a slight movement of his jaw, indicated that I should leave.

The next day I went up to the university and was just in time to switch from the science program to arts. I changed every course I could, and in a moment went from science to English literature and creative writing.

This was a huge relief. Not only was I no longer carrying the burden of certain failure in biology, chemistry, and math, but had a whole new world of soul to explore. I bought some albums: Leadbelly, Memphis Slim, Sonny Terry and Brownie McGee, the Paul Butterfield Blues Band. A heavy weight had fallen from my shoulders, and I hardly gave marine biology another thought.

I also grew impatient with my meditation. The shared beliefs and pious harmony that the other meditators seemed to enjoy eluded me. The great promise of inner peace was not being fulfilled, and the insidious formation of an organization with its hierarchy and marketing agenda had quickly overshadowed the original intention of the practice. I became disillusioned with the Maharishi's silly giggles and constant pretense to be in some 'higher' state. I investigated the origin of his name: 'Maharishi Mahesh Yogi', and found that 'maha' and 'mahesh' both mean 'great'. A Rishi is one who has wisdom and insight, and a yogi is one who has attained union. Apparently he had bestowed these grand titles upon himself, perhaps as a marketing ploy. It was clearly working! At about the same time that TM began to gain wide acceptance, I left it, disgusted.

At that time, the revolution in consciousness that had begun in San Francisco in the early sixties finally reached Victoria, in the form of LSD made by a man called Osley. It was still legal. I heard about it, and decided to try it. I only knew one other person who had done it, and he was able to provide me with the required dose. Fortunately, it was pure and powerful, and I took it in the familiar safety of nature. I had no idea what to expect, beyond some kind of change in consciousness similar to what I had experienced on the mountain, and perhaps similar to meditation.

And in some ways, this was correct. It gave me a day of freedom from conditioning and fear, a happy time when the internal barriers that limited my consciousness were dissolved.

Of course there was a price. The high induced by LSD was a state of consciousness not connected to my heart. Whether this was a reflection of my own lack of maturity, or an inherent limitation of the chemical, is perhaps not for me to say. At any rate, after a few experiences, I could no longer deny that although the initial sense of unity was quite wonderful, it left me even further separated from other people. After so many years of hiding in shyness and feelings of inadequacy, I suddenly went to the opposite extreme of trying to raise everybody else's consciousness! In fact, my capacity to relate to others in a balanced way, which had not been much to begin with, became even more fragile. One day while I was holding forth to a friend, he stopped me and said:

"Man, you bring me down enough to listen to you, and then you go on to say the most irrelevant things!"

Soon after this I gave up using chemicals altogether. It was clear that drugs were not the way for me to find inner peace. It took a year to regain any grounded center within myself. I resumed my habit of meditation, but made no attempt to re-join the TM group. I added yoga asanas to my daily routine, and began reading books about spirituality, such as *Autobiography of a Yogi*.

In the summer of my twentieth year I was working for the Dept. of Highways in Kamloops, B.C. It was 1967, and jobs were still plentiful. My total lack of confidence with girls and sexuality was becoming a real problem. I decided to seek medical advice on the deformity of my penis that continued to cause me so much anxiety. Fortunately, on my first attempt, I found a young doctor from Italy who was just starting practice here. His response was totally supportive and sympathetic. I was also fortunate at this time to have good friends among the crew I worked with. They were all a bit older than me, and were able to accept me in spite of my obvious eccentricities. I decided to confide in them the nature of my coming surgery.

This became a huge joke, but now the teasing was good-natured, and I actually enjoyed it. By the time the fateful day arrived, even our boss, the engineer, knew about it, and I was given the day off with pay. In an all-male crew who often worked 10 hours a day, any excuse for a celebration was welcome, and it was decided that we would meet in the pub that evening for what was called "a bodango straightening party."

The surgery was quick and, thanks to a skillful local anesthetic, quite painless. When it was done, I looked down at the 10 black stitches in my bloody penis, and said: "What a mess."

The doctor looked a bit sad, and the nurse said: "You have hurt his feelings!"

"Avoid getting an erection for at least a week!" the doctor kindly advised: "The stitches will dissolve by then. Come back and let me know how it works!"

That night, in the bar, we all got drunk. From time to time, someone would get up and go to another table, and begin to whisper the story behind our celebration. There would be an intimate silence while the tale was told, and then everyone would erupt in laughter and cheers. Eventually, the whole place knew about it, but I was too drunk to care.

The next morning I awoke, as usual, with an erection. There was just no way to adhere to the good doctor's advice. This painful event took place every morning until the stitches were gone.

Shortly after this I was posted further north, to Mica Creek, and so lost contact with the doctor. Six months later, back at University, I finally got to try out my new organ.

That year was something of a turning point for me, and I found the beginnings of self-confidence. The fellowship of the highway construction workers had been very good for my spirits, and I was looking forward to my third year of university.

It was a careless time, but not carefree, as I entered a phase of ungrounded elation. I began expressing myself in poetry, and found myself quite at home in the new world of literature and art. The influence of my parents now became an advantage, and with the success of the Beatles and Rolling Stones, it was even quite fashionable to be English.

One evening in the student union building I found myself sharing a table with a young woman who seemed to find me interesting. I gave her a ride home in my Austin A-50, and we smoked some pot and found our way into bed together. It was quite wonderful at first. I saw stars! She got pregnant! And so I was initiated into the all-consuming paradox of human sexuality. I got to enjoy ten weeks of blissful ignorance, and then she told me: "WE are going to have a baby."

I was once again plunged into despair, this time not just for myself. I counted backwards and understood that she had become pregnant before I had even known her name. Dawn insisted we get married and start a family. Four years my elder, she was more ready for this than I was. Torn apart, we eventually agreed to give the baby up for adoption. The following summer, while I was away working on road construction, our daughter was born. I was told she resembled her mother, with big brown eyes and dark hair.

No one understood why I volunteered to work in Fort Nelson that year, five hundred miles North of Prince George on the Alaska Highway. We worked ten hours a day, six days a week, and I saved all the money I could in order to help support Dawn through her last year at University. After work there was nothing to do except hang out in the bar, and a good-natured co-worker from Jamaica introduced us to a drink called a "wild

Brazilian". It had four ounces of liquor in it, mostly rum.

The place was full of working men who were a long way from their wives and families. Life was simple: work, eat, drink, and then sleep. And talk about women. I discovered that within every tough Canadian working man was a secret soft place where an illusion about some woman was carefully guarded and worshipped in darkness. It was dangerous to touch that illusion. While the juke-box played "your cheating heart" and they drank beer and boasted of their conquests, each would have one special sweetheart, somewhere, who was different, who in fact was saving that lucky man from all the rest. That was sacred ground, and God help the foolish student who trespassed there.

A huge fist was held under my nose: "So! Have you been to Uni-fucking-varsity? How many fucking years of uni-fucking-varsity do you have?"

"Three," I confessed:

"Then you can answer one simple question, can yuh? With three fucking years of uni-fucking-varsity can you answer one simple question?"

"I can try." I suggested.

"All right then," the fist clenched harder and seemed to expand before my eyes: "Tell me: do you have more facts in your fucking head than I have right here in my fist?"

I had no choice but to admit that he did indeed have more facts in his fist.

"All right then! So have a beer!"

In this way I continued to make friends and gain acceptance. And the friendships were real. For some reason that I have yet to understand, I was given the role of confessor. One night a fight broke out in the beer parlor. Soon everyone was either fighting, or leaving in a hurry. The police arrived, and in the end the man who had started the whole thing was left alone in the middle of the wreckage and spilled beer.

I was still sitting there, alone and secure in my role, just watching. I stood up to leave, and the man came staggering over and cried on my shoulder. I just waited until he was finished pouring out his tears and his confession. There was nothing to say.

August came to an end and it was time to return to the University of Victoria for my final year. I hitched a ride down to Vancouver with a truck. It was after midnight when we stopped to pick up a young woman who stood under a street-light with her thumb out, and a cat on her shoulder. The truck driver joked about the possibility of me getting laid. About 1 a.m. he dropped us both off near the greyhound bus terminal, on a street with some cheap hotels. They were all closed. I asked the girl if she knew anywhere where I could stay that night. She looked at me for a moment, perhaps decided I was a safe person, and said I could crash at her place. I noticed that she had green eyes, like her cat, and that she was small and slender, also like her cat. I walked with her through the empty streets, into a run-down part of town with some empty buildings. I think it was Water Street. She led me into an old warehouse and up some stairs to a vast, dark space on the third floor. A temporary wall had been built all around this space, and there were doors in it that were decorated with wild art. She stopped at one of these and knocked. The door opened and a shaft of yellow light greeted her, followed by a small, dark man with a face like a hawk.

That was how I met Ivan. The girl's name was Juliet, and Ivan was a friend of hers. She was a student at the Vancouver school of fine arts. Ivan was a native from Oaxaca, from the Mazatec people. He had been born near a town called Huotla de Jiminez. Everything else about him was a mystery. He spoke good English, had taken the name 'Ivan' and traveled North via San Francisco to Vancouver, where the artist community had taken him in. He was small, but seemed very powerful. His hair was long and black, and his eyes were piercing –I felt as though he looked right through me. Juliet made us some herbal tea, and they talked about their travels while I just sat there. That was something I knew how to do: just be present, awake, and interested. It turned out this was a quality Ivan was not used to finding in gringos. After about 30 minutes he turned his attention to me, and asked who I was and where I came from.

The next three days were like an initiation for me. I listened while Ivan talked. He told me the story of his people, of the life he had known in Oaxaca, about the persecution and suffering his family had endured. He also told me about special powers that he said he had, and that were available if I hunted them. From time to time he would stop and we would smoke some marijuana. He called it "medicine". It was very strong, and I listened and he talked some more. He used the word "medicine" in a way I had not heard before: it seemed to mean anything that helped us connect with spirit. He was the first person I met who was seeking spirit, and who had found something. It was his energy and his faith that impressed me most. His words were like a fresh, wild wind from some remote country that I longed to explore for myself.

"Learn from the four directions," he told me: "You can trust the number four: it lets you go. Go to the four directions."

It made sense at the time.

"You're different," he said: "most people I meet argue with me, but you just listen." I listened for three days. From time to time Juliet would come into the room, and from time to time we would go out to eat. I was riveted to Ivan's words. He spoke about magic, of miraculous healings and people he knew who could transform themselves into animals and birds. He also spoke about the source of this strange power, a special kind of mushroom that only grew in the mountains near his home, and that was sacred to his people.

At one point, while Ivan was out, Juliet told me about her life as an artist, her classes at the art school, and added: "There is more going on around here than Ivan." She hinted that I should leave soon. I realized that I had crashed at her place for three days, and had all but totally ignored her. I was still very shy around women, and had no intention of coming on to her. I was unable to understand whether she was relieved, or disappointed. It never occurred to me that she could have any interest in me. These shortcomings on my part left me available to give my full attention to this mysterious and powerful native man.

When the time came for me to say goodbye, Ivan gave me a strange knife. It had a long blade, and a very small handle carved into a horse's head.

"My people are very small," he explained: "Their hands are small, and the horse is sacred to them. You will get something good from this knife. My only other possession is my guitar. I have not yet met anyone worthy of it."

I was very glad to be considered worthy of this beautiful knife. A year later I did indeed get something good from it.

Returning to Victoria after the clear, simple life working in the north was like jumping into quicksand. I soon discovered that there was nothing I could do that could heal the pain of a woman who had just given up her first baby. Dawn had changed her mind at the last minute and wanted to keep the baby, but of course it was too late. The adoptive parents had a legal right to her. And it was all somehow my fault.

I was twenty-one and having my first experience of what for lack of a better term is called "mental illness." From somewhere within the unexplored levels of my unconscious a huge and all-consuming guilt arose: guilt for the suffering of women. I felt as if it really was my fault. The pain was unbearable. My mind became a womb that carried that baby, endured labor and delivery, and then lost the beloved girl again and again and again. It was an obsession that gave me no rest. In this condition I offered Dawn what comfort and support I could, but our relationship had been fragmented beyond repair. Feeling that I deserved only suffering and pain, I stayed and endured her rage and grief.

My attempts to meditate were futile. My mind continually played the tape of a labor and delivery I could never experience, and so never bring to resolution. A black cloud of guilt hung over me that was out of all proportion to my actions. Finding the source of this torment later became one of my most difficult quests, and it led me into confrontation with forces that were far beyond my imagination.

This downward spiral hit bottom with a desperate attempt to "transcend" my pain by taking a final dose of LSD. I was unaware that in the three years since my first experience with the drug, things had changed, and the original, pure form of LSD was no longer available. A friend had just got out of jail, where he had been serving a two-year sentence for trafficking marijuana. He also wanted to get high, and celebrate his freedom. He had met a young woman who had just come up from San Francisco with some acid. I was in a self destructive state and willing to take extreme measures to end my mental anguish. I can remember the scene so well! I was driving, and we stopped outside the house where she stayed. My friend went in, and came out with two large, orange pills. It was October, and the leaves on the trees were dying and falling in the streets. He handed me my pill, and I swallowed it down without thinking. Then I noticed that he was carefully cutting his pill in half. At that moment the woman came out of the house and stopped to talk with us. My friend must have told her that I had just taken the whole thing, because she leaning into the car, and asked: "Did you just take a whole one?"

"Yes." I replied.

"I feel sorry for you!"

With these comforting words she walked away. Apparently what I had just taken was called a 'California Goof Ball' and they did not know of anyone who had taken a whole pill before. A quarter was enough. My friend took a half. It was a mixture of LSD, STP, speed and all kinds of other shit that was supposed to produce hallucinations and generally rip your head out of shape. That it did!

We quickly realized that we needed a safe place to trip out, and found the house of a mutual friend whose parents were away. By the time we arrived I was 'rushing' and in no condition to drive. Fortunately we were welcomed there, and I lay on my back on a carpet in the middle of the living-room floor while all hell broke loose. At some point in the night FM radio was on, and I heard Janis Joplin singing "Piece of My Heart" for the first time. It was a live recording, and I could hear every swig of Southern Comfort that Janis took and then hear the bottle smash on the floor as if my ears and my heart were there in the crowd feeling everything –every nerve, every need, and every desire wide open and raw. The song ended. A voice said: "Cheap Thrills."

The next eight hours were a wild ride. I was congratulating myself on surviving, and expecting the drug to wear off, like LSD. But the STP just went on and on, and the next morning I was still high, stoned, whatever: totally without center or ground under my feet. I could not face going back to the apartment that I shared with Dawn in that condition, so I went home to my long suffering parents.

I was expert in hiding my troubles and moods from my parents –or so I thought. Years later my mother told me they had known a lot more than I suspected, and it turned out to be they who were good at hiding their true feelings. The overwhelming fury of hallucinations had calmed down, and I was able to accept my father's invitation to go sailing with them.

It was a day of clear sky and fair winds between two storms. It was perhaps the last sail of the year for them. My father was a strong man with black hair and tanned skin, very well educated and intelligent in an old-school way. He seemed to be unaware that the world and human consciousness was changing so fast: his values and understanding were deeply rooted in the traditions of England. My mother was more aware of the social turmoil her children were growing up in, but she shared the same deep roots, and no storm ever blew them over, or blew them apart. I sat there, almost useless as a sailor, while my father navigated us through the dangerous waters and my mother acted as crew, following his orders and pulling on ropes. I helped her, and took my turn at the tiller as we sailed back and forth in the choppy waters around Trial Island. My father's eyes were brown and far sighted, his gaze forever searching for things just beyond the horizon. My mother's blue eyes saw what was right in front of her, and she kept things together as my father steered the family towards his vision of freedom and happiness. As for myself, I had not yet found any roots in the society into which I had been transplanted.

By evening, I was exhausted, and had been stoned for more than 24 hours. At about ten I decided that perhaps some pot would help me to relax, and I smoked a joint of Mexican marijuana that had flakes of hashish in it. Then I swallowed some downers that a friend had given me for emergencies such as this. My happy idea was that I would become drowsy, and float softly away into sleep.

The opposite happened. I did not know that benzodiazapam and STP, when combined, created a poison that had proved fatal in some cases. As the effects of the drugs be-

gan to come on, and my fragile world began to spiral upwards again, my heart began to beat faster and faster, and my
breath became restricted as the poison took effect. I blasted
off into the unknown like a rocket. My last coherent thought
was that I had mixed some bad shit, and had to get out of my
parent's house.

It had been my intention to leave quietly and unnoticed.
I came downstairs from the room that they kept for me and
was walking towards the front door when my father came
out of his room and looked at me with total love and concern. "Where are you going?" he asked. There was no blame
or judgment in his voice, just a tenderness that pained my
heart.

"I can't sleep...I'm just going out for a walk...." I kept
moving, not wanting him to see the insanity that must have
shone from my eyes.

"For a walk?" His voice sounded sad and helpless behind
me as I hurried off into the abyss.

On the street the wind was blowing again. From time
to time a break in the clouds let the light of a half-moon
down where I walked among the shadows and falling
leaves. The marijuana and hashish that I had smoked was
still coming on strong, in spirals of mental anguish that
spun in my head like vomit being flushed down a toilet.
My heart rate increased to what sounded like the continuous firing of a machine gun somewhere in the cage of my
ribs. It was too fast to count and I expected that at any
moment my heart would burst. At the same time my head
was on fire and a black wind of insanity blew the burning
embers of every useless thought I had back onto the raw
nerves of my brain.

Suddenly everything was still. The wind in the trees
stopped, and for a few minutes the demons within me took a
break. I was able to rest near a grove of oaks in a park beside

the sea. From far away I heard the approach of the next gust of wind. It was like a live thing tearing at the trees. When the branches around me began to move I could see long purple flames as the life that had been given was taken away. It was somewhere near midnight and the streets were empty as I waited for my turn. Then the wind stopped and another cycle of madness began, more powerful and fearful than the first. I saw the white line down the center of the road, and began to walk on it, wanting something that would just be there for me that night. Just to keep walking was the best I could do. Thoughts of suicide came and went, but without any purpose or plan.

Eventually I noticed a slight decrease in intensity within the cycle. The calm places lasted longer, and my heart rate began to slow. I found myself walking through a park on an empty road. It was strange that I saw no cars or people that night. At last my mental storm just blew itself out, and a black calm held the darkness. I had survived, and with this a strange elation came over me. My awareness seemed to have merged with the night, and the core of suffering was gone.

At this point I turned towards home. An unfamiliar energy filled my body. All my senses had a supernatural capacity to know what was around me. At one point while passing an old house set back in a large yard, I noticed a cat sitting on the lighted porch. The moment I stopped to look at it, the cat looked back at me with a flash of red from its eyes. We seemed to share the same mind. It ran towards me in a strange spiral over the grass, and then circled me. The cat, too, was without conscience or emotion that night, just dancing with power and life. It followed me for miles as I walked home, and then was gone. I found shelter once again and just as dawn broke was finally able to sleep.

It took about a year to recover from that bad trip. I lived devoid of emotion or capacity to respond to life and love. Dawn became increasingly unhappy in our relationship, but we were unable to let go of our failure and move on. I was able to finish my B.A. in English and creative writing, but had become a bit of a zombie. I avoided all drugs and alcohol, and worked out regularly in the YMCA in a determined effort to repair the damage. The experience had left me with a clearer understanding of the value of life, and the opportunities that I had.

When spring came I returned to work for the Dept. of Highways, and was posted to Dawson Creek. My plan was to save some money during the paving season, and then go somewhere far away. The routine of working outdoors far away from the pressure of classes, family and relationships was good for me. When summer ended, I returned to Victoria, determined to finally break off with Dawn and leave the place that was so heavy with unhappy memories.

Chapter 3: *Long Journey*

I left Victoria in November of 1969 on a greyhound bus bound for San Francisco. The only thing clear to me was that I had to get away, and that I wanted to go south. The bus reached the Bay area terminal at 10:30 p.m., and I got down into the dark, strange city with no plan and very little money. The YMCA and the Salvation Army were closed. While asking around I was picked up by a gay man who took me back to his place, saying I could crash there. He gave me something to eat, and came on to me as I was making up my bed on the floor and preparing to sleep. I explained to him that I was straight, and that I was grateful for the hospitality. I knew very little about the world of gay sexuality, in fact I knew very little about sexuality, period. It seemed to be making everybody crazy and had certainly caused me enough misery already. We talked for a while, but he was not interested in anything else, and always led the conversation back to sex. Later in the evening his partner came back, and I heard them yelling at each other. It took me a while to understand that his partner was in a jealous rage, having assumed that I was another gay man. I got up to explain the situation to him, but by this time he was at the bottom of the outside stairway that led down to an alley. My host had picked up a gallon wine bottle, and hurled it after him while yelling "bitch" into the darkness of the city. The bottle smashed on the pavement. I somehow felt responsible for their unhappy evening, and lay down to sleep with the cockroaches.

Next day I left in a hurry. I found my way to the corner of Haight and Ashbury, like a lost pilgrim. The streets were empty and gray. A young man came by and stopped to ask me for spare change. I asked him what had happened and why there was no-one around and his answer was to explain the advantages of mixing speed with gasoline.

I found my way up to Berkeley, without plan or purpose. I just kept walking up the canyon, and spent that night under a log in the trees, as far from people as I could get. I spent one more day drifting around Berkeley, one more night under the log, and then moved on. I wrote the word "south" on a piece of cardboard, and stood by the road with my thumb out.

It took all day to reach a place called Fresno. A truck driver let me off near a highway intersection.

"Fresno sucks!" These words that some traveler had written on a highway sign said it all. I crawled under an overpass and spent the night listening to the traffic rumble over my head. In the morning I walked to the nearest truck stop, and found a driver willing to take me farther south.

The next night I was the guest of an old man who lived in a dump. He found me standing beside the road and asked if I would like a cup of coffee. It was late and I was lonely so

I followed him to the shelter he had made out of the hoods of old cars that had been left in a vacant piece of land near town. He slept on a car seat that he had pulled out of a 1951 Ford. The remains of the Ford served as his kitchen. He started a small fire and brewed some coffee in a black pot. It was strong and black. I pretended to drink and then poured my coffee out when I thought he was not looking, but he noticed:

"Something wrong with my coffee, kid?"

"Sorry. I don't usually drink coffee. It keeps me awake at night. I just wanted some company."

"Don't worry. I don't mind. I've been working the cans all day. Found half a chicken…can you believe it? What some people just throw away!"

Perhaps he had not had anyone to talk to for a long time. He told me about his life. He had been in the merchant marine and seen every port, even Calcutta. He never told me how he had come to end up homeless, and I did not ask. Seems he had never married. I asked him about Calcutta.

"City of dreadful night," he quoted "There were people everywhere, living on the street, with nothing. Could not see how they were making it, but they were making it somehow. There were whole families just sleeping on the street under rags. I don't have it so bad." He gave me a quick look from under long, white eyebrows that curled over his watery blue eyes, like he was looking to see if I understood. How could I? But there I was, listening, and that must have counted for something. He let me unroll my bed near the fire.

"Don't worry, no-body comes here, no-body will bother you. I work the cans in the morning, early."

I heard him crawling into his shelter. In the morning I was alone, and continued my journey south. After hitching all day I was let down at the edge of a small town. It was too late to go on, so I walked into a field of trees and went to sleep. I woke up to find myself in an avocado orchard. The sun was shining through the leaves and green fruit hung everywhere. I was beginning to feel better. Later that day I crossed over into Mexico at Tijuana.

It was a huge relief to be out of both Canada and America. Some invisible weight, a sense of guilt and failure that I had been carrying, was left behind at the border. Only when it was gone did I get to know about it. In my own country I had been nothing, an unknown who had not joined anything, and so escaped finding a social or personal identity. In Mexico I was just another gringo, and yet I felt at home: the people did not judge me. There was too much life going on all around for that.

I kept going south, to Ensenada, and there I learned about the Baja peninsula. It was 500 miles to the next town, La Paz, and the road turned into a dirt track over the desert. My last ride was with a farmer in an old GMC pickup. The motor overheated, and he stopped to check under the hood. I did not speak Spanish, and he did not speak English, but he seemed to be asking me if I knew anything about motors. I tried to stop him from unscrewing the radiator cap, but he went ahead and hot water exploded up about twenty feet. The radiator was now almost empty, and he did not have any water with him. He walked back along the road towards a farm we had passed, and I sat on a rock beside the road to wait.

Sometimes having nothing to do but wait is a good thing. I noticed the dry beauty of the landscape and felt the stillness and magic of the desert. To the east a long range of mountains rose out of the haze and continued on south as far as I could see. To the west there was nothing but cactus and some grass on a flat horizon. I could hear the gentle music of surf when the wind was right. This wind was warm and touched my skin with the promise of freedom. I saw the farmer walking back towards the truck. He was carrying a can of water that pulled his body to the right. His eyes were tired and worried. The truck refused to start, and he got me to help him push it off the road. I thanked him for the ride, and walked in the direction of the surf.

Closer to the ocean, the cactus gave way to grass that grew out of the sand in tall clumps. When the wind was towards me, the waves sounded close, but then the wind would change and they would sound very far away. I walked for over an hour until the grass just stopped, and I stood at the edge of a wide, empty beach, with the waves still far away. Red light from the sunset touched the foam as it curled and fell in a slow, gentle rhythm. I lay down on the sand and slept in the ancient music of the sea.

Perhaps that was when my journey was transformed from a blind, desperate escape to a pilgrimage filled with magic and purpose. I had no water or food with me, not even a map. I made it back to the desert road in the morning, and waited for a ride to show up. A group of men passed me on their way to work in the fields. They were laughing, and I heard one of them singing as they walked away. It was soon quite hot, and I began walking south on the long road to La Pas. The mountains that had seemed so clear and close at sunrise began to fade away in the haze. I passed the field were the men were working, and they waved to me. Finally I heard a noise behind me, and saw a cloud of dust approaching. It was a truck loaded with irrigation pipes. Two Mexican men sat in the cab. The one driving was large and overweight, while his partner was lean and wiry. Both had bushy, black moustaches, and they looked like bandits out of an old western movie. The driver spoke a little English, and he asked me where I was going:

"La Pas." I replied.

"La Pas! La Pas!" they both repeated, laughing and pointing down the endless desert track: "Take me to La Pas!"

They both went into the desert to piss. When they came back, the driver motioned for me to sit in the middle. I did not know it at the time, but La Pas was five days hard driving away.

The first thing they did was to offer me a drink from a glass bottle. I could just about see the life that thrived in the tepid water. But I was so thirsty I forgot about amoebic dysentery, and drank. Shortly after this, we pulled up in front of a group of shacks. One had a veranda made of baked dirt, with a table and chairs set out. We had breakfast there, and I ate a large quantity of corn tortillas with huevos and frijoles, or eggs and beans. The driver insisted on paying for me. We drank some coffee, and then they suddenly got up, and we continued our long journey.

After a couple of hours my stomach began to churn. These men were serious truckers on an obvious mission to deliver irrigation pipe. The driver had told me at breakfast that they were in fact going all the way to La Pas, and joked about it in a way that let me know it was a very rare thing for any vehicle to drive all that way on such a rough road. I knew that I would be very unlikely to find another ride. So the onset of a major bout of dysentery was the last thing I needed. I wondered how long it would be before I exploded. The pressure in my stomach moved down and became painful. I was getting ready to try and tell them that I needed to get into the desert, fast, when something wonderful happened. A length of pipe fell off the back of the truck. When they stopped to pick it up I ran a few yards into the cactus and got my pants down just in time. Yellow liquid shot out behind me about twenty feet. By the time I got back they were ready to go.

How many times this sequence of events repeated, I lost count, but all that day, pipes kept falling off the truck, and I kept going into the cactus. The truck lurched and rattled down the road through the heat and dust, and finally there was nothing left in my gut. The pipes stopped falling off the truck. The truckers, who had noticed my problem, had finally got them tied on right. Soon they stopped at another tiny village, and ate supper. I had to decline the food. Then they pulled off the road and we unrolled our bedding and slept under the stars.

Very early next morning they woke me and we drove on in darkness. The truckers had friends in the few settlements along the Baja road where we stopped for meals. My dysentery cleared up, and I was able to enjoy the steaming, soft corn tortillas that were the main food. At night we slept beside the truck. Sometimes the truckers would sing songs in Spanish, harmonizing in a way that was very moving and beautiful. They looked rough and fierce, like bandits, and yet their songs touched my heart. They tried to learn more about me, and I tried to learn some Spanish, but most of the time we just drove on over the endless desert in silence.

One night we slept with a group of road workers. In the early morning darkness, they lit a fire and made some coffee. While we drank, they passed around a special mug, each man taking a swig and then passing it along. When it reached me, everyone watched to see my reaction, with teeth and eyes flashing in the firelight. I took my swig, and found that the coffee was spiked with tequila. No one took more than one gulp of this special cup, and I felt for the first time how good it is to sit on the ground in a circle of kind, very poor people who are happy to share what they have.

Slowly the desert changed and gave way to scrub with a few palm trees. The long range of mountains to the east became less steep and remote where the flat desert changed into hill country. Our last night on the road was spent near a town in an oasis on the east coast of Baja. The following day we reached La Pas before dark. They left me near the center of town. I did not know any way to express the gratitude and respect I felt for those two men. That night I had a warm shower and a real bed to sleep in.

I was still without any plan or direction in my travels, beyond just drifting south. From La Pas I went down to Cabo San Lucas on the southern tip of the Baja peninsula. I walked out from the town and found a hidden beach surrounded by a half-circle of cliffs. It was beautiful and isolated. For three days I just watched the rise and fall of the sun and moon and swam in the warm water. Each day I walked into town for dinner, and carried back food for the next day. After the full moon had passed, I decided to take the ferry to Mazatlan and then continue on to Mexico City.

In Guadalajara I experienced the first of many solitary Christmas days. I was alone in a cheap room in a *pension*. It was strange to me how that special day, once the most magical day of the year, had become my saddest day, the one day when loneliness and exclusion became almost unbearable.

A recurring dream told the story of my life: I would find myself flying high above a city at night, and be attracted to the lights in the windows of the houses below. I would float from window to window, peering in at the comforts of family life, as people prepared for bed. There was no sexual feeling in the dream, just an overwhelming longing to be human, to be accepted and loved, and to have a home. I would get tired of peering into the lighted rooms from the darkness, and always tried to return to somewhere far away in the abyss of night, but I had forgotten the way. I would awake feeling lost between two worlds.

In Mexico City I again found a cheap *pension* to stay in. I liked the old style architecture, with a courtyard surrounded by rooms on inner balconies. It was quiet and cool. During my travels I kept up my practice of meditation and yoga, and avoided alcohol and drugs. I had a sense of purpose that kept me focused, but had no idea what that purpose was. I suppose I was looking for God. I never doubted that there must be some deeper meaning and value to life and that the blind suffering that I saw everywhere must have a cause. I was determined to find a way out, and to share whatever I found with other people.

While in Mexico City I visited the museum of anthropology. A large section of the museum was focused on the original peoples of Mexico –the many different communities that had lived there before the Spanish invasion, and the few that had survived. While wandering among the exhibits and displays, I became aware of a strange music playing in the background. The rhythm and melody was unlike anything I had ever heard, and yet it was familiar to my soul. I followed the sound to a display that looked like the interior of a village hut filled with ritual objects. It was all very simple and everything was the same color as the earth. The music was coming from a small speaker above this window. I noticed that a drum, a flute and a stringed instrument were included in the scene. There was a small table with a clay pipe and a leather pouch that seemed to be filled with herbal medicine. The music continued to hold my attention as I stood there in a trance. The scene was at once strange, and deeply familiar to me. A sign read: "Velada ritual of Mazatec Indians of Oaxaca". When I read this, I remembered Ivan, and what he had told me. He had been a native of Oaxaca. It became clear to me then that I must find him and his people, and learn about them.

While I stood there, wondering where these people lived and how I could get there, three people came up beside me to look at the display. They looked Mexican, and spoke Spanish. They appeared to be a few years older than me: a woman and two men, all with long, black hair. One of the men had a beard. I asked them if they knew any English.

"Yes, a little." replied the man with the beard.

"Can you please tell me about this ritual?"

They exchanged glances. It was clear that something here was very important to them, and they were slow to talk about it: "What does this scene represent? What is this music?"

They spoke among themselves in Spanish before the man with the beard answered: "This is an initiation ceremony. It is from the mountains of Huotla de Jiminez." He pointed to the bag of herbs: "See, that is the medicine, the hongitos."

When I heard the name of the town that Ivan had been from, my determination to go there became stronger.

"That is where I am going!" I replied: "Can you tell me how to get there?" Again they consulted together before the bearded one told me: "It is not possible for you to go there."

This I could not accept. I had already been excluded from too many experiences that were part of growing up in my own culture. The music continued its hypnotic, timeless melody. The pipe, the herbs, the ritual instruments of the display seemed to be alive with power. The moment was a doorway of opportunity into the unknown freedom that I longed for. "Please help me," I appealed to them: "I know I must go there."

Again they spoke among themselves. There seemed to be some disagreement between the two men and the woman. Finally the man with the beard turned to me: "No foreigner is allowed to go there. It is a big risk for you. The federales will arrest you."

"I will take that risk."

He looked back at his companions, and then told me: "We are going there ourselves!" At this point he introduced himself:

"I am Roberto. This is Miguel, and Illamo." I shook their hands. Illamo looked at me with fear in her eyes. She did not trust me.

We went to a café to make our plans. They were going to leave the next day by bus, after spending the night at Roberto's house. As the bus left very early, Roberto invited me to spend the night with them. We took a taxi back to my hotel, and then drove out to the suburbs of the city. Roberto's house was three stories high, with small balconies decorated with planters on each level. I thought his family must be rich, but it turned out they all lived on one floor. I left my things in a tiny room with one bed, and then we went out to have dinner.

Roberto seemed to be the leader as he had been to Huotla before. Miguel was a friend of his who lived close by, and Illamo was from Brazil. After dinner they took me to a club where there was live music, and they offered me marijuana. I wanted to keep my mind clear, and was still in recovery from my bad trip, so I declined. Miguel got sick and had to rush to the bathroom. Later when we got back to Roberto's house, I discovered that I was to share a tiny room and single bed with Illamo. She did not speak any English, and Roberto translated for me: "Illamo says she does not want any…trouble." He was embarrassed at having to explain something delicate: "Do you know?"

"Tell her she has nothing to worry about from me," I replied. I did not find her attractive, and was so grateful for their accepting me into their group that nothing would have tempted me to risk their trust and friendship. The small bed was just wide enough for the two of us. While she was undressing to get ready for bed, I noticed that her body was covered with scabies, a parasitic skin infection. She spent the whole night scratching while I did my best to stay as far away from her as possible. I had experienced the maddening itch of scabies already, and knew how difficult it was to get rid of.

After that night, Illamo was more trusting and friendly towards me. I wondered what her experiences with men had been to make her so wary.

We began our journey in the dark of early morning. Throughout the day we changed buses several times, and then spent the night in a cheap, noisy hotel near a bus station somewhere to the south. The next day it was the same thing: an early start, changing buses, sitting in cafes and bouncing along over rough roads in the heat. Then we entered an un-inhabited desert region, and after a few hours, Roberto got up and asked the driver to stop. We got down, and the bus pulled away in a cloud of dust, the sound of its motor fading away into the vibrant silence of the desert.

It was early afternoon, and hot. I did not know why we had got off the bus there until Roberto told me that in the next town there was a federal check point, and I would not be allowed to go any further. His plan was for us to walk across the desert and meet the road again in the foothills. That was when I realized what these people were doing for me. We began walking towards the hazy, blue mountains in the east –the Sierra Mazateca.

After a few hours the sun began to set, and it got cooler. There was no shade anywhere, and we had very little drinking water. They had only light packs, but mine weighed about forty pounds. We were all tired when we reached the hills. We found a creek among the rocks, and my friends drank from it. I hesitated after my experience in the truck, but my thirst was too much, and so I also drank. I could not see any dwellings above us on the hills, and so imagined that the water might be pure.

As we climbed the desert gave way to the more fertile terrain of the mountains and first bushes and then small trees appeared. At last we were able to see a road winding up from the flat country and disappearing into the mountains above us. A few moments later a cloud of dust appeared, moving towards us. We just made it up to the road in time to flag down a bus.

It was getting dark when the bus stopped for us. There was no room inside, and so we climbed the steps at the back and sat on the luggage rack. Even there, it was so crowded with people, luggage, chickens, baskets and bundles of cloth that there was no room for me, and I found myself sitting on the curved edge of the bus, holding on to the luggage rack to keep from falling.

We passed through wonderful scenery as we went higher and higher into the mountains. The trees became larger and larger until we were driving through thick forest. I could see long beards of lichen hanging from branches. I clung on for about two hours, while night fell, and then someone got down and I was able to join my companions on the relative safety and comfort of the wooden rack. After another couple of hours, we were able to find seats inside the bus. At about two a.m. Roberto woke me from an exhausted sleep and told me we had arrived.

We got down from the bus into total darkness. I could hear the sound of a stream beside the road, and noticed a couple of dim lights among the trees higher up. Roberto led us to a hut that was built on stilts right over the stream. We each took a wall, unrolled our bedding, and immediately fell asleep.

I became aware of the sound of the stream under the floorboards, and then the snoring of my companions. It was dawn in the mountains, but when I climbed down the ladder from the hut, I found myself in thick fog. I followed a path among the stones beside the stream until coming to a pair of railway ties that formed a simple foot-bridge. The place had been named after this feature: Ponto Del Fuego, or "The Iron Bridge". I followed the path up the hill, and came to a hut with a veranda where a man sat beside a brick cooking fire and a large, black kettle. He called me over, and I had coffee and some sweet rolls. All around thick fog rolled like a river, at times letting me see perhaps a hundred feet, and then closing in again. I saw only a few huts, some large trees, and a few rows of coffee bushes. Everywhere I looked the land seemed to rise steeply. I could hear children begin to cry as they woke up hungry.

It was ten a.m. before the clouds began to lift. When they did, a magical land of dreamlike beauty was revealed. The steep mountainsides were covered with thick jungle that contained huge trees hung with moss and flowering vines. There were fruit trees in bloom, and waterfall that burst out of the green tangle to fall singing into deep pools. Above these pools hung flowers shaped like bells, and brightly colored birds flew in and out of the shadows. When the sun finally broke through, I felt as though a beloved king had finally returned, and everything became warm and filled with joy. As the clouds rose higher, more and more of the mountains was revealed until all traces of mist vanished in the blue heat of the day.

Soon my friends joined me in the little café, and spoke to the owner in Spanish. They were cheerful and excited about being there. A plate of hot tortillas arrived, followed by eggs and potatoes, and more coffee. We were very hungry. It was New Year's Eve, and the reason they had traveled to Ponto Del Fuego was to meet with friends and celebrate by taking "los hongitos" together. Apparently it was an annual event, this pilgrimage to the land of the sacred mushrooms.

I did not like the idea of taking the mushrooms at night in a party atmosphere, and so I decided to walk the five miles to the town of Huotla, and search for my friend Ivan.

Before departing on this trip to Mexico I had cut my hair very short in an attempt to avoid unwanted attention. My appearance, together with my decision not to join their celebration, caused my friends to consider me a bit of a "strawberry". This was their expression for a "straight" person. Illamo seemed convinced that I was a total strawberry and had no idea what I was doing there.

The road to Houtla curved up through coffee plantations and areas of forest towards the top of a mountain. By the time I reached the town, the clouds were already coming down and the air was cold and damp. I found a small hotel near the town square and took a room for the night. The people there were a bit wary of me, and seemed to know that I was breaking the law by being there. When I went out to find something to eat for supper, I saw a column of soldiers crossing the cobblestone street below my hotel. They did not see me, and soon vanished into the mist. After dark there was nothing to do but sleep, so I returned early to my room and sat in meditation for an hour, wrapped in rough blankets. This was my bedtime routine, to sit until sleep overcame me, and then lie down for the night.

The cold awoke me at 6 a.m. My room had no windows, and I could not see or hear anything. I dressed quickly, wrapped myself in a blanket, and went down to the street. Everything was hidden in thick fog, and I could not see across the town square. I walked around the rows of old stone buildings that fronted on the square until I found a little coffee shop that had been made by enclosing the veranda of a building with boards. The fire was going, so I went inside.

An old man came out, and offered me coffee and a plate of sweet rolls. Then a young native man came in, and asked if he could sit with me. He was small, with huge shining black eyes. He spoke good English, and asked why I was there.

"I am looking for a friend. Perhaps you know him: his name is Ivan."

"I do not know anyone by that name," he replied: "Is he a gringo?"

"No, he is native of this place: he was born here."

"How do you come to know him?"

I told him of my meeting with Ivan, and how he had given me a ceremonial knife from his home in Houtla. Then I told him of my experience in the Museum, and said:

"I feel that I have been led to this place for a reason, and that it is related to the sacred mushrooms used in that ceremony."

He was silent for a while, and then told me:

"There was good medicine in that knife." He paused again, and then said: "In just four days I will be sixteen years old. It is our custom to be given the hongitos on our sixteenth birthday. That is when we become men. It is our initiation."

"We have lost our rituals where I come from," I told him: "The people have lost their connection with the Earth."

He looked into my eyes, and replied in a serious tone: "I am very sorry!"

"Is it possible for me to receive the hongitos?" I asked him.

"Possible, yes….but our curanderos, our medicine men will not give it to you. It is very sacred. We are only given the hongos once in our life. Only those who are to become healers take it more than once. Only the elders speak the name of the god of the honguitos. I have been preparing for this day for a long time."

His eyes held a depth of ancient wisdom together with the bright joy of youth. I wondered what it would be like to experience such an initiation, guided by the elders of his people. Perhaps it would heal the pain in my heart. I said goodbye to this young man, and wished him "vaya con Dios".

Once again I walked out alone into the fog, not knowing where I was going. I just followed the road that led on through the town up into the coffee plantations beyond. As I walked, the clouds lifted and once again the warm sun was revealed. Groups of native women passed me. They were tiny, and glanced at me with suspicion from under their shawls. A native man approached me, speaking in Spanish, and showed me a bundle of dried mushrooms that he had. He kept looking around in a furtive way. I did not trust the situation, and kept walking, but I was beginning to understand that it was dangerous for me to be there.

On my way back to the hotel, I met two young Mexicans with long hair who spoke English. They greeted me cheerfully, and then warned me: "You must not be seen by the police. They will arrest you. Come, will you have coffee with us?" I followed them back to the same little café.

"Are you staying here?"

"Yes, in the hotel. My friends are back in Ponto del Fuego."

"It would be better for you to go back there. Here, there are police and an army post. Many foreigners have come here. They had to close it a few years ago. How did you get in?"

I told them about our trek across the desert. One of them lit a joint and offered it to me. I was tired of being alone, and in a moment of weakness I took a couple of careless tokes, expecting it to be quite mild, like the pot I was used to. But this was a far more potent variety, and I soon found myself ripped out of shape. I asked them about the mushrooms: "Is it a trip? The hongos, I mean, are they powerful?"

They both looked at me as if I had asked a really stupid question, and then looked at each other and began to laugh. One of them leaned closer to me. He took both my hands in his, looked deep into my eyes, and said: "You bet they are!" For what seemed like a very long time he held my gaze, and then smiled and added: "Go back to your friends. They will help you with the hongos. But be careful!"

At that point I felt afraid. There seemed to be no limit to the power of that marijuana. I remembered my original reason for coming to Houtla, and asked: "Do you know a Mazatec man called Ivan?"

They spoke in Spanish. I could see their words swimming through the air like tropical fish.

"Yes, we knew him. I am sorry. He is dead."

"What happened?"

"He became very mystical. He was becoming a curandero of the hongos. Then one day he died. He left his body and never came back."

I was feeling very small and alone. These people seemed far beyond me, and their medicine too strong. Somehow I had counted on finding Ivan, and being guided by him on my journey, but instead I had been led to the source of the sacred mushrooms. I was convinced that Ivan had wanted me to take this medicine.

At that point I noticed that one of the men held an ancient key in his hand. It was huge, heavy, and carved into a design with two snakes for a handle. He noticed my gaze, and handed the key to me. It must have been for a very large door.

"From the key you can tell the kind of house we stay in!"

It was as if I could see their ancient house with its heavy wooden door and ornate lock. I had the thought that they might invite me back to stay with them, but then I remembered my friends and the room above the stream, and I got up to leave.

"Good bye, friend," they said: "May God be with you."

I paid for my night at the hotel, packed up my things and began walking back down the dirt road to the village. I felt very obvious and vulnerable: the only white face, and a foot taller than anyone else. There was no traffic on the road, just occasional native people. The men and women walked in separate groups. The men dressed quite plainly, but the women all wore white cotton dresses with glowing embroidery. I saw birds, flowers, and even mushrooms in the designs. I felt out of tune with the place and the people, like I did not belong there, a stranger in this magical paradise. My god, if the pot is this strong, what would it be like to take the mushrooms?

About halfway back I noticed some caves in the rocks beside the road. I went over and peered into one that expanded in the darkness before me. Although I had to bend down to enter, I was able to stand upright inside. The light from the entrance faded and I felt a line of rocks across the ground at my feet. Without thinking, I stepped over it, and continued on into the darkness. Suddenly there was nothing under my feet. I crashed onto my back, and the stick I had been carrying clattered down far below the narrow ledge I had landed on. My pack had broken my fall, and when I regained my breath I was able to slither back up to level ground. On the way back out, it was clear that the line of rocks were intended to act as a barricade and warning.

It was a narrow escape, and served to remind me of my original purpose in making this journey. I had not forgotten my bad trip, and it was with some fear and doubt that I had reached the decision to take the mushrooms. I had recovered some degree of inner health and peace by keeping sober and focused, and now I was about to take another step into the unknown, and give up control of my consciousness to a plant that had mysterious powers. I did not want to make any more careless mistakes, but I was determined to continue my inner journey. So far, everyone I had met who had any experience with these mushrooms spoke of them with the most profound respect, if they spoke at all. There was a whole religion built around them here. They mentioned peyote also, but when it came to the hongos, it was either total awe, or silence.

In a sober mood I arrived back at the room on stilts. There were three sleeping figures snoring gently in the shadows along the walls. I put my pack down against the fourth wall, and went back to the café to look for something to eat. It was mid-afternoon, and everyone seemed to be asleep. I sat there on the porch, looking out at the trees and coffee plants that surrounded me. Clouds were already beginning to form around the tops of the mountains.

For perhaps an hour nothing moved in the village. Then the sound of a child crying came from the hut across the path from where I sat. The little voice was very weak at first, but soon became filled with urgency. I heard a woman's voice, then a man's. Soon, the child was only sobbing, and then there was silence again. Smoke began to rise through the leaves on the roof at one end of the hut. A child ran down the path, turning briefly to glance at me from huge, black eyes. A woman walked slowly by, carrying a bundle of firewood on her head. Her long dress was covered with embroidered mushrooms of all colors and sizes. I felt like a ghost, longing to be part of a world that I had no means to touch.

Illamo, Roberto and Miguel came up the path and joined me at the table. Miguel called out in Spanish, and the old man called back. Miguel looked at me with a smile, and said: "Tortillas! He is making fresh tortillas." The family who owned this little café were the only people in the village who had any visible means of livelihood.

The three of them were very happy. They told me about the ceremony on the night of the New Year: "We sat in a circle around a fire. Everyone took the mushrooms. It was wonderful."

Roberto asked me if I had found Ivan.

"I heard he had died. They told me also that I should be careful not to get arrested here. I have decided to take the mushrooms."

"Wonderful. You are safe here, but don't go back to Huotla. We will find mushrooms for you."

They consulted together in Spanish, and then Roberto said: "Miguel will stay with you for your journey with the hongos." I looked at Miguel, and he nodded his agreement. I was glad of this, because I had an instinctive trust of Miguel. He was grounded and clear. Illamo did not quite trust me, and Roberto was a complicated man with things in his eyes that he did not communicate, but with Miguel I felt totally safe.

We ate our tortillas and beans. After dinner, my friends sat there, drinking coffee and smoking marijuana. I declined both. It was still a mystery to me why, even here with such good friends, I felt like a stranger. I wondered if I was holding back from life too much, if I would be less lonely if I just said yes to everything. But I knew this would not work. It was as if the drugs and caffeine did not affect them in the same way. If I had coffee, I would be awake all night: if I smoked as much pot as they did, I would be incapacitated.

Illamo and Roberto were sitting close together, and had become a couple overnight. The glow of love and intimacy that surrounded them was so beautiful, and yet unknown to me. My heart ached.

I slept deeply that night and the music of the stream under the floorboards was there to welcome me to the new day. I was surprised to find myself alone and the sun already shining. Illamo and Roberto were sitting together in the café. They told me that Miguel had gone to ask the local people about mushrooms for me. He also advised me not to have anything to eat.

Soon Miguel came up the path, a bit out of breath but with a wide smile. He spoke only a few words of English, and Roberto had to translate for him: "It is good news. He has got Dherumbas. They are the best kind of hongos."

He took a small packet of green leaves out of his pocket. Gently, he unfolded the leaves to reveal five tiny mushrooms with long stems. The caps were almost white, the gills dark brown, and the stems a pale gold. He folded the leaves again with care, and presented the bundle to me. Roberto explained that Miguel had paid the equivalent of ten dollars for them, and so I paid this amount to him. They all looked at me.

"Well," said Roberto: "Vaya con Dios!"

I realized they expected me to eat them on the spot, without any further ceremony. The moment had finally come. I placed the five little mushrooms on my tongue, chewed them slowly and then swallowed. There was a bitter taste, more like a sensation, similar to lemon juice at the back of my tongue. I was told that this bitter feeling was a good sign, and meant that the mushrooms were strong. Mushrooms that had no power in them were called "awa" or water. Roberto again advised me not to eat anything. I asked them again:

"Is it ......is it a trip?"

I immediately felt stupid, as they first looked astonished at my question, and then laughed. Miguel, for the first time, took the initiative to respond to me: "Si...yes!" he said. At this they all laughed even louder. Then he added: "Estas bonito! –it is beautiful!"

I thanked them, and asked Roberto to let Miguel know that I wanted to go into nature, someplace where we would not be disturbed. Roberto replied: "Go with Miguel, he knows a good place. Have a good trip!" As we got up to leave them, I noticed a bemused look in Illamo's eyes, like she knew I was in for a big surprise.

I followed Miguel back to the road, and then along a trail that led up the mountains in the opposite direction to Houtla. It was a narrow trail, and did not look as if any vehicle could use it. He led me down an almost invisible path to a beautiful place where a waterfall leapt out of the jungle to join a larger stream. I sat on the grassy bank with my feet beside the water. Miguel just let me be. I think the first hint I had that something very powerful and wonderful was indeed happening was when a bird flew past and left a trail of colors hanging in the air behind it. They glowed there against the living green of the jungle, and then returned to their origin...I would have said faded out, but it was no longer true. I closed my eyes to listen to the sound of the waterfall, and saw to my amazement total, pure darkness for the first time. No confusion of blurred shapes and patterns, just absolute blackness. Then an amazing creature made of jewels appeared, shone with inner light for a moment, and vanished back into inner night. Another and another appeared more brilliant, detailed and shining than the last, until I opened my eyes.

Then the beauty of the world that I was sitting in finally got through to me. It was awesome. No hallucination could equal what was right in front of me. It was only about thirty minutes since I had eaten the mushrooms and already I was in unimagined realms of perception. There was a strange current, like electricity, but also like water, rushing through me. It seemed to be coming from the earth I was sitting on, and then it seemed to be coming from the base of my spine, and then I could not find the difference between the two. At this I laughed and looked over at Miguel. Our eyes met for an instant, and he said just one word: "Bonito!"

"Bonito!" I repeated, and then looked away. We were the same, and both of us were alone with the creator. I knew I could trust him absolutely.

Very gently and with irresistible power the spirit that had been invited into me through the mushrooms opened my heart. There was no longer any experience of separation from anything. I looked at my own hand with utter wonder.

The ages of evolution that had taken place in order for me to receive that gift were clear. The life that shone within my hand and within everything else was known, and was the creator as well as myself. This opening had been swift, smooth, and natural. For a moment I saw the face and shining eyes of the native boy who was so eagerly waiting for his sixteenth birthday, for his time to experience this, and carry within him for the rest of his life the sure knowledge that the Earth was a living being with whom he was forever related, and to whom he owed the deepest respect and gratitude.

I thought for a moment of my own people, the white folks of the modern world, who had all but lost this connection. It was at that moment that the spirit of the hongos gave me a clear vision, an inner direction that came from my own heart, but also from the creator. I, too, was not meant to repeat this experience with the mushrooms. My vision was to find my own way, using only the god-given gifts that all humans have, and whatever grace I could find, to verify this experience without the help of any outside medicine. This was our natural human condition. I made a clear intention not to forget this vision, and to celebrate this gift of a sure direction and focus for my life I threw off my clothes and plunged into the deep pool under the waterfall.

I came up laughing, and called again to Miguel: "bonito!" I was aware that my usual habit of shuddering when going into cold water was not there. The cold was wonderful, refreshing and renewing, so that when I came out it felt as if I had just been re-born. One spirit lived in everything: the rocks, the trees, the lizards that basked on the rocks, and also the amazing human body where this awareness of "I" was formed by the capacity of consciousness to know itself.

The warmth of the sun was the manifest love of god on my skin. A gentle wind came up the valley and the trees all spoke to me with the voices of ancestral spirits. There was only one message in everything, the simple message of unity and love. My gaze found a large tree growing near the waterfall. Its roots embraced the rocks in their search for the soil and water of the earth. The trunk where it rose above the rocks was the same silver gray, and the same shining consciousness that was in the rocks continued up into the tree. The branches and leaves were bursting into the sky with joy and gratitude. The spirit of the tree just rested there, patient and strong. All were my relatives.

The inner view of jeweled formations that appeared in the flawless darkness, glowed for a moment, and vanished, was waiting for me whenever I closed my eyes, but it was the world of sun, earth, water and sky that held my attention. I saw for the first time the beauty and the mystery of my life, and the world I lived in, and it was so sacred I wanted nothing more.

I walked over to a flowering bush that grew beside the stream. The blue flowers faced up into the light. A small butterfly landed on a flower in front of me, and began to probe for nectar. It had blue circles on its wings, the same color as the flowers. Suddenly a large wasp-like insect dived in with deadly speed, pounced on the butterfly, and stung it to death. It had strong jaws, and devoured the dead insect in seconds, leaving only the wings to drift down in spirals of blue towards my feet. The buzz of the huge wasp hung in the air, loud and harsh, and then slowly faded as the insect flew away. In that moment innocence fell away from my mind as I realized that every living thing in this beautiful creation eats and destroys other living things. The only difference between myself and the wasp was the gift, and responsibility, of choice. The huge weight of human history with its endless cycles of violence and destruction rested on this difference alone.

This moment of sobriety began the very gentle return of my familiar habits of thought and my limited capacity for perception. There was no sensation of "coming down," just a soft closing of magical doors. The afternoon had passed, and the clouds were beginning to form again as I turned to look for Miguel. At the same moment, he appeared, coming up a path beside the stream. I put my clothes back on and in silence we walked back to the café to join our friends.

A deep peace and joy stayed with me. Everyone was delighted with my good experience, and nobody said a word or asked about it. They knew and accepted. The old sense of alienation was gone, and I felt strong and confident that the purpose of my journey had been accomplished.

The next day Roberto told me that federales had been seen in the area, and that they were probably looking for me. He advised me to stay out of sight. I decided to return to the waterfall, and pass the day peacefully in nature. My plan did not work. I was sitting quietly beside the path when an old Ford truck suddenly came bursting up the trail and stopped beside me. I did not think it possible for any vehicle to navigate that path, but there it was, with three federal police jumping out of it. They did not speak any English, but that did not prevent them from communicating to me that I was under arrest. I was searched, and my pocketknife was confiscated. At first they were quite rough and aggressive, but I was still very much at peace within myself, and their attitude soon changed. Using mostly sign language, the oldest and perhaps ranking officer let me know they needed to see where I was staying. I led them back to the room on stilts. Roberto and Miguel were inside, asleep. They did not stir as the three police searched every corner of the room, and then searched my pack. They did not find anything. I knew that the mushrooms were not illegal, but if they had found any pot, I would have been charged. They indicated I should pack up all my things, and come with them.

By the time we got back to the truck, a group of Mexicans had appeared and were sitting on the ground, waiting. They put me in the back, and then motioned for this group to climb in also. The police seemed to be in a hurry, and we were soon rattling down the road away from that enchanted place. After about a mile they stopped to pick up a group of Mexican hippies, and when they joined us, I recognized Illamo. One of them spoke English, and asked why I had come there. I did not know if any of the men crowded into the back of the truck were police, so I just repeated my story: "I am a tourist"

Illamo added: "And you are a little strawberry, no?" There was nothing to say to this.

The mountains and jungle finally gave way to the dry hills, and at sunset we passed the place where we had first found the road after our trek across the desert. I was being expelled from paradise. When we reached the town, all the Mexicans got down from the back of the truck, and it was only then that they realized that I had been arrested. A few young Mexicans who had also gone to Houtla for the mushrooms pleaded with the police on my behalf, and then they all waived goodbye as we drove away. We stopped briefly at the local police station, where a man waited for the return of his truck. Apparently it had been commandeered for the journey into the mountains. The three federal officers and I all transferred to their waiting car and began the long drive to Mexico City.

I fell asleep in the back of the police car. Although my circumstances had changed dramatically, my state of mind had not. The magical beauty of the mountains was gone, but my experience there had been so powerful and so real that even being shown into a dark jail cell at about 4 a.m. did not concern me. I felt no anger or resentment towards the police, as it was clear they were just doing their jobs. A flashlight pointed out an empty metal bed, with no mattress or bedding of any kind. My pack was returned to me, so I unrolled my sleeping bag and fell asleep.

All too quickly I was awakened by the sound of someone vomiting in the darkness. I fell asleep again until a clanging of metal doors awoke me. A bit of daylight came in through a single high, barred window, and revealed a stream of vomit running down the floor from the other end of the cell, and pooling right under my bed. I could see it clearly through the rusted wires that were all that kept me above it. There were four beds in the room, and the one at the other end held a man who must have been sleeping off one hell of a drunk.

Breakfast time came and I joined a line up of men in the central courtyard. To my surprise, the breakfast was quite good: coffee, rolls, and beans. I was very hungry. A young man sat down beside me and introduced himself. He spoke good English. His name was Maturo, and he was from Guatemala. I asked him how he had ended up in jail:

"Drink," he replied simply: "too much tequila. I woke up in here."

"What will you do now?" I asked.

"Nothing…. they will send me back to Guatemala. This is a federal prison for non-Mexicans. No one stays here for long. They either transfer you to a regular jail, or deport you. It is better here than other jails. What is your story?"

"I was in the mountains, someplace where I was not supposed to be. They found me there."

"Have you been charged with anything?"

"No. Not yet."

"If they found any marijuana on you, you will be charged. Do you have any money?"

"No. They took it all." This was partially true. When they arrested me, the police had taken my wallet and passport, but I had two US twenty-dollar bills sewn up in a secret pocket in my coat. It was my emergency money, and I did not want anyone to know about it

After breakfast we were allowed out in the courtyard. It was just a square of bare ground with cell blocks on three sides, and a high brick wall topped with barbed wire on the fourth. I was still in the dark about my situation, and had no way of finding out anything, as none of the guards spoke any English. There were about twenty men sitting around on the ground, smoking.

At lunchtime we were all lined up again, and then given tortillas and beans in the canteen. Then we hung out in the courtyard all afternoon. At about seven p.m. we were given a simple dinner, and then locked in our cells for the night. I was relieved to find that the man who had been sleeping in my cell had gone, but no one had cleaned up the mess. There was nothing to do but lie down in the foul smelling darkness and wait for sleep.

During the night I was jolted awake by the clanging of the cell door as another man was put into the cell. He lay down on the same bed as the first man, and soon he, too, began puking his guts out onto the floor. The room sloped down towards my bed. The morning light revealed two converging streams of puke right under my head. The new stream was a slightly brighter yellow than the old. It stank. He, too, disappeared during the day, and that night I was alone in the cell again, with no way to clean it up.

I asked Maturo about finding some way to clean up my cell, but without pesos to offer the guards, nothing was possible. It was not even possible for me to buy a soft drink so I had to trust the water. With each passing day more of my familiar habits of mind returned as the effects of the mushrooms faded. Soon, I began to worry about my future. As the familiar patterns of resistance and anxiety about life returned, I felt an overwhelming loss, as if my own mind had become the cause of exile from paradise. It was then that the clarity of the vision I had been given sustained me. I knew that I must somehow find a way to verify the experience, and to get out of jail was the next step.

One day a group of us were taken to a headquarters in the city. Our cases were up for processing. We sat on the floor at one end of a huge room full of desks, and waited. I could understand nothing of what was being said. Far away in the mountains the eyes of the people had shone, but here the light had all but gone out. Finally I was called into an office where an imposing man with a mustache sat. He spoke in English:

"We think you are an addict of the hongos. You will be sent back to your country." His words were final, and even as I began to protest with my 'innocent tourist' routine, I was escorted back to my place on the floor beside Maturo.

A few more days dragged slowly by in jail. The vomit had dried up, and did not stink so badly. No more men were put into my cell. Maturo was gone. I longed to be on the streets, free to buy fresh orange juice.

I was awakened in the middle of the night by a rattle of the door and the command: "Canadiense!" I quickly got dressed and packed.

The two officers that drove me through the night to the airport seemed in a hurry. They drove right onto the runway and up to the boarding stairs of a plane, just as day was breaking. My passport was returned to me at the foot of the stairs, and I was shown an empty seat just before the announcement came to prepare for takeoff. After the plane was in the air, I turned to the woman sitting beside me, and asked where the plane was going.

"Toronto." She said, with a touch of irritation. Perhaps the smell of my recent cell had followed me.

This was a shock, as it was January, and I was in no way prepared for winter in Ontario. I had only sandals for my feet, and a light, summer jacket with my last forty dollars hidden in it. Well, they were sending me back to Canada at their own expense, and had not charged me with any crime, so this four thousand mile discrepancy was no big deal. Soon, breakfast was served: the ordeal was over.

The plane droned down through endless clouds to land on the snow swept runways of Toronto airport. The outside temperature was twenty degrees below zero. Everything seemed gray, frozen, and lifeless –even the people. I found ground transportation into the city. At the last stop, I asked the driver directions to the train station, and then wrapped myself in my blanket and walked as fast as I could. At the CPR counter I was told that the cheapest ticket to Vancouver was sixty-five dollars. I explained my situation, and was directed to the CNR counter, where I got a ticket for 42$ that included onward bus and ferry transportation to Victoria. The exchange left me with 3$ for food during the long train journey across Canada.

Chapter 4: *Journey to India*

A few days after I arrived back in Victoria I became very ill. It was far worse than any flu or cold –every part of my body and mind felt exhausted. I began to vomit and lost interest in food. First my eyes turned yellow, then my skin: the doctor said I had infectious hepatitis, and I was hospitalized. Soon my piss was brown and my shit was pale green as my liver lost the capacity to process bile. I became too weak to stand, and had such a high fever that I had trouble recognizing family and friends when they came to visit.

In hospital my ears were tormented all day by the sound of a radio coming from the next bed. The endless commercials, the forced cheerfulness –even the music was painful. Nurses and doctors came and went like phantoms at the edge of a nightmare. My thought process drifted beyond the reach of any comforting or familiar subject, as if my brain was as diseased as my liver.

My abdomen became swollen and tender to the point that I could not bear even the weight of a blanket. It was explained to me that treatment was "symptomatic", which meant that there was no treatment beyond rest. For the first week I did not even have the strength to stand, and never left the bed. As the pain from my liver subsided an infernal itching began as my skin took over some of the functions that my liver could no longer perform. I learned that the liver has over 400 known vital functions. Hepatitis was my first real taste of mortality. I must have contracted it in Mexico, perhaps in the desert, or in jail.

I was fortunate to have a very caring doctor who found me a private room on the infectious diseases ward. It had a window, and I could look out at the trees, where the first signs of spring were beginning to show. The fever left first, then the tenderness in my liver, followed by a return of my appetite. The itching persisted for a month. Once a week the doctor came and took a blood and urine sample, and announced that I should stay in bed for another week. During the two months that I was in hospital, three people on the ward died of hepatitis.

During the second month of my rest there I had nothing to do but reflect on my recent adventures, and on the vulnerable nature of my health and freedom. After studying the biology and functions of the liver I decided to become a vegetarian. I explored the spiritual literature of the world in a search for some direction that would help me fulfill the vision that had been given to me in Mexico.

The hospital was called St. Joseph's, and was part of a Catholic complex that included a convent, a church, and a nursing school. Once a week the Mother Superior would visit, and inquire if there was anything I needed. She was always kind and caring. I would ask her questions about whatever path I was studying at the time, and she always expressed interest without departing for a moment from her own beliefs. I felt drawn to the teachings from the East, and it never occurred to me that any real spiritual path could be close at hand.

The day finally came when the levels of bile in my blood were low enough for my doctor to recommend I be discharged. It was spring and I felt elated to be out of hospital, but soon my weakened system came down with flu and I was back in bed. When this passed, regaining health became an obsession. I began a raw food vegetarian diet, and began to exercise a little every day, going for walks and doing yoga postures.

Spring came and I was re-hired by the Dept. of Highways and stationed once again to Kamloops. It was healthy, outdoor work that consisted mainly of running survey points for road construction in different locations around the province. Every Friday we would drive back to Kamloops, and I would explore the country and camp out during the weekends in order to save my living allowance. My favorite spot was near Williams Lake, beside a beaver pond. I would sleep under a cedar tree on a small hill, and just sit and watch the beavers. Once I saw a black fox with a white tip on its tail. Sunday night I would hitch back to Kamloops and sleep in the gardens of the general hospital. There was a place were they piled the grass cuttings and it was always soft and warm. On Monday morning I would report for work again. I followed my routine of yoga and meditation, and ate raw fruits and vegetables. My body became light and healthy, and my mind became clear and focused.

The crew found my behavior a bit odd, but my boss happened to be from India, and we got along very well. His name was Jaswant Chauhan, and he rekindled my interest in the wisdom of the East by telling me stories about India. I became determined to visit that country and search for spiritual guidance there.

Towards the end of the season I began to relax my strict raw-food diet, but remained a vegetarian. The food served in the truck stops and restaurants along the highways where we worked did not interest me, and one day I invited Jaswant to have dinner with me at the motel where we stayed. My idea was to cook a vegetarian meal, but he quickly took over, and began to teach me Indian cooking. Every day after work we would get together and cook up curries, make chapattis, and talk about India.

In September of 1970 I left Victoria with a friend, Peter, whom I had met on the highway crew. Our flight from Edmonton to London on a charter jet cost just $108. This included unlimited free drinks, and most of the people on board were headed for October fest in Munich. It was a wild flight, with Peter and me remaining sober and serious in the midst of the party. We were both into yoga and meditation, and at that stage in our journeys, did not even drink tea or coffee.

It was morning when we landed in Gatwick airport. The sun was shining. Perhaps my blood recognized the land of its origin, for I felt a deep love for the land. We walked a short distance from the airport, and fell asleep under a tree in a quiet field. The most difficult part of the journey was over.

Our family had never fitted in very well in Canada, and now I began to understand why. England was different. This hit me at our very first stop: my godfather's school in Surrey. It was only a short hitchhike from the airport through countryside that I found amazingly beautiful. We passed small farms surrounded by stone walls, wooded hills, valleys, streams, and villages that blended in with the landscape. The driver who had picked us up went out of his way to drop us off at the gate of Kingham Hill School. We were deep in the Surrey countryside, and the school stood like a castle alone on a hill surrounded by playing fields and gardens. An old Rolls Royce drove out from the gatehouse and quietly passed by. It was driven by a lady of dignified appearance who turned out to be my godmother, Ann Hall.

Fortunately they were expecting us, as to just "drop in," in a rural Canadian way, would have been out of the question. We were soon shown in to the headmaster's study, where my godfather, John Hall, awaited us. He was genuinely pleased to meet me, and extended his warm welcome to my friend, Peter. The word that describes him best is 'refined'. He had the same accent as my father, the same relaxed confidence that came with the Cambridge education and background that they shared.

We had time to wash up and change before joining them for lunch in the school dining room. The boys were all there, in identical gray-flannel uniforms, but of many different races, as this school was where the rich from many countries sent their boys. We attracted some attention, and the room was buzzing with conversation until John simply clapped his hands twice, lightly, bringing instant silence. It was not fear, but respect that moved these students. I understood why my father had given up teaching in Canada after only one year.

In London, we crashed with a friend of a friend, a musician from Victoria who had made it in London with a group called "May Blitz". We stayed there just long enough to find a cheap room in Earl's Court, where we stayed for the next two weeks. Our purpose in London was to collect the various visas we would need for the overland trip to India. In the Afghanistan embassy, I was offered the longest ride in my life as a hitchhiker: London to Calcutta. This was from a real eastern "salt" –an Englishman of about 60 who had spent most of his life in India. He was lean, tanned, and cynical.

"Do you want to know what the East is like?" he asked me: "well, it stinks."

I declined his offer, but there were times during my over-land journey that I regretted this.

Peter had his own inner journey, and one day we hunted for an address he had of a man called Asiz Balleau, reputed to be a Sufi from Persia. We finally found his humble two room suite on a quiet street in Earl's Court. A sign outside his window read: "Sufi Singh Society." Peter requested that I stay outside while he went in alone. I faithfully waited on the opposite side of the street and looked with longing at those mysterious windows where the first wise person of my search lived. I imagined that Peter was indeed having some wonderful experience from which I had been excluded, but then he came out and waved for me to join them.

"He is asking for you."

I was momentarily elated, thinking that perhaps I was the 'chosen one' instead. My search for a natural way to reach the same state of consciousness that I had experienced in Mexico on the mushrooms had led me into Eastern spiritual paths where the guru was considered essential. Peter and I both held the stubborn conviction that some powerful, saintly person was going to bless us and point the way towards God.

"Welcome, welcome," said Asiz when I entered his room. He sat on his narrow bed, with his feet folded under him on a carpet. He was small and frail, with huge, dark eyes. I felt at once the presence of an extraordinary man. He asked about our journey, and listened with great interest to all that we told him. When the time came for us to leave, he invited us to visit him again.

The next day, while waiting for the Turkish Embassy to open, I saw a poster advertising a concert of classical music from Pakistan. There was a photo of two men called Salamat and Nazakat Ali, with three other musicians backing them up on sarangi, harmonium, and tabla. I wrote down the address—it was happening the very next evening.

Peter accompanied me to the small concert hall across the Thames. It only held about two hundred people, but every seat was filled, mostly with men from India and Pakistan. I did not know what to expect. The musicians were greeted with warm applause. The Ali brothers sat in front, on either side of a small stage that had been covered with a carpet, while the other musicians sat slightly behind and between them. The Ali brothers were short, round men with wonderful smiles. They wore long shirts, woolen waistcoats, and very loose, flowing trousers. They sat cross-legged, with their instruments held on their laps. Salamat Ali played a harp like instrument called a delharubar, and Nazakat played the tamboura while they sang.

There are no words to describe the music that I heard that night. I was transported somewhere that must have been close to heaven. I found myself gasping, unable to think, with tears streaming down my face, beyond shame or any other known state of mind. They sang long ragas that started very slowly and then uncoiled, spiraling ever faster towards an ecstatic climax that left the whole hall in stunned silence for a moment before applause erupted.

The following day I tried to tell Asiz about my experience, but he knew, and stopped me with the words:

"They lifted you up to the feet of God. What can you say? Just thank you....thank you!"

I felt that I was alone with him that day. He told us a few things about his Sufi path, and his own music. He showed us his guitar, and said that he had first trained on the piano, and had given concerts, but had left it for the guitar. We learned later that he had doctorates in both music and literature. I told him that my journey to India would take me through Iran.

"Take the time to walk from Shiraz to Isfahan," he suggested: "It is an ancient route, and often the friend appears to pilgrims there."

"Who is "the friend"?" I asked.

"Khidr, the one that helps us find God."

He offered us tea. Peter and I exchanged glances, and I went on to say: "We don't drink tea."

"Oh," he replied gently: "you are better than me!"

I have few regrets in life, but to this day I would give anything to have that cup of tea with Asiz Balleau! I never made the journey from Shiraz to Isfahan. Years later I saw a photo of Isfahan, with the turquoise blue domes of its mosques set like jewels in the desert, and my body shook with a grief that seemed to have no end.

We left London with the necessary visas and hitched our way to the ferry across the channel. Between rides we found ourselves standing beside a road on the perimeter of Canterbury. I could see the famous cathedral, and the school where my father had been sent at the age of thirteen. He had told me that it was a good preparation for life: after that, nothing worse could possibly happen. I was passing through, a wanderer who looked down briefly on those green fields and gray walls, while waiting for the next kind driver to carry me away. The traditions and rites of passage that had helped form my parents' consciousness had been left here, and I had not found anything in Canada to replace them. I was without social identity.

Peter and I separated in Venice. He wanted to explore more of Italy and Greece, while I wanted to be in India. Even the lovely canals and architecture of Venice held little attraction for me. It was not until reaching Istanbul that I felt any real excitement. This happened in the middle of the night when my flight from Athens touched down at the airport outside Istanbul. I was always trying to save money, so I searched for a cheap hotel and ended up in the artists' quarter of the city. Even at that hour I could hear hammers and chisels at work. My room was small and filthy, with a wooden cot covered with old woolen blankets. A single barred window looked out onto an alley filled with yellow rectangles of light. I fell asleep to the sound of metal on stone.

That night I lost my first encounter with a persistent enemy: bedbugs. I awoke with a vicious itching all over my body. The bites all became infected, took weeks to heal, and left me with small, round scars. Nowhere did I encounter such vicious bedbugs as in Istanbul.

There is electricity in the air of Islamic countries. Perhaps it is the mystery of the hidden feminine, the quick flashes of beauty from behind a veil, or the sublime architecture, or the constant call to prayer. Sources of water always seem sacred and scarce, and the desert whispers around with the voice of death just too close for boredom or carelessness.

Istanbul to Ankara was the longest bus ride of my life: 36 hours on a hard seat designed for people much shorter. We stopped for a few hours rest in a place called Eskisahir. I joined the little group of foreign travelers in the café-bar of the hotel where we waited, and drank Sahlab, a non-alcoholic drink made with hot milk. It was crowded, and I found myself sitting next to two women in black burkhas. I could not tell anything about them, but a low and sultry voice spoke to me in English, asking where I was from. I turned my chair around by way of joining them at their table. Nothing was visible through the finely stitched veils that covered their faces in such a way that they could see without being seen. My mind just stopped, it was such an unexpected invitation into the unknown. They asked me the usual questions about my occupation and the purpose of my visit and how I liked Turkey. They remained utterly feminine and mysterious, and I could not think of anything to ask them in return. I was awkward and inhibited around women even in my own country. Then one of them slowly pulled back her veil and revealed her beautiful, smiling face. I felt intoxicated. It was perhaps the most seductive movement I had ever seen. She was quite young, perhaps my own age, and her eyes sparkled with life.

So it was that a vast and complex world, with a diversity and length of history that far exceed the west, welcomed me with wonder after wonder. I saw little of Iran until reaching Mashad, and there I spent most of my remaining money on Turquoise and an old carpet. In fact I was only able to put a down-payment of $100 on the carpet, and promised to send the dealer the balance later, at which time he could kindly mail the carpet to my address in Canada. When it finally thumped onto my doorstep two years later it was a small miracle that proved many skeptics wrong. The turquoise could be sold for a big profit in Japan, or so I was told, but I never reached Japan, and eventually sold it to a native artist in Canada where it became the eyes of wooden animals and birds that he carved.

I wrote to my bank and requested that my remaining funds be sent to the American Express office in Kabul, Afghanistan. Every capital city surely had to have an American Express office. When I finally reached Kabul, with about fifty dollars left, I found there was no such facility. I was slowly being removed from the insulating security that money can provide.

1970 was one of the last years of glorious freedom and peace for that proud country. If I had known what was coming, perhaps I would have stayed longer, and just been witness to the ancient ways that survived there. Camel caravans crossed the desert with slow majesty, floating like dreams above the quivering sands. Far away, the blue domes of the mosques gave the first promise of shade and refreshment, and it was a thrill to see them, even through the windows of a rattling bus. I took the time to read a bit about the history of these countries, and inquired about their prophet, and his teachings, but I learned very little. It was loneliness that led me to befriend the local people on my travels, and I was met with warm hospitality and uncritical acceptance again and again. Men were happy to share their hookah with me, sitting in the shade of a tree or in front of a small shop. The barber would pause between snips of his scissors to take a puff of hashish, and go on to tell me that he was saving his money in order to take a second wife.

Once I bought a pomegranate from a man with a cart made from bicycle wheels. I picked through the red fruit carefully, trying to find a good one, while a group of men in turbans looked on. I made my selection, paid the vendor, and immediately cut the fruit in half. The inside, instead of being full of juicy red kernels, was brown and full of insects. The men all began to laugh and the vendor smiled in a cautious way. Like a fool, I got angry and accused him of cheating me. One of the men walked over, and with a kind smile, said simply: "The joke is on you!"

There was nothing to do but laugh with them. Then they showed me the tiny hole where the insects had bored into the fruit, so that next time I would know better.

There were also times when the East seemed like a desert filled with scavengers waiting to take anything and everything, and I held on to my passport, ticket, and money as if my very life were at stake. I met a traveler who had lost everything, and was just surviving day to day while waiting for help to arrive. I heard the story of a young man who had gone to a clinic to sell a pint of blood, only to be discovered dead, having been drained of every drop. There were days when it felt as if every bit of my health, innocence, and energy were being sucked out of me by the endless poverty and suffering that I saw. But then my perception would change, and all I could see was happiness and beauty.

The carefree cheerfulness of some of the very poorest people amazed me at first, but in time I came to understand that they were not as poor as I thought. When the day finally came that I had no money or return ticket left, I felt a strange and unfamiliar freedom, as if the creator had just lifted me out of a prison I had never known was there.

I entered India from Pakistan in early December. I had twenty-five dollars left. It was necessary to cross the border on foot so I shouldered my pack and walked alone to the immigration desk at Kasur, where a woman in a colorful sari waited. Outside, under a tree, she received me graciously and asked for my passport. Very slowly, she looked through my passport, and then put it on the desk in front of her, and called to a servant who brought us two glasses of chai on a tray. She said simply: "Take tea."

We sat there sipping tea while she inquired about my journey, my purpose for visiting India, what places I planned to see, and what countries I had already seen. We finished our tea, and the servant removed the empty glasses. We both just sat there, while a warm and gentle wind sang in the branches of the tree that shaded us. Eventually I asked if everything was in order, and if it was all right for me to proceed.

"Of course," she replied with a smile: "I just don't want to see you go. You may stay in India as long as you like."

She pushed my passport back to me.

"Thank you." I said.

"Welcome to India."

And so I set foot for the first time in the land that was to become my home. I took a local bus to Firozpur, from where I planned to catch the train for New Delhi the next morning. I found a cheap hotel room near the station, and went to the bazaar to find something to drink. I was feeling quite ill, and found a vendor selling fresh orange juice. He squeezed them for me, but when the glass was full, suddenly added a spoonful of salt, and handed it to me. Apparently that was how they drank orange juice there. I settled for a couple of bananas that cost only twenty-five paise.

I felt worse the next day, and used my last strength to board a third class carriage on the train to Delhi. I was so weakened by fever that I needed to lie down, but there was not even any place to sit. Eventually I crawled under a seat and found rest among the beedie butts and spilt chai on the floor. My fever became worse throughout that endless day and night. By the time the train pulled in to Old Delhi station, it was so crowded that a solid wall of legs kept me pinned under the seat. Only after everyone had got off was I able to crawl out onto the platform. I found a seat on a bench, and bought a glass of chai from a man in a turban who was walking up and down the platform, shouting: "Chai! Garum chai! Meethai garum chai!" It was nectar!

I had the address of a missionary from the Baptist church of Maryland, who had been a friend of Jaswant Chauhan's years ago. Edward, my younger brother, had reached India a month before me, and was waiting for me there. I took a taxi to Patel Nagar and found the simple apartment of the Reverend John Dorsey. His servant, a local woman who was preparing food, let me in and showed me to a room with two cots. On one of them I recognized some things belonging to my brother, and I collapsed onto the other. It was cool and quiet.

At some point my brother came in, and found me there. It was a huge relief to see his familiar face. Later John came back from his work, and welcomed me to his home. While they had dinner, I slept.

For two weeks I lay on the cot, recovering from fever and exhaustion. During that time I experienced India mainly through the sounds that came to my fevered brain. All day I could hear a symphony of life passing on the street below. At night, the strange calls of the chowkidors floated in the darkness as they let each other know where they were. Somewhere a loudspeaker on a Mosque called people to prayer five times a day. In the early morning, another loudspeaker from a temple played Hindu devotional music. It was enchanting, and I longed to regain my strength and explore this new world.

I was curious about a strange transformation that had taken place in my brother. He was quite serious, and had a routine that included several hours of volunteer work with John. He seemed at ease both in India, and in the Christian environment of John's home. When Sunday came, he accompanied John to church. Finally he confessed to me that shortly after arriving there, he had joined John and some of his friends at a prayer meeting, had a powerful experience, and become a Christian. This was the last thing I had expected, given Edward's secretive and antisocial behavior in the past. But there it was, and I could only be happy for him, and observe with interest. I had grown up so close to him that I never noticed things that were quite obvious to everyone else.

After two weeks I felt better and we said good-bye to John and caught the train to our first destination, Varanasi. On the way, we stopped to see the Taj Mahal. I went alone at night, crossed the Jamuna River and sat on the bank to see the light of the full moon glowing on this most beautiful of tombs. Another twelve hours on a train and we entered India's holiest city through the vast cavern of metal that is Varanasi station.

In Varansi we stayed at the home of an Indian missionary friend of John's. My brother was fast becoming irritable and critical of everything Indian, while I was fascinated and feeling quite at ease. I loved the pagan richness of the Hindu religion and the diversity of peoples that make up North Indian society.

On Christmas Day we went for a walk along the bank of the Ganges. At one point we stopped to watch a curious ceremony. A small group of Indian men and women in western dress were standing waist-deep in the river. An albino Indian in a suit and tie was conducting baptisms. His pink skin and white hair contrasted with everything around him, including the brown water of the river. One by one he pushed the heads of the converts under the water while reciting prayers in Hindi. It was a solemn event, and seemed sad and lifeless in comparison to the colorful chaos of devotion that crowded the riverbank.

A second event finally ended Edward's brief encounter with Christianity. I had accompanied him to a Sunday church service during which a few children came forward to repeat verses they had memorized. After a couple of small girls had rattled off their lines perfectly to polite applause, a much larger and older boy got up to take his turn. He was unable to remember a single word, and stood there silent and shaking with agonized self-consciousness while the priest hovered over him and the congregation waited.... and waited.... and waited. My brother and I exchanged glances and quickly left this unbearable scene.

Two experiences remain in my memory from that first exploration of India. We had reached Mysore in the south, and I was climbing the many steps to visit the Chamunda Devi temple on a hill overlooking the city. Near the top was a huge statue of Nandi, Shiva's bull, sitting beside the path. I stopped to rest and enjoy the sunset, and then went to take a look around. Behind the statue I saw a cave among boulders on the side of the hill. I never could resist a cave, so I went over for a closer look, and found a small fire burning at the entrance. I peered into the darkness, and saw that there were candles shining in the back of the cave. The entrance was low, but inside was a dry and spacious cavern. I crawled in and sat on the sand and waited. Slowly my eyes adjusted and the candlelight revealed an extraordinary figure on a low shelf of rock. A man sat there in the full lotus posture, with his back straight and a mass of black hair falling down around his bare shoulders. His eyes shone with a powerful but gentle joy. His posture was so calm that his body seemed to float in the darkness. There was no trace of care or suffering on his face, just a relaxed smile. While I sat there the silence of the cave and the powerful presence of the yogi turned my attention inward, and I remembered why I had come to India. Here was a man who perhaps embodied the very state of consciousness I was seeking. I was still doing a little meditation, but during the long months of travel, and then the weeks of sickness and fatigue, I had been so busy with the struggle to survive that I had forgotten my original vision. There was a big difference between my shallow, scattered state of mind and the calm, clear consciousness of this yogi. I left the cave with the feeling that I had lost my way, but I never forgot those eyes, so wild, gentle and free.

The second event happened in Madras. I had come down with an ear infection after swimming in the ocean at Cape Comorin, and by the time we reached Madras I had blood coming out of both ears. The pain and the heat had kept me awake for two days and one evening I lay down naked under a fan and fell asleep. When I awoke it was dark, the electricity had gone out, and the fan had been stopped for hours. The fan had been cooling me a bit, but, more important, it had been keeping the mosquito from settling. There were 150 bites on my left arm alone, and then I stopped counting. It was clear that I would get no rest until the itching stopped, so I went out to walk it off. It was about eleven at night, and the streets were almost empty. After walking for about an hour I sat on a bench near a street light to rest. I saw three small boys walk out of the darkness across the road to stop near me in the dim circle of yellow light. They exchanged whispers and then came over to ask me my name and where I was from. Their eyes and teeth gleamed in the hot city night. They had no shoes and wore only a loin cloth. We talked for a bit, and when it came time for them to go, I gave the eldest boy a five rupee note. Again they talked in their own language for a bit, and then the smallest boy took the money and ran off into the darkness, leaving the other two to keep me company. Five minutes later the boy returned, holding a little parcel in his hands. He handed it to the eldest boy, who then passed it on to me. A page out of a school book had been wrapped around a package of Turtle brand mosquito coils. Then they gave me the change.

"You keep this money." I said.

"No. You are our friend."

With this they turned and walked over to a narrow space between two buildings behind us. They each pulled out a piece of cardboard that was hidden there, and vanished into the night. The cardboard was what they slept on in some corner of the city, and was perhaps their only possession. They had seen the mosquito bites all over my skin, and had done what they could for me without thinking of themselves. I had been touched by something wonderful and my suffering became nothing. What more can I say?

We left India for Sri Lanka. There had been a few moments of magic, but I had slowly become a wanderer without purpose, always looking for the cheapest room, the cheapest way to travel, and I was beginning to think about going home. We dragged ourselves from town to town, country to country. My brother flew home from Bangkok while I forced myself to stay on and try to find some value in a trip that had become hollow and pointless. I hitched all over Thailand, reaching Chiang Rai near the Mekong River and the border with Laos. At least it was cooler in the mountains. I saw the files of orange robed monks on their morning begging rounds, but I had no interest in Buddhism. I kept peering into other people's lives, but had no real life of my own. I returned to Bangkok in April, when both the humidity and temperature are extreme. I had a standby ticket, and waited at the airport, but there was no room and it was a week until the next flight. I hitched up to Udon Thani in the north east of Thailand, just to pass time until the next flight. There was no room on the next flight either. So I paid some extra money to ensure a seat and quickly returned to Chiang Rai to wait yet another week.

I arrived back in Canada in time to sign on with the Dept. of Highways once again. Clearly, my trip had been a failure. The original vision given to me by the hongos, and my search for a way to verify it, had been lost somewhere between Istanbul and Bangkok. All I had to nourish my spirit was the memory of those street kids in Madras, and the eyes of the yogi in the cave.

Chapter 5: *Prayer*

The paving season began again and I was stationed in Duncan on Vancouver Island. Once again the highway crew assembled at a motel where we were assigned rooms. It was a dismal living situation, and after work I searched the town for an alternative. I found a room in a boarding house, but this was also depressing and isolated. Then I met a young woman I had known at university. Her name was Shirley, and she had just graduated from the registered nursing program in Vancouver. There was a new hospital in Duncan that had just hired her and four other women from her class. They had rented a big house near the hospital. Five of the rooms were occupied, and they were looking for someone to rent the sixth. For once in my life I did not hesitate.

This turn of fortune began a year of happiness. I was living in a beautiful, rural house with five beautiful, young women. We were all employed, optimistic and healthy. I became the envy of my co-workers on the highway crew. They were forever looking for reasons to visit me, and would then try to make time with the nurses. I soon had to tell them to leave us alone.

At the beginning of the week, we would each put twenty-five dollars into a kitty, and this would pay for groceries and other household expenses. I would cook curries for everyone, and leave them on the stove for the nurses when they got home from their shifts at the hospital. There was a constant flow of life and creativity in the house, and with the shared trust and respect we had a happy community.

Over the course of the summer the nurses came and went, some formed relationships, and some moved on. Fritz Perls, the creator of Gestalt therapy, had lived in the area for a time, and founded an institute. A man called Ray Wollens, who worked with Dr. Perls, began leading his own seminars on personal awakening at a local pub, the Maple Bay Inn. These weekend seminars had a profound and liberating effect on Shirley, the original occupant of the house, and finally she, too, moved on. Eventually I found myself alone in my room on the second floor, uncertain about the future of my new home.

While Shirley and the other nurses were making their exit, I heard that the house had been rented again. I continued to live in my room, and work for the paving branch. One day after I had been alone there for almost two weeks, I heard that the new tenants were on their way over. I can only guess that my natural optimism allowed me to just be in the house when they showed up, trusting that somehow things would work out. They arrived, having been warned of a "squatter" who refused to vacate their new home. I heard strange voices one Sunday morning followed by the sound of footsteps coming up the stairs. I emerged from my room to find four young men and a woman standing there, all looking quite nervous.

"Hello," I began: "my name is Mark. I come with the house!"

I had intended this to be a joke, but they remained quite serious and resolved. Their leader was a very kind looking man, perhaps in his mid twenties, who looked at me through large, round glasses, and did his best to sound grim:

"Well, I am afraid that just won't do," he said: "we need you to vacate the house as soon as possible. We are opening a meditation center here, and have to get to work right away."

"What kind of meditation?" I inquired.

He looked a bit annoyed with my question. At this point, one of his friends who had been exploring emerged from Shirley's room holding a cardboard box with some empty hypodermic needles in it. She was, after all, a registered nurse, but they did not know this, and took this for evidence of drug use and clear proof of my depravity. They consulted together, and then confronted me once again with renewed determination:

"Look here," someone began.

I had already decided that these were good people, and was convinced that somehow that house was to remain my home.

"Would you like to have chai?" I asked. I did not know it, but Gordon was a meditation teacher who had just re-turned from India. Protests were murmured, but I was already on my way to the kitchen where I prepared chai for everyone.

They turned out to be students of TM, and Gordon had attended a three month retreat in Rishikesh and was now qualified to teach that technique on behalf of the Maharishi. I explained that I was already an initiate, and would be delighted to live with them in their new center.

At this point the subject of the needles and suspicion of drug use was raised, but my explanation that nurses had recently occupied those rooms was accepted, and I was welcomed aboard.

This unlikely meeting began some of the deepest friendships and happiest times of my life. The innocent faith and enthusiasm that my new friends had for their Guru, and the meditation he taught, inspired me to begin meditating again myself, although I never recovered faith in the Maharishi. Gordie occupied the downstairs bedroom. Steve and Loretta, who were engaged, moved into a room upstairs –fortunately at some distance from my own. A quiet man called Cliff occupied another room whenever he was not away working in a logging camp. A young man called Mike who rode a Harley moved into another room. The energy in the house changed, and I adapted. I was determined to demonstrate my sincerity in yoga and mediation as they worked to redecorate the living room in preparation for initiations and group meditation.

And yes, for a few months anyway, our house became the quiet, spiritual sanctuary that Gordie had envisioned. Then, gradually, parties became more frequent than initiations. While we remained faithful to our routine of starting the day with a group meditation at six a.m., drinking beer began to replace the evening meditation. We were a crazy household. We shared the vision of some blessed state of freedom that would one day result from our meditation and yoga. We were all too willing to project this vision onto questionable characters that were capable of reflecting our illusions back to us. Titles such as "His Holiness" and "His Divinity" were readily ascribed to teachers from the East by people who would have been very quick to notice the obvious absurdity of such titles had they become attached to a westerner. While my friends in the meditation center remained devoted to their Guru, I kept my doubts to myself, and continued my own practice.

At this time I met a native man, Charlie Joe, who stayed with us for a few weeks. He was looking after a young relative who was being initiated as a dancer in the tradition of the Cowichan people. The process was secret, and Charlie would not talk about it. He was gone much of the time, returning only to sleep and eat. I learned that the initiation focused on the new dancer having a vision, in which the spirit of an animal or bird would teach him a song and a dance. At the conclusion of the ceremony, the new dancer would demonstrate this song and dance to the elders, who were able to tell if it was authentic or not. Once a novice received this visit from the spirit world they were recognized as dancers, and would perform during traditional ceremonies. The native people believed that the creator communicated with us through animals and birds.

During this time Gordon became very friendly with Charlie Joe and his people. They even invited him to become a dancer, which was a rare honor for a non-native person. Gordon later told me that he had felt that he could not accept this invitation for the sake of the people whom he had initiated into TM, who would begin to have doubts if their teacher took another path.

The one thing I learned from Charlie Joe was that every morning during the training period, the new dancer would take a ritual power bath in the Cowichan River. At a protected place, they would enter the water four times, and then dry off without using a towel. I went to the river one morning to try this practice, and found it very refreshing. It became part of my routine to run to the river first thing in the morning, go in and out four times, and then run on the spot until dry. Refreshed and awake, I would then return for morning meditation. I continued this practice into winter.

One cold morning, while I was jumping up and down naked in the snow, a fisherman suddenly appeared coming up the path through the trees. Our eyes met and we both just had to laugh. I said nothing, and he continued his way upstream, shaking his head inside a warm parka.

Once again, the community in the house began to disperse. Steve and Loretta got married and moved into a place of their own. Cliff left for a logging camp in the north. Gordon began a career as a reporter and moved to Ladysmith as editor of the Ladysmith Chronicle. I decided to try something new and registered for a month in a Gestalt residential facility that had opened nearby.

It was a dismal experience. The group consisted of twelve men and two women. It was lead by a man called Brian who insisted he was not the leader. He and his wife had rented a farmhouse for the year as an experiment in Gestalt community living. She did not participate in the groups, and appeared to be always in a bad mood. We would meet twice a day in the living room for.....I was never quite sure what. Any attempt to define what we were doing was frowned upon by Brian. Any suggestion that he provide leadership or guidance was called "copping out". A few people there, including Brian, his wife, a beautiful young girl of 15 called Lisa, and her boyfriend, Tom, had lived in a similar community with Fritz Perls. They were all very good at defending themselves, and at attacking others. Lisa was really exceptionally relaxed, and radiated natural, healthy sexuality. Tom, who was about 30, was the only happy man in the house. He bragged openly of "his power", and was quick to confront others with "their bullshit."

Meanwhile the farmers had moved out into the guest cottage, and continued to run the farm. They needed the money from the rent of the main house. We all spent some time each day helping around the farm. I milked the goats.

'Group', as it was called, consisted of us all sitting around in a circle, waiting for something to happen: something called 'Gestalt'. Whatever that was, it had happened in Fritz Perl's groups, but was clearly not happening here. I infuriated the other members by continuing my yoga and meditation, and by refusing to be violent or confrontational in group. The only other woman present got in my face one time and said: "You are such an asshole! Such an ASSHOLE!" I felt that in some way perhaps she was right, and was trying to tell me something, but I just could not get it. One day a young man from New York attacked me and tried seriously to hurt me. With an effort, I threw him off, but he had managed to bruise my ribs. Yes, years later when I finally got in touch with my anger and dropped the spiritual persona I understood what had pissed them off. The end of our month came, and I left the place without a single meaningful experience...except for the warm memory of my time caring for the goats, and a few honest moments spent with the farmers.

I moved from Duncan to Victoria, and applied for unemployment insurance. I lived in a two room cottage on a rock beside the sea. The sound of the waves and the gulls reminded me of my childhood.

That winter I met Lucille. She lived in Duncan and I had first met her when she came for meditation classes. We met again at a blues concert. She put her arms around my neck and said she missed me. Enough time had passed for me to be ready to risk intimacy again, but I had not forgotten the pain of my last relationship. It soon became clear that we were on a collision course. Lucille had a street-wise sense of humor, and one day while I was attempting to express my feelings, she said simply: "It's bigger than both of us!"

Just prior to becoming intimate, I explained my fears and told her of my recent heartbreak. In summary, I said I would rather we never had sex than go through another unwanted pregnancy.

She assured me that she was taking the necessary precautions, and we immediately had wild, wonderful sex. At some point the bed broke, but we hardly noticed. I was only too happy to leave the responsibility of preventing conception to her, and never inquired exactly what precautions she was taking.

Lucille found work in a greenhouse near Victoria. I began desperately looking for work in the area, but could find nothing. Some friends had a tree planting contract near Lake Cowichan, so I joined them at their camp at the north end of the lake. It snowed, planting was impossible, and we agreed to return in a week, at which time it snowed again. The third time it snowed, we decided to plant anyway. I was put on a crew called "the slugs." We each had a quota of a thousand trees a day, but this was impossible, as snow, rock, and piles of slash covered most of the ground. Inspection was minimal, and perhaps we set a record by putting five hundred seedlings in a single hole. It was healthy but brutal work, and so I decided to take my chances with the Dept. of Highways once again.

For the first time, I felt the void where meaningful work needed to be. I had lost sight of my vision, and there was only Lucille to take its place. This was dangerous ground.

I was posted to Prince Rupert. We spent our last night together and then I drove to Port Hardy to catch the ferry to Rupert, leaving Lucille in the cabin by the sea. It was a gray and dismal journey. I reported to the highways office, and was shown to the motel where the crew stayed. It rained all the time. My mood was as bad as the weather.

The others were all long-term highway employees, and I just did not fit in. Living at that motel with the rain falling on pavement and nothing but the sound of traf-

fic or the television next door was just too depressing.
When the day's work was done, I once again drove around
town looking for alternative accommodation. My circles
got wider until one evening I found myself beside a lake
about 20 miles out of town. It was near the gravel pit that
we would be using for road construction. On a small hill
behind the pit the roof of a cottage was just visible among
the trees. The snow was three feet thick and covered everything but the road. I trudged up the hill and found an
open door framed in snow-laden branches of evergreens.
The roof of the place had caved in under the weight. Near
the front door was a woodshed with a supply of firewood.
Inside everything was new, but damp and abandoned. The
shelves were stocked with food, there were pictures on
the walls, carpets on the floor, but the broken roof sagged
down into the living room. I imagined myself living there,
cleaning the place up and perhaps fixing the roof. Outside, the rain poured down into the heavy snow. It was
a crazy idea. The cottage was full of sorrow and broken
dreams.

I went outside and looked around, trying to imagine
who had lived there. It was an isolated and beautiful spot. I
ploughed on up the hill to see what I could find. There was
a small clearing at the top and an older, smaller cabin. The
door was open, but inside it was dry and empty. There was
a front room with a window that looked out over the lake,
a table and two chairs. A smaller back room held a large
wooden bed. There were a few shelves and a chimney pipe
sticking through the roof above the place where a stove
used to be. I could see myself living there.

When the weekend came, I began my search for the
owner of that property. I asked around, and the trail ended
at the door of an apartment above a bar. The woman who
answered the door was about forty, and looked as if she had

been crying. Perhaps she was younger, but sorrow was heavy on her face. I told her that I was new to town, employed, and wanted to rent the small cottage.

"What, with the roof fallen in and all this snow?" she replied.

"No, the other one....the cabin on the hill."

"Oh, you want to live there?" She looked at me more closely. "Sure, you can rent it. Come on in."

We agreed on fifty dollars per month rent. She had no keys or lock for the place, but promised to come and visit me sometime.

I quickly checked out of the motel, told the crew chief were I would be living, and suggested that he assign me to be the "crusher man", as the guy who inspected the gravel coming out of the pit was called. This idea must have gone over well with the engineer, as it was clear that I was a misfit on that crew. I packed my things into my station wagon and drove out to the cabin. I had to leave the vehicle at the bottom of the drive and carry everything up through the snow. It was brutally cold that night, but I was happy to be away from the motel and the highway crew. I had Sunday to fix the place up and make myself comfortable.

Finding a way to keep warm and dry was the first challenge. The other cottage had a free standing fireplace in it, and I lugged it up the hill and installed it as best I could, but it smoked and produced very little heat, so I put it back. I searched the area around the gravel pit, and was standing on a rise to look around when I noticed what looked like a stovepipe sticking up black above the snow. I ploughed over and discovered a collapsed cabin buried in a deep drift. Sure enough, when I followed the pipe down, digging with my hands, I found a stove under a pile of shingles. It was an old 'Charmer', made of cast iron with a decorated front and a silver handle. Somehow I got the thing onto my back, and stumbled back towards my cabin. I had to crawl up the hill on my hands and knees.

An hour later my 'Charmer' was blazing, the cabin was warm, and I was beginning to dry off. That night I slept well for the first time since arriving in Prince Rupert.

A month later the snow had melted and I was at work in the gravel pit. Except for a daily visit from the crew chief, I was left alone. I had an electric heater in the trailer where I ran a series of tests on the gravel to make sure it was crushed right. I put in a couple of benches so the men who worked in the pit had a warm, dry place to hang out.

On those rare days when the sun came out, everything just glowed with life and beauty. A small creek sang through a valley behind my hill, and I could hear loons calling on the lake. I learned to imitate their calls, and they would swim over to check me out.

Without electricity or telephone it was difficult to communicate with Lucille. After I had been there for about two months I received a letter from her, saying she was planning to come up and visit me. This was good news, as I was quite in love with her.

The day came for me to pick her up at the ferry. I was looking forward to her companionship during my lonely days and nights in the cabin. It was full summer when she arrived, but she was as cold as ice. I went to kiss her on the lips, but she turned her cheek. Something was wrong, but she would not tell me what. My confusion and frustration grew when it came time for bed, and she prepared a place for herself on the couch. I did not sleep much that night.

During the days I worked and in the evenings I came home to a very unhappy woman. This continued for about a week, and then one Sunday morning she told me that she had just had an abortion.

"But why didn't you tell me you were pregnant?"

"Don't you remember that big ultimatum you gave me when we first met, before we had slept together?"

I had forgotten. Like a fool, I said: "But I would have been happy to have a baby with you!"

Our relationship never recovered. Lucille soon returned to Victoria, and the rain poured down on the gravel pit and the gray, loon haunted waters of the lake.

It was my habit in the evenings to walk through the campsites in the park beside the lake and see if anyone was there. I had made friends with the park ranger, and occasionally I would find him there and we would talk. Usually, the campsites were empty. Soon after Lucille had left, on one rare, sunny evening I saw a man walking towards me on the road. As he approached I saw a very intense, almost crazy look in his eyes. I thought to myself, this guy is either a criminal or a saint.

It turned out he was a Christian evangelist from the southern USA. He was on a mission in the area, and was camped out with his wife and daughter. He introduced himself as the Reverend Billy Corbett. He asked me where I lived and if I knew of any places to rent in the area.

"There are only two houses out here," I replied: "The cabin I live in, and a cottage near me that has a broken roof."

"I am sure God has something for me!" he replied in a southern drawl: "He has not let me down yet! Can you show me this cottage with the broken roof?"

We walked back to the foot of the hill and up the driveway to the cottage. With the snow gone, it looked quite comfortable. The roof sagged, but it did not leak.

"This looks just fine to me! Just fine! I can fix this place up, no problem." His face just radiated faith and conviction.

"Well, I will be happy to have some neighbors." I told him: "It gets lonely out here"

I gave him the name and address of the woman who owned the property. A few days later I came home from work one day to see smoke coming from the chimney of the cottage. The door was open, and inside, Billy was frying fish on the large propane hotplate in the kitchen.

"Come on in and meet my wife and daughter," he said when he heard my knock.

The whole place had been cleaned up, and looked very much like a home. He introduced me to his wife, Margaret, and his daughter, Emily. Margaret was about 35 and had the same look of intense faith and devotion in her eyes as her husband. Their daughter was a girl of sixteen. She had long, brown hair and blue eyes. I had never seen such calm and confidence in anyone so young.

They invited me to join them for dinner.

Over the weeks that followed I had many conversations with Billy, Margaret and Emily. Often, I would come home from work, take my bath using a bucket of hot water, change, and join them for dinner. They overflowed with hospitality and enthusiasm for life. Billy often drove into town to teach and give sermons.

One evening, the dreaded question came: "Are you a Christian, Mark?"

He held me with his piercing blue eyes. There was just no doubt in his mind: if I was not Christian, I was bound for hell!

"I don't know," I replied, rather weakly: "I would describe myself as a seeker."

"What are you seeking?"

"Inner peace….truth….reality."

It all sounded so vague in the face of his unwavering certainty. I was lost and miserable, and no doubt it showed on my face and in my eyes.

He let me go that time, but a few days later he confronted me again: "I will tell you this, Mark: the devil is widening the gates of hell to welcome you in! Hell is just opening its gates wider and wider every day to welcome you in!" He pronounced "wider" as "waaahdah", drawling it out in a threatening way. His eyes became even more intense, and focused squarely on my squirming soul.

"If you get down on your knees and pray...right now! Get down on your knees and pray for Jesus to come into your life you will be saved from the very jaws of hell! Will you do that? I will pray with you. Right now....don't wait another minute!"

This I could not do, but I thanked him for his concern and friendship, and promised to reflect on what I had heard that day.

"Think it over. Jesus will be waiting for you, just waiting for your call, your prayers, and Jesus will come into your life and show you the way. Just you ask!" He held my hands in his. I could feel the genuine friendship, the concern of a good man who really believed he could make the difference between my salvation and an eternity of torture. While I could not accept his beliefs, I could not refuse his kindness.

Chapter 6: *Victor Smith*

I looked out over the lake and hill that seemed so close and friendly on a clear day, but had once again become remote and indifferent in clouds and mist. With the rain pounding on the shingles I finally got down on my knees and prayed that God come into my life in whatever form was best for me, in whatever way I might need. It was the first time I had really opened my heart and asked the creator for help.

That night I had a very clear and powerful dream. I was standing at the foot of an immense, old growth Douglas fir tree that stood beside the ocean. I was gazing up through the brown and green branches of the tree into a blue sky. I was waiting and watching for a golden eagle. A speck appeared, spiraling down towards me. It was clearly a large bird, and when it came to land on one of the higher branches, I could see the white tail and head of a bald eagle. This was disappointing, but again I turned my gaze towards heaven and waited. Another speck appeared, spiraling down larger and larger, and a magnificent eagle landed on the branch directly over my head. The sun gleamed on feathers of gold. The head and tail feathers were golden, and golden feathers covered the bird's legs. It was a golden eagle. I then looked down into the ocean where the shadow of the tree fell. The waters were deep and dark where green waves rolled in and out of the shadow. Suddenly a white whale came up from the depths and breached. Its huge body surged out from the shadow of the tree into the sunlight, and then crashed back into the water, sending up a wave that rushed towards me and broke, covering me with foam and salt water. Soaking wet, I followed a path beside the ocean until I came to a small cave in the rocks. It was a fertile place of earth and water, surrounded by moss and flowering plants. I could not see anything in the darkness of the cave, but it seemed to contain some sacred mystery and with great reverence I bowed my head to the ground.

This dream was like a visit to a familiar home of beauty and meaning from which I awakened into exile in Prince Rupert. With each day I was becoming more impatient with the duties and details of my work and my life. The trailer in the gravel pit was surrounded by noise and pollution. A huge jaw crusher, a cone crusher, and then a roller crusher reduced boulders to gravel in three deafening steps. My job was to collect samples of crush from the conveyor belt where it carried the gravel from the crushers to the loading bin. I then tested these samples for their capacity to produce strong asphalt.

The emotional pain of another failed relationship had rekindled my longing to explore the promised freedom of the world of spirit. I gave notice and prepared to leave the Dept. of Highways. By quitting before the end of the paving season, I was burning this bridge behind me in a reckless attempt to escape boredom and routine.

I decided to look for work on a fishing boat. In desperation I drove around town searching for a skipper who would take me on. I was driving through the rain one day when I saw a native man standing beside the road with his thumb out. I stopped and he got in without looking at me –impersonal like the rain that came with him. I introduced myself and he said his name was Jim. I asked him if he knew any fishermen who were hiring deckhands. He was silent for a while and then said slowly:

"My uncle Vic might take you on."

The idea of working for a native fisherman appealed to me:

"Yeah? Where does he live? I'd like to meet him."

"That's where I'm going."

Jim navigated as I drove out of town towards the Skeena River. We ended up driving down a dirt road overhung with alders. When the road ended I turned off the motor in the dripping green music of a coastal rain forest.

"This is my uncle's place," said Jim: "His name is Victor Smith, but people call him Vic."

I followed him through the mud towards a clearing with open sky beyond it. There was a small house built on pilings. I could see the river gleaming beyond the darkness under the house. We went up the front steps into the porch, and then Jim stopped, as if afraid to go any further. I could hear a big, male voice booming inside the house. Then he pushed open the door and stepped inside.

"So it's you, eh? You bring any beer?" the big voice asked.

"No, Vic."

"So what do you want here?"

I stepped in to stand beside Jim. Victor Smith was as big as his voice. He sat at the far side of the kitchen table, leaning his elbows on the red, checkered plastic. He did not move his eyes from Jim as he said:

"So instead of bringing beer you drag in some lousy, long-haired hippie!"

With these words he fixed his eyes on me. He had a broad, flat face and his eyes were kind and trustworthy.

"He wants to go fishing with you," said Jim by way of explaining my presence.

"The hell he does."

There was another man seated at the table: a short, gray shape slumped over among empty glasses, ashtrays, and a plate of chicken bones.

"Wake up, Charlie," Vic shouted at the sleeping form: "We got company."

Charlie looked up and smiled at me. For a moment I saw the kind, clear eyes of a man who had lived a long time close to the land and the sea…and then his face clouded over again. He tried to take a drink from an empty glass.

"Have a drink, Charlie! Everyone have a drink!" Vic stood to fill the glasses. He must have been six feet four and over three hundred pounds. There was no arguing with him.

Jim took a glass of whiskey. The smell, the taste, even the thought of it made me sick.

"Hey Jesus Christ –have a drink." He was not swearing, just calling me "Jesus Christ".

"No thanks, Vic… I can't drink alcohol… doctors orders."

"To hell with the doctor's orders! I'm the chief here, and I say everyone have a drink. Wake up, Charlie, and have a drink with Jesus Christ!"

Jim had left me to fend for myself, so I said: "My name is Mark."

"The hell you say! What kind of man needs all that hair unless he is Jesus Christ? You don't look like a man at all, covered in hair like that does he Charlie? Does he, Jim?"

Charlie and Jim had no answer, and after a moment's silence, Vic bellowed: "So you there all covered in hair: what are you, an asshole?"

After another silence Vic repeated: "Well, what are you?"

He poured himself a drink. Jim was laughing, and Charlie had gone back to sleep with his head resting on his arm, still holding his glass. I never did get to answer Vic's question. The door opened and a burly young man in a red, checkered shirt pushed past me into the room. He was followed by a woman who must have been his girl friend. They were both smoking, had both been drinking, and for the first time I sensed danger. They ignored me while Vic motioned for them to sit in the two empty chairs. Jim walked out without a word.

I needed to find some clarity and purpose for being there. With Jim gone, there was no-one between me and the awesome Victor Smith. I just repeated that I wanted to go fishing with him. He ignored me and set about offering the new arrivals drinks. I looked past the table, through clouds of cigarette smoke, and saw a figure standing just beyond the open door into the next room. Two dark eyes gleamed at me from the shadows, and then a native woman stepped forward just far enough for me to see her without Vic seeing her. She motioned for me to come so I walked over and followed her into the next room. She turned on a light and revealed her kind and worried face.

"Are you hungry?" she asked.

"You bet I am."

She took some cold salmon out of a huge fridge, cut me some bread and sat me down at a small table beside a window. It was just getting dark and I could see the gleam of the river and the dark shape of a gill-netter at anchor with her bow pointing upstream into a night that had already swallowed the mountains.

When I had finished the salmon Mrs. Smith gave me a bowl of rhubarb preserve with slices of orange in it that tasted good. Then she sat down and looked at me with deep, serious eyes:

"You know, Vic is a good fisherman. He doesn't take any booze out with him when he's working. He's a good man."

It felt good to have somebody on my side. I knew I was going fishing with Vic. I never paused to ask myself why.

Then we heard shouting in the front room and with a weary look at Mrs. Smith I got up to see what was happening. The stink of whiskey and cigarette smoke warned me of danger as I stood in the harsh light of that room. The young man and woman were both shouting at Vic, but I could not make out the words. When the man noticed me, he turned and strode up to stand on my toes and snarl in my face: "Take off your glasses!" His eyes glinted, showing the steel ball that filled his skull. He did not look native, and his girl friend, pale and blonde behind her cloud of smoke, egged him on: "If he won't take his glasses off, just make contact lenses out of them for him, Lenny... Haw haw haw!"

Victor's huge voice boomed out just in time: "Leave him alone! He is a guest in my house."

She was relentless: "These kind of bums are just looking to take advantage of you, Vic." She continued.

Lenny moved even closer: "Take off your fucking glasses!" His breath stank.

Sometimes doing nothing and saying nothing is the right thing. Lenny could have dropped me with one punch. His arms bulged with muscle. Victor was standing up, leaning on the table and telling him to leave me alone. Lenny took a reluctant step backwards, and was joined by his girl friend who sneered at me as they walked out together: "Come on, honey. If we can't have any fun here, let's get the hell out!"

Lenny gave me one last backward look of hatred as they walked into the night.

"So you want to come out fishing," said Victor as I sat down beside Charlie, who was fast asleep.

"Yeah, I do."

"Have you ever been on a gill-netter before?"

"No"

"So you're green, huh?"

"That's right. I'm green as grass."

"Well, don't worry. There is nothing to it. You just do what I say or I throw you overboard. That's all there is to it!"

He roared with laughter at his own joke. I felt so relieved that Lenny had left without turning my glasses into contact lenses that I laughed, too. Victor's wife appeared suddenly, cleaning up the table and smiling to herself.

"Can you believe he wants to go fishing with me?" He gave his wife a surprised look.

"Sure Vic.... maybe he'll bring you luck."

We all helped carry Charlie over to the couch. He lay there, still sleeping, with his tired old face looking like a child.

"We leave tomorrow morning." With this, Vic went into the back room.

She looked at me, concerned about where I would sleep.

"Don't worry," I told her: "I'll sleep in my car."

I did not want to miss my chance to go fishing by being asleep in my cabin when Vic left, so I felt my way back through the rain and unrolled my foam and sleeping bag in the back of my wagon. Big drops of water knocked gently on the roof as I lay down.

The rain stopped during the night and I awoke to silence. I got dressed awkwardly in the vehicle and sat on the tailgate to pull on my boots. At first I was afraid Vic had left without me, but nothing stirred in or around the Smith household. Beyond the house I found a lawn with some flowering bushes sloping down to the riverbank. Victor's boat was at anchor about a hundred yards offshore. There was a small dock with a dingy floating at the end of a long rope that was stretched out on the incoming tide. At the center of the half-mile-wide river fishing boats were speeding out to sea. The season ran four days on, three days off. Vic was sleeping away the morning of the first day.

I stood there gazing out at this vast, silent flow of water. A faint murmur of motors was all I could hear until a quiet voice at my side said:

"Will you help me, mister?"

A short native boy had come silently to stand beside me. I could not tell his age: maybe ten, maybe fourteen. He was heavy, but not fat, and had the same dark eyes as Mrs. Smith.

I sat down on the riverbank. "Help you with what?"

There was a long silence. His expression did not change, and he did not look directly at me. Eventually he said: "Will you help me with my dream?"

His small voice came from some far away place that I did not understand. He sounded unsure, and yet unafraid. I turned towards him and for a moment he searched my eyes like a caged bird looking for freedom. Perhaps I saw my own reflection.

"What is your dream?"

"Come. I will show you."

His words came slowly, as though each one was powerful and to be used with care. He led me along a path through thick woods downriver from the house. After about five minutes he stopped in a grove of yellow cedars. We stood silently in the shadows while a single shaft of sunlight appeared, slanting down among the ancient trees to illuminate a small patch of earth. The amber light was full of insects and floating jewels of dust.

"I'll show you…. just say yes or no."

He continued his purposeful advance down the path. I began to worry that Vic might leave without me, but the boy seemed to read my mind, and said: "Uncle Vic won't get up before noon."

The path ended on a patch of open ground on the bank of the river. We were standing about ten feet above the water where the current circled slowly in the shelter of a small point of grass and mud. Just offshore a few old pilings stuck out of the river and a few remaining crossbeams and planks suggested that there had once been a boathouse here. The boy stopped beside a pile of grey lumber and looked out at the decaying posts in the river. He waited a long time and then, with a shadow in his voice, quietly said: "Will you help me build my own place here? I need my own room. It is quiet here."

I thought he meant to build a cabin on the riverbank, but he pointed out at the bleached boards that hung from the black pilings: "We can finish this boathouse. This is my dream. I can't do it alone…. just say yes or no."

I remember the scene from the night before with so much shouting, smoke and drinking in the harsh light of the room where Victor held court. Those dark, silent eyes were looking at me as I struggled with the unbearable weight of his dream. A gentle wind moved the cedars and then loneliness and sorrow blew through me like a ghost. The blue water of the river shivered. No one could build anything on those few rotten posts. I looked again at the pile of sun-bleached lumber he had collected, the fragments of his precious dream of a safe place to call his own. He had not even told me his name. The trees breathed again. Then I said simply:

"No."

I was about to go on, to explain my unworthiness, to apologize and say it was impossible…anything to avoid feeling responsible for his dream.

"I understand." He said. He meant it. "You don't have to say anything. I know someone is going to help me."

We looked into each other's eyes. I felt shallow and lost. The feeble voices in my mind were stilled by an ancient silence. He and I were the same. For a moment I stood there in two bodies, looking at myself. Then I turned and hurried back up the path to the house. I thought I could get away from myself at sea.

It was one o'clock before Victor came lumbering out of his room. He was in rough shape. Mrs. Smith had given me breakfast, and together we had loaded supplies onto the dinghy. She was almost protective of me, as if she hoped I could help Victor in some way. Again an imagined weight of responsibility fell on me. I got into the front of the small boat and prepared to row as Victor came lurching down to the dock. He was unsteady, but he did not fall. Nothing was said. His wife stood back at the house, watching. She had done her part. I untied the rope and backed the boat up to the dock for Victor to step in. His weight caused the bow to rise so much that I had trouble rowing, and the water was inches from coming in over the transom. Slowly and carefully I pulled out to the gill-netter. Victor appeared to be drifting and was about to lurch to one side when he steadied himself, and growled:

"Not like that. Head up beyond her bow and the current will take you to her."

We reached his boat, and I looked for a name, but she did not have one –just a number. When Vic stepped onboard, water sloshed in over the stern of the dinghy. I passed him the boxes and he stowed them in the cabin. I had no idea what to do, so I tied the dinghy up to the stern, thinking that we would tow it with us.

"What in hell!" yelled Vic, suddenly emerging on deck: "Tell me how in hell I can use a gill net with that thing dragging behind us! Tie it to the float when you cast off. Make damn sure it will be there when we get back."

Moments later we were roaring out to sea. His boat had an aluminum hull, and was light and fast. Victor promptly fell asleep on his bunk in the forward cabin, leaving me at the wheel as we speeded out from the river mouth into the ocean. The other boats had left long before, and I had no idea what course to set among the islands offshore. From time to time Vic would emerge, like a bear from hibernation, and point out the next beacon or landmark to aim for. In this way we reached the fishing grounds, and Victor finally took over. He showed me how to unroll the long net from the huge drum on the stern of the boat. It became calm as the sun set, and we could see the long line of small floats, and the big, red one with an electric light that marked the end of our net. Victor went back to sleep in his cabin. He had not told me how or when to bring the net back in, but I did not need to know that yet. The water turned pale blue, like the sky, and then began to burn with the fires of sunset. For hours I sat there alone on the calm water, watching the lights on the water in the long, slow fall of night.

I must have fallen sleep on deck, and awoke when Vic's huge hand shook my shoulder. It was dark, and he motioned for me to go below and get some rest.

The next day was hard for both of us. While Victor slept and worked off his hangover, I learned about commercial fishing by making mistakes and getting yelled at. He never told me anything until it became necessary, and I slowly accepted the fact that, out there, I did not know anything. It was peaceful when he was asleep, and my mistakes went unnoticed.

We fished day and night, and slowly Victor became a different man. The fog of alcohol burned away to reveal the skilled fisher and leader of his people that Victor was. He had been generous enough to take a green stranger like myself onboard his boat and share his chances. When the fishing was good, he got on the radio and told his friends that he had "Jesus Christ" with him, and it was bringing him luck. But when the net came in empty, he would call up his friends and tell them that he had a lousy, long-haired hippie with him that was scaring all the fish away. He would make sure I heard him yell: "I think I'm going to throw him overboard!"

On the second night he showed me how to cook a pink salmon by boiling it with potatoes and onions to bring out the flavor. After eating in silence, I cleaned up the galley, and we sat and talked: "Do you usually fish alone?" I asked him.

"Now I do. Charlie used to work with me, but he's retired now. I took Jim out once, but he was no use, just puked and slept all the time. Now I fish alone, most of the time. It gets lonesome out here. Maybe I'll keep you on, just to keep me company, eh?"

By the third night we had become friends. For the first time he spoke of his wife: "Rose is a good woman. I don't know why she stays with me: if I was her, I would have left long ago. Sometimes I wake up early and the sun is shining on her, asleep in my bed, in my house, beside me all through life. Imagine that, a good woman, a Christian woman, too, staying with a fat, old Indian like me! Can you help me understand why she would do that? Are you married?"

"No, Vic."

"Do you have a girl-friend, then?"

"I did until a week ago!"

"Was she a good woman?"

I thought for a long time: "Yes, I would guess she was a good woman."

"What do you mean 'you guess'! Don't you know a good woman when you find one? I knew Rose from the moment we met. You know…. in that first moment before your cock comes up and hits you on the head so you can't think straight anymore, that's when you know."

"Well, then I would have to say she was a good woman." I said, but it felt like a lie. I had tried hard to prove to her, and to myself, that I was 'not like those other jerks' that she complained about, but had clearly failed.

"Then why did you let her go!" thundered Vic: "Don't they teach you anything useful at school? If you find a good woman who will put up with you, don't throw it all away!"

Later that night I stood alone on deck. A silver path rippled from the stern of the boat over the darkness under the moon. For the first time my mind stopped and I realized where I was. No job and no girlfriend –I was alone on the ocean with a hole in my heart. After about thirty minutes Vic came quietly up on deck and stood beside me. I could feel his warmth and his strength, close, like a mountain. Something sweet seemed to flow into me, like a warm wind from a meadow of summer flowers. It was so familiar, so powerful, and filled the void inside me as we stood there silently on the rolling belly of the sea.

All that night the sockeye slammed into the net and at dawn, when we pulled in for the last time, Victor had his wages.

We stopped at the fish buyer's dock where Victor sold his catch, and once again told his story about Jesus Christ bringing him luck. I could see the men who worked there sizing me up behind their smiles, and wondering how long I would last. They found a steelhead in our catch, and pointed out how its thick tail gave it away. It was not worth much. Everyone knew Vic, and was glad he had a good catch. He sang the same song over and over again in his native language as we headed home.

It was another rare, sunny day on the mouth of the Skeena. After four days without much sleep I was light headed, clear and happy. We came in with the other boats and, one by one, the tired fishermen pulled away from the center of the river to tie up and row in. At last we passed the black pilings, the sad little pile of lumber, the tall yellow cedar grove, and nosed up to the dinghy that waited for us at Vic's float. Rose Smith stood by the house, watching, but she did not come down to greet us as I rowed in to the dock.

During the trip I had never said anything about staying on, or not. At times Vic had talked of keeping me on all season, and at other times, of throwing me overboard. When we reached the house he paused, and seemed lost for words for a moment. I kept my pack on my back, and held a sack with six under-size salmon in it.

"This is all I want," I told him: "these fish are my wages."

"Yeah....you sure?" he looked into my eyes. That warmth was there again. His silence let me know I was worth more than that, and my silence let him know I had already been given far more. I just turned and walked away. We both knew I would not be going out again.

Chapter 7: *Return to India*

It was a long drive from Prince Rupert to Victoria, but I was riding a wave of energy and once again felt clear and strong about my inner journey. The simple, hard life in the cabin followed by the adventure with Victor had cleared the clouds away and my vision was once again shining with clarity and purpose. I had no doubts that I must return to India to follow the promise of the spirit that I had caught a glimpse of there. I remembered the wonderful welcome India had given me, the inner peace that shone from the eyes of the yogi, and the joy of devotion that had seemed to be everywhere.

A friend had given me the address of a Hindu ascetic called Harish who lived in the Himalayas and was interested in starting an ashram there. I had written to Harish and told him I was interested in joining his ashram. After a few weeks his reply had come. He had called himself a "sadhu", the name given to people in India who renounce worldly life to search for god. This was very exciting, as I had read *Autobiography of a Yogi* and my head was filled with absurd and romantic ideas about spiritual life. In October of 1972 I returned to India, this time with a one-way ticket.

From the airport I went directly to Chandi Chowk, the heart of Old Delhi. I took a room in the Chandi Hotel that overlooked a crowded market. After showering and changing into light, cotton clothes I went out to have my first cup of chai. The air was warm and alive with the chaotic rhythms of India. Vibrant colors and sweet scents greeted me everywhere. I found a tea-stall near a row of flower-shops and sat there, alone but at home in that ancient, complex world.

My destination was a village called Tung in Himachal Pradesh, where Harish lived. An overnight train took me as far as Pathankot, and from there I found the bus to Dharmshala. My pack was cheerfully placed on the roof rack by a boy who then demanded payment. I found a window seat near the front of the bus and waited. The sun rose and the air became hot and sticky. The conductor banged on the metal seats with his ticket-puncher as he collected fares and the driver started the motor. People came running from tea shops and crowded in. Then the driver turned the motor off. This routine was repeated until the bus was full and we suddenly lurched onto the street and began blasting our way at reckless speed through the crowd of trucks, horses, bicycles and cows. After an hour we turned onto a narrow road and began to climb the foothills of the Himalayas. After three hours we stopped for tea. The wheels of the bus were inches from a chasm that held a river of white water hundreds of feet below. Everyone got down on the other side of the bus without a downward glance. The road followed the river valley towards the North. I saw what I thought were clouds floating in the sky beyond the hills. Then, with a chill that rushed up my back, I realized I was seeing the Himalayas for the first time. They were shining with the promise of freedom.

For two more hours we climbed towards those mountains. The bus shook and the motor roared fit to burst. The road was so narrow that every time we encountered an oncoming vehicle, it was a major incident, with drivers shouting and arguing about right of way. At times I looked straight down into canyons that were littered with wrecked vehicles. Everyone else seemed relaxed and unconcerned. I began to understand why the windshield was all but obscured by pictures of gods and goddesses. On that journey, to trust the creator was the only way to find any peace of mind.

We finally pulled in at the State Transport station in Dharmshala. Boys swarmed the bus to unload luggage and by the time I got down, my pack was waiting for me. The five rupees I offered to re-claim it were not enough, and so I paid ten. He smiled at this as the other boys looked on with envy and competed for the one or two rupees the locals were willing to pay for their services.

I stood there in reverence and gratitude. The air was cool, and the setting sun shone softly on the dust and pollution we had just left behind. A steep, forested hill rose above the town, which was perched on a ridge between two valleys. To the north a long row of mountains glowed red as shadows filled the narrow streets of Dharmshala. As I walked through the town, looking for a place to stay, a cool wind came down from the snow and touched my face.

I was directed to the Tourist Bungalow by a kind old Nepali man who asked me to save any stamps I might have for him.

"You can find me sitting here each afternoon," he said, tapping the stool where he sat in front of a vegetable stall.

The tourist bungalow was an old English house on a piece of flat land above the bazaar. It had four spacious rooms, all with high ceilings and large bathrooms decorated with ceramic tiles. The manager was out and a small, silent man in the ancient uniform of a doorman showed me to my room, and then vanished. He did not ask for any money or to see my passport.

My room opened onto a balcony with a view to the west where the embers of sunset smoldered. Slowly the crickets stopped singing and a silent darkness welcomed me to the Himalayas.

The following afternoon I found my Nepalese friend at his place by the vegetable stand. His name was Ranu. I gave him a few stamps and asked about the village called Tung where Harish lived.

"Tung?" he replied: "That is near Chamunda Devi. You can take a bus from the ST station. Ask for the Chamunda Devi bus, and get down at Tung. Here schoolteachers and postmasters always know English, so they will help you."

"What is at Chamunda Devi?"

"It is a very powerful temple of the goddess. We Nepalese worship goddess Kali. Chamunda is, how to say, a sister of Kali. I go there sometimes myself."

At the station I learned that there were only two busses a day to Chamunda, and I decided to take the bus the next morning. For the remainder of the day I wandered the streets of Dharmshala and sat on the balcony of the tourist bungalow. I was anxious to meet Harish and confirm that I had really found a safe, spiritual retreat.

The road to Chamunda followed the foothills of the Himalayas to the East. Each valley held a stream that rushed down under bridges built of stone. To the North stood a range of snowy peaks, and to the South the hills rolled away towards the haze and smoke of the plains. The narrow road passed through villages of mud houses with slate roofs that had little streams of fresh water running by their front doors. Every hillside was a mosaic of terraced fields separated by lines of yellow bamboo.

The bus shuddered to a stop at each village and finally the conductor signaled for me to get down, and I was left standing on the road in a cloud of diesel smoke in the tiny village of Tung. There were two tea stalls and a shop selling dry goods and school supplies. I approached the small, fierce man who sat at the front of the shop, and asked if he spoke English.

"Yes, yes, of course!" he replied: "Speaking! How are you? Have a cup of tea." he immediately began shouting towards the little tea stall near his shop, and then turned back to me: "Please sit down," he said, indicating a sack on a bench in front of his shop: "What is your country? What is your purpose?" He was still shouting.

I told him I was from Canada, and was looking for a man called Harish.

"Harish Swami. I know him: he lives near here, behind the school. I will take you."

The tea arrived, far too sweet, but courtesy demanded that I accept it. I insisted that I find Harish on my own. This friendly man with the fierce eyes was exploding with restless energy, and I was looking for peace. He pointed to a meadow that came down to the road: "He lives there, behind the school."

I left the road and walked up the field past a small, brick schoolhouse. There were groups of children sitting on the dirt floor and a buzz of small voices. I hoped to get by unseen, but they noticed me with obvious glee at the welcome distraction. A teacher leaned out to see what the commotion was about, and then tried to restore order in a sharp voice. About a hundred yards beyond the school I saw a small stone structure surrounded by a hedge of thorn bushes. Beyond this, on slightly higher ground, was a mud hut with a bamboo pole in front of it. A white flag at the top of this pole floated gently against the dark background of a mountain valley. Perhaps a mile away a solitary hill was illuminated by the mid-day sun. Two temples stood on this hill, their ancient stones glowing as if lit from within. Beyond this rose the remote and inaccessible beauty of a mountain from which a white plume of snow blew away into a dark, blue sky. Rows of similar peaks were visible to the south and the north, but this one mountain stood alone and magnificent at the head of a valley. The village, the huts with their hedges and stone paths through terraced fields all seemed so tiny and fragile against this immense background.

There was a bamboo gate in the hedge that bordered the land where the stone hut stood. As I pushed the gate aside to get through, I noticed a man in the orange clothes of a sanyasin, or renunciate, reclining on the grass in front of the hut, listening to a portable radio and smoking a cigarette. He furtively turned off the radio, put out his cigarette, and then pretended to notice me for the first time. He approached, oozing holiness from big, brown eyes framed in black hair and a beard.

"Harish?" I asked.

"Yes, yes," he replied: "Welcome, Mark....welcome." He took my hand in both his and held it for a moment while he gazed into my eyes. His voice was very soft, like his hands. He wore a scarf around his head and a long shirt over tight pants. It was the style in the mountains for men's pants to have an immense waist but be skin tight at the ankles. Everything was orange.

"Come, let us take tea." He said.

He locked the door to his room and led me back down over the field. The students pointed and giggled as we passed. There were two tea shops in Tung, one on each side of the road. The first was a pleasant spot, set back from the road and with a table on a verandah surrounded by bougainvillea. The second was a small, dark room behind a coal fire and a glass case full of insects and tin plates containing deep fried snacks. It was to this second shop that Harish led me, explaining that the lady who ran the other shop was not to be trusted. I met Chumney, the young man who owned the shop, and Krishna, a small, homeless boy who worked there all day, then slept on the floor at night. He had nowhere else to go.

After tea Harish showed me around his home, and pointed out the bed where I would sleep. There was a simple altar with a photo of a naked man with a huge, round belly and incredible eyes that looked right through me. On the wall above Harish's bed was a picture of goddess Durga sitting on a tiger. The floor, walls and flat, concrete roof of his single stone room were all unfinished. A separate kitchen and bathroom stood at one end, also unfinished. Apparently he had run out of money. He was careful to refer to the place as "our ashram". I made every effort to like and trust Harish, and tried hard to see him as a genuine holy man at the beginning of a worthy enterprise.

After an hour's rest I was awakened by the sound of a kerosene stove. Harish was making more chai. I looked around the room as we sat on our cots, sipping the sweet, milky tea. He had a metal trunk under his bed and a table made from a wooden crate at one end where he kept his radio. There was dust everywhere. Rays of sunlight slanted in through barred windows and glowed in the cool shadows within those thick stone walls.

"There is a festival tonight," began Harish: "If you like you can come with me to the temple." He spoke very good English and I later learned he had a degree in English and Hindi literature.

"That sounds good. What temple is it?"

"There is a temple of the goddess Mother near here. We will go there after tea."

We walked to the temple through the magic of sunset in the Himalayas. The snow peaks glowed red above us, and below us the wooded hills sloped gently down towards the plains. Just beyond Tung was the valley of a stream called 'Iku Nala' that flowed over huge boulders down a series of waterfalls into pools that looked deep enough to swim in. We passed two more villages, with their tea shops and food stalls beside the road. Everything seemed soft, warm and gentle. After an hour we arrived at the path leading down into another stream valley, and I saw the temple of Chamunda Devi for the first time.

Goddess Chamunda Devi had originally been worshipped at a small temple in a remote place in the mountains. There was a path that followed the stream up the valley to the original temple. A famous yogi had lived there and had persuaded Chamunda Devi to relocate for the sake of devotees who were unable to make the difficult climb. In this way the temple before us had come into being. A red flag hung from a bamboo pole above the tower of intricate carvings that formed the roof of the shrine. The kailash, or final decoration that crowned this tower, was plated with gold. Lower down beside the stream I could see the dome of a Shiva temple with its white flag, and blue spirals of smoke that rose from the fire that was kept burning there. Across the stream was a group of mud huts that looked like a small ashram.

We had a quick supper of puris and channa at a tea stand near the entrance to the temple, and then Harish led the way down to the stream where we washed our hands and feet before going to meet the goddess. It was later explained to me that this ritual, called darshan, or 'seeing', was not just about me seeing the goddess, but also the goddess seeing me. The room was full of women and girls who sat on the floor, chanting mantras. Chamunda Devi looked very fierce, holding weapons in most of her eight arms and riding on a tiger. I made my offering of two rupees and some flowers, and received prasad in return. Prasad is an important part of temple worship in India, and the sweets and pieces of coconut that the priest gives to visitors are believed to contain the blessing of the deity. I bowed my head to the floor, and then stood back for a moment while Harish had his darshan. Although I had once again entered a world that was new and unknown, the joy of recognition rushed over me like a cold wind once again. I knew in my heart that something good had just happened.

We walked home by the light of the moon. Even with the occasional kerosene lamp in a hut or shop beside the road, there was always the feeling that I was walking close to an immense wilderness. Beyond the peaks that rose above us there were just a few passes through the mountain ranges that separated India from Tibet.

That night I had the first of a series of powerful encounters with goddess. In my dream I was walking alone on the hill where the old temples stood. It was a desolate and empty landscape. The tall figure of a woman approached, wearing a long blue robe with a hood that hid her face in shadow. She stopped before me and stood for a moment, shimmering like water in moonlight. Then she asked the simple question: "What do you want?"

Without hesitation I replied: "I want to know the mystery of love completely." I clearly remember saying that extra word "completely".

The goddess responded: "Ask the sky."

I turned my gaze towards the sky where immense, dark clouds floated. A bolt of lightening came down and struck me in the top of the head. At the same instant I awoke to a state of sleep paralysis, with an overwhelming rush of energy coming from the base of my spine up and out the top of my head. I was both transfixed by the power of this energy and filled with joy. I could hear a sound like a conch shell being blown. When I felt I could bear it no more, I made a great effort and moved my head slightly, and the rushing stopped. In the same moment the voice of the goddess said: "When the time comes, look towards heaven."

I lay there peacefully for a long time before drifting away into deep, dreamless sleep. I awoke to the sound of birds calling from the trees and Harish making chai.

Later that day I walked through the fields to visit the abandoned temples on the hill. They were made of stones that had been carved and fitted together with wonderful precision. The deities had been removed after a major earthquake had damaged the temples beyond repair. It was a perfect place for me to be alone with the memory of my dream. Just beyond this hill was a valley filled with shadows that led to the foot of the snow peaks. It was all so close, and yet seemed so remote and dangerous.

Later that day Harish took me to the house of his friend Prem Chand, whom he always referred to as "surpanj," which means "village head man". Apparently Prem Chand had held this position at one time. His wife served us lunch of rice and lentils. It was the custom in the hills for people to eat twice a day. First the children were fed before they left for school, then the men ate before leaving for work in the fields, and finally the women had their meal. This routine was repeated at the end of the day.

That evening was the final day of Navaratri, which means nine days and nights for worship of the goddess. Harish described the ceremony to me briefly and advised me to bring two blankets—one to sit on and one to wear, as we would be up most of the night. At sunset we returned to the temple. For the first time I felt real devotion for the mother goddess, and was certain that there was a connection between Chamunda Devi and my recent experience. I had come to India with no clear plan to plunge in Hindu worship, just the feeling that this was were I needed to be for the unfolding of my journey. The experience of the power of the goddess came to me before I had any concepts or expectations. I was trusting, ignorant and young, and good things were happening.

The temple grounds were crowded with local people, all wearing their best clothes. The area around and inside the temple was a riot of color from the women's bright saris. The men wore long, white shirts with woolen vests and tight pants. Everyone carried a shawl. The Gaddis tribes-people wore their traditional long cloaks of white handspun wool. They had bare legs, and ropes of dark wool wrapped many times around their waists. The men wore turbans of white, and the women covered their heads with their shawls. Children ran and played everywhere. The air was filled with the sound of devotional singing and the ringing of bells from the temple.

All this celebration of life and faith was set in a landscape more beautiful than I had ever seen. That this was to be my home for an indefinite time, and the fact that the spirit of the place had already visited me in such a powerful way caused me to overflow with joy.

That night we gathered in the central compound of the small ashram across the stream from the temple. The buildings were made of mud, with red tile roofs. There was no electricity, and kerosene lanterns hung from the corners. A central veranda had become a stage covered with white cloth where the musicians and the guests of honor sat. I sat in the front row on the floor, with Harish on one side and Prem Chand on the other.

I had heard that the real depth of Hindustani classical music can only be experienced in live performances, and that the best music could be heard in the temples. That night, this was proven to be true. The featured musician was an old man called Master Rattan. I had never heard such a voice. He went through three octaves with ease, at times holding a high note, dropping one octave, and then another, still holding the same note, while the crowd sighed and gasped with pleasure. Master Rattan's face was deeply lined, his front teeth were missing, but his smile was angelic. Everything about him spoke of a long, hard life, filled with suffering that his music now transformed. The old men of the mountains especially appreciated him. They sat with great dignity on their blankets, and wept.

In the weeks that followed, I settled in to the simple routine of village life. Harish began to spend more and more time smoking and listening to his portable radio. Some dark shadow was haunting him. It soon became clear that the village people did not regard him as a "holy man", and for the most part they just left him alone.

His one friend, Prem Chand, soon became my friend too. Although the women in the village always had plenty of work to do, the men were busy only at planting and harvest time, and often had nothing to do but hang around tea shops or sit on the ground and play cards. In the next village about a mile away was a small liquor shop next to a place that sold meat and eggs. At night I would hear howling and yelling coming from this direction, and believed it was the local drunks going wild with boredom and frustration. Later I learned that this noise came from packs of wild dogs. These dogs were so furtive that in all my time there I saw only one when it crossed the path in front of me and vanished without a sound.

From time to time Harish would speak with reverence of a man called "Baba", whose full name was Swami Muktananda Paramahamsa. He considered Baba his guru, and attributed much grace and good fortune to a year spent in

Baba's ashram at a place called Ganeshpuri in Maharashtra. I believed that for self realization to happen, the grace and guidance of a guru was essential. Perhaps Baba would turn out to be my guru, and I asked Harish if it was possible for me to meet him. In November, my chance came. Harish received a card inviting him to join a camp in New Delhi, where Swami Muktananda was coming to stay for a week at the house of a devotee. A few days later we were on our way.

We spent our first night in New Delhi in the home of one of Harish's relatives. The Guptas turned out to be a large family, and there had been a time when they had ruled Northern India. These urban relatives did their best to treat Harish as a "holy man", perhaps only because of my presence, but it soon became clear that they considered him a dropout. We spent an uncomfortable night sleeping on the floor of a small apartment. In the morning we showered, put on our best clothes, and left to meet the mysterious Baba.

Lodhi Estates is a wealthy suburb of Delhi with grand houses on large, treed lots. The quiet streets provided a rest from the endless crowds in the city. I followed Harish up a long drive that ended at the verandah of a wide, single storey house. Near the house was a multi-colored tent large enough to hold a wedding party of many hundred people. On the veranda a group of Indian men and women sat in silence, intently focused on a man in orange robes who sat in an arm chair at the far end. As we approached, they cleared a space for us to come forward. Harish went up and bowed his head to the carpet before this awesome figure. A deep voice said something to him, and space was made for him to sit near the chair. Then the swami's eyes were on me. Perhaps instinct, or perhaps some buried memory carried me forward, and I touched my forehead to Baba's feet.

"Bahut accha!" said a golden voice. It meant something like "Very OK."

I joined Harish on the mat with the devotees. My mind had stopped its neurotic chatter and my whole being was held in the Swami's electric aura. His eyes flashed power through dark glasses. This was no ordinary man.

With a quiet sense of satisfaction I noticed that there were no other westerners present. I wanted very much to find something authentic that had not yet been discovered by the west. We sat there in silence for about ten minutes, and then the Swami suddenly stood up. The movement exuded power. We all stood to make space for him to leave. He stopped in front of me, tapped me on the chest, and said in Hindi:

"Tumara bhojan hamare pas khao."

This was translated for me by a thin, elderly woman also dressed in orange: "Baba says you are to take your meals with us."

Later I understood that in the language of sadhus, this was a very significant statement. Finding enough to eat was often a difficult challenge for people in India who had renounced family and friends and had no income. Baba had welcomed me to his path, and that night I discovered just how much power there was behind this simple statement.

A room in a nearby school had been made available to the devotees who had come long distances to meet Baba. There were six simple wooden cots in a row, and Harish and I bedded down for the night. I lay on my back and listened to the night sounds of Delhi: the distant whistle of a train, the rumble of trucks, and the lonely cries of the night watchmen. Sleep came like a soft hammer.

That night I had my second visit from the goddess. I found myself in a vast darkness, facing an awesome figure with huge eyes that shone with fire. I felt wide awake, but was unable to move or open my eyes. The goddess advanced towards me, her arms and legs shimmering with jewels. Her fierce eyes looked into my soul as she came closer and closer. At first I was filled with fear, but when I remembered the Guru I had just met, the fear vanished. The jeweled goddess kept advancing in the darkness and finally walked right into my heart at the place where the Swami had touched me. I was released from sleep paralysis and lay there drenched with cold sweat while currents of energy surged through my body. Sleep was impossible so I felt my way past the other beds to the bathroom and had a shower. I put on fresh clothes and sat on my bed to meditate. Perhaps it would be more accurate to say I just sat on my bed, happy in the conviction that I had not only found my Guru, but received a powerful initiation from the goddess as well.

The pre-dawn darkness in India is filled with sweetness and the mystery of the creator, whose presence can be felt and heard everywhere. Devotional music began to play from the loudspeakers of a temple, somewhere a donkey brayed on its way to the river with a load of laundry, and the wheels of a hand cart rumbled on the pavement outside the school. I heard Harish awaken with a soft "Jagadambe ma!" He passed me on his way to the bathroom. By the time he returned, it was getting light, and we went out together to find a chai stall.

The first chai of the day is best! It was the habit of seekers in India to get up very early, sometimes at 3 a.m., to begin their sadhana. This practice I was happy to join, and soon I felt that the early morning darkness belonged to me. Most Indian people shunned the night hours, just as they shunned wild places. In such a crowded country, I found solitude in the night hours, and in the jungles and abandoned places. Everywhere an ancient wilderness could be felt, beckoning from just beyond the noise and lights of clustered humanity. This wilderness penetrated the cities in the form of wandering, homeless peoples. The family who had pushed their cart to the gateway of the house where Swami Muktananda was staying looked as if they had just emerged from the jungle, and were untouched by modern civilization. The man stoked up the fire of charcoal in a burner made of mud, while the woman prepared our chai, and a little girl with gleaming eyes stared at me from under the cart. I smiled at her, and she turned away, giggling into her hand. The chai was flavoured with fennel seed. To this day, the taste of fennel reminds me of that little girl.

We joined a small group of people sitting in the tent, meditating near a small platform where a photo of the Swami had been placed on the cushions where he would sit. A rare feeling of belonging and being welcome comforted me as I sat there. The question of how or upon what to meditate did not bother me: I was in the honeymoon phase of a new spiritual path.

After a long time we were called to the verandah of the house to join the devotees for breakfast. We sat in a row and a young swami passed out plates made of leaves and plastic cups. A woman in white then served upma, a special dish made from semolina, vegetables and spices. The young man who came around next with a kettle of chai recognized Harish and said something to him in Hindi. Harish then translated for me:

"Baba himself made the upma. It is Prasad.... do not waste any."

When we were finished I followed the others to a place behind the house where a cow was eating the leaf plates that were thrown to her. This was Hindu India, and I loved it. I had not yet seen another white face. I wished to avoid anyone who could remind me of myself.

In the afternoon Baba gave darshan again, and I had another chance to go up and meet him personally. He smiled in recognition as I came up to touch his feet. There was such an aura of power surrounding him that my mind simply stopped and all questions vanished in the clarity and fullness of being that seemed to be his gift.

The woman called "Amma" who wore the orange robes of a sanyasin spoke to me in English, and invited me to the ashram. Her assurance that there were other foreigners there did not interest me at all. I was convinced that once back in Tung I would continue my solitary meditation, and reach that elusive state called "enlightenment." I was convinced that the grace of a Guru was necessary, and that I now had it.

That evening there was a concert of Hindustani classical music in the tent. I sat near the front and we waited for Baba to arrive while the musicians tuned their instruments. We all stood up as the powerful figure of Swami Muktananda walked quickly up and sat on his throne. He wore an orange toque and dark glasses. He joked with the musicians and then swung his glance around the room like a search light, looking at each of us for a moment. His presence made any occasion feel magical, as if some great miracle was just about to happen.

I was fascinated by the tabla player, who wore jewels on his fingers that sparkled as his hands danced over the drumskins. He seemed to be really enjoying himself, and had an obvious appetite for life. Years later, when my interest in renunciation had gone, I remembered how this man had touched something inside me that would not be denied.

The next morning Baba and his group of devotees left, and the camp was over. In the evening we caught the night train back to Pathankot. Harish was silent and withdrawn. I was filled with the conviction that I had received a great blessing and my meditation would now deepen. The Himalayas were to be my new home. I felt grateful to Harish for introducing me to Swami Muktananda, and for offering to share his tiny ashram with me. We seemed to have some things in common: we were both "drop outs", or, as we preferred to see ourselves, seekers who had renounced worldly life, and now we had the same guru. I was far from being able to find my own way, and did not have much faith in myself.

I sent for the five-hundred dollars that I had left and we began work on my cottage. It was to have a single room, a small verandah, and a kitchen. If we had used the mud-bricks and slate roof that the villagers used, the whole thing would have cost just a few hundred dollars. Harish insisted on a "pukha" construction, using bricks and a concrete slab for a roof. He had a sophisticated distaste for rustic things.

We made a trip to Pathankot to buy bricks. Harish invited Prem Chand to go with us. His idea was that Prem, a big man of imposing countenance, would be helpful in dealing with people. It turned out that the city intimidated him, and he was useless. We went from one plinth to another where the bricks crumbled in our hands. Finally some good quality bricks were found, and we ordered two truck loads. We sat and drank tea while the trucks were loaded.

Harish and Prem rode in one truck, and I rode in the other. The trip back to Tung took about four hours, and the trucks got separated. I arrived about thirty minutes before the others, and had to find a place for the truck to unload the bricks. It did not occur to me that it could drive right up to the building site, and so I had them dumped at the edge of the road beside the school. It seemed that at least half the bricks broke in transit. When the other truck arrived and came snarling up over the meadow to dump its bricks right in front of Harish's place, I felt stupid.

It became part of our routine to spend about an hour carrying the bricks up from the road after tea in the morning. It was quite tedious work. One morning we were surprised by the sound of laughter and the crunch of bricks being dropped outside the window. A small army of school children had been put to work on our behalf, and it took them just an hour to transport all the bricks. When the work was done and the kids returned to class, the headmaster came over for a visit and we had some more tea.

Finding cement was hard as it had to be bought on the black market. A government project that required ten-thousand bags of cement would result in five-thousand being diverted into this underground market, leaving a structure that was weak and vulnerable to earthquakes. We needed a hundred bags for our project, and these Harish found ten or twenty at a time.

Perhaps the only material that arrived smoothly was the sand. It was carried up from the stream on the backs of two donkeys that a local man kept for this purpose. He had a quiet, dignified air as he earned his living in this stress-free way.

Harish hired the same mason who had built his cottage. He was paid ten rupees a day, his helpers three. Ten rupees equaled about one dollar.

During the winter months while this work went ahead, I lived with Harish in his small, dark room. In January a few flakes of snow fell and the temples on the hill just a few hundred feet higher turned white. I began to feel weak from lack of nourishment, and was always cold. There was nothing to do but meditate. My money began to run out. One day I passed out while on my way to the temple. For a moment I had no idea where I was or how I came to be lying on the ground. But I would not give up my romantic notions of spiritual life in the Himalayas.

In March I took the bus to Dharmshala to get some clothes made. It was only just beginning to warm up. The tailor needed two days to stitch my shirt and pants, so I took a room in the tourist bungalow. The next day I decided to walk up the mountain above the town. There was a narrow track that led up among the houses on the hillside and continued on through a forest of pine and rhododendron. A group of silver, black-faced langur monkeys crashed away through the branches. I went higher and higher with no idea what lay above. After about an hour I found myself walking through thick fog. Then I noticed that the path was once again paved, with a wall of rocks on the uphill side. I seemed to be arriving at a village on the mountaintop.

At that moment a strange figure in maroon robes suddenly appeared out of the mist and stood in front of me. He bowed once, touching his forehead to my arm, and then motioned that I should follow him. I was seeing a Tibetan monk for the first time. The young man in the robes had a round face and a natural radiance. His eyes searched mine as he stood before me, waiting. But I had no desire to follow him and returned his greeting with a bow of my own. He looked concerned, stood for a moment in silence, and then turned quietly and vanished into the mist, leaving me to continue my solitary journey.

The path ended in a small town square surrounded by stone buildings with doors painted yellow or red. I could hear the sound of bells coming from a little temple that contained a prayer wheel. People went in, turned the wheel to the tolling of the bells, and then continued on their way. Everyone was Tibetan. It took only a few minutes to walk around the town. Every building faced the square, and one had a simple sign that read: "Tibetan Hotel". I went upstairs and sat at a long table with a view of the fog that filled the valley. There was no-one there. At one end of the room was a desk beside a complex altar. Incense was burning before a photo of the Dalai Lama, and a statue of an impressive figure in gold that I later learned was Padmasambhava, the guru from India who helped bring Buddhism to Tibet.

I had stumbled into McCleod Ganj, or Upper Dharmshala, and the atmosphere was quite different from the town below. This was the new home of the exiled Tibetan leader and a growing community of Tibetan refugees. While bamboo and flowering trees surrounded Dharmshala, here, 1500 feet higher, it was all pine and rhododendron forest. The buildings seemed to defy gravity, and were perched along a narrow saddle of the mountain that continued on up to Dharmkot, a forest rest house at 10,000 feet, then Larka, a group of stone shepherd's shelters at 11,000 feet, and finally the Toral pass at about 14,000 feet.

A Tibetan man wearing a down parka bought me a glass of milky tea, and asked if I wanted a room. Even in the middle of the day it was cold, and the night would have been even colder, so I decided to return in April or May to explore some more.

Soon after my discovery of the Tibetan refugee town, I broke my only pair of glasses, and had to learn to get along with reduced vision. Harish had developed a habit of noisy, forceful breathing during meditation. He claimed it was the result of kundalini moving within him. For an hour every night, beginning at about one a.m., his panting breath filled the night. Sleep was impossible, so I began to get up and meditate with him. I suspected that, as my cottage was nearing completion, he had no further use for me, and was trying to drive me away. I had spent most of my money on the cottage, and was hanging on to a fading illusion and my gleaming innocence as best I could.

At this time I had a pleasant surprise one day while watching people get down from a bus on the road in Tung. My friend Peter appeared. He had been traveling through India with a teacher called Namjal Rimpoche, and had come to visit me. He was my first contact with a westerner in six months. We sat in the teashop under the banyan tree and told each other of our adventures. Peter noticed how short-sighted I was, and urged me to send for a new pair of glasses, offering to pay for them if I was broke. I felt shocked when he ordered two more cups of chai and another plate of snacks: I had become accustomed to austerity and poverty. Finally I told Peter my big news:

"Peter, I have found my guru."

He sat back and looked at me, eyes wide and smiling: "I never thought I would hear you say those words."

After tea I took Peter to meet Harish, who held his hands and gazed into his eyes with the same melting look of holiness that had once so impressed me.

After staying with us a few days, Peter announced his intention of going to Ganeshpuri to meet Swami Muktananda at his ashram, and urged me to go with him. This idea scared me: for one thing, it was early April, and the plains were sweltering; for another, I dreaded having to get along with other westerners, and wanted to continue my solitary meditation. But Peter's enthusiasm overcame my doubts and a few days later I said good-bye to Tung and we boarded the bus to Dharmshala on the first stage of another long journey.

Chapter 8: *Ashram Life*

The mountains seemed to rise higher and higher behind us as we got closer to Pathankot. Six months of tranquility in the dream-land of the Himalayas was over –it was hot, humid and polluted as we waited for the night train to Delhi. We were fortunate to find two sleeper berths in third class. In Delhi we stayed in Pahargunj, opposite the New Delhi station, an area crowded with small shops and cheap hotels where low-budget travelers stayed. Then another long train journey took us to Bombay. Peter knew a place there with two cheap hotels, Stiffles and the Rex. It was hot and very humid. We had cool drinks at Dipti's juice stall. Everything in Bombay seemed very expensive. My long hair and beard were always itching.

From Bombay we took the local commuter train as far as Vasai Road, where we waited a long time in the afternoon heat for a bus to Ganeshpuri. The local buses were red and yellow, and always seemed to be going too fast. Clouds of dust rose into the hot, still air, and crowds of people pushed on and off at the same time. Finally someone told us our bus had just pulled in, and we joined the scrimmage at the door. It was standing room only, and we bounced and lurched over the country roads for about two hours until the bus stopped in front of the tall, pink temple at the ashram gate. We arrived tired, hot and filthy.

We were taken through a courtyard and over a field of papaya trees to a hut made of reeds that stood on some raised, red ground surrounded by mango trees. The hut was filled with a dozen cots made of wood and rope, with thin, lumpy mattresses. There was no fan and only a single bare light bulb hanging from a rafter. A shower stall stood under a palm tree nearby where we washed and changed our sweaty rags. I saw a few western men working in a garden at the edge of the jungle. Green, forested hills surrounded the ashram on three sides. To the north, beyond a wide river valley a red mountain with tall pillars of stone shimmered in the haze. It was all quite beautiful.

That evening we were given a simple meal of chappaties and dal, and then everyone gathered in the courtyard. It was dusk, and a warm breeze rustled the palm fronds above us. About forty people sat waiting on the flat stones in front of the little porch where Baba would sit. The door into his apartment was small, so he had to bend down when he came through. We all stood up briefly as he took his seat on the orange cushion, at ease in the lotus posture. It was a truly magical time for me. The air was sweet with the perfume of a tropical summer night, and the atmosphere charged with spiritual power. Baba spoke in his deep, golden voice. As new arrivals at the ashram, Peter and I were taken up to be introduced. Perhaps we were both hoping for some sign that we were special cases and would somehow avoid the struggle and suffering of ordinary human life. He smelled of sandal-wood, and said "welcome."

The next morning we were awakened at 3:30 am by the sound of a bell. I was amazed to find that the other young men in our hut were already up and had left for medita-tion. This was the time of power, the time of personal prac-tice. There was an underground room near Baba's apartment called the meditation cave. It was opened at three a.m.

Even in the cities, night in India always feels like a wil-derness, as if the darkness conceals an ancient mystery so vast and unknowable that our lives become small and frag-ile in comparison. In this darkness rises the spirit of human longing and devotion: small lamps are lit, and incense is of-fered to the many forms of the creator. This perfume of faith fills the night and reminds the pilgrims of their journey.

The next few weeks were hard for me. My inner feeling of having found the spiritual community where I belonged collided with my fears of being with other human beings, in particular the other westerners in the ashram. My first con-tact had been with an American woman called Chandari. I had a cut on my foot, and she was called in to treat me. She made it clear from the very beginning that this duty was far beneath her. She had an aura of power and determination around her —a cold force that just about paralyzed me. Half the people there were like her to some degree, and I learned to avoid them. The rest were delightful, open-hearted peo-ple from just about every country in the world.

It was the Australians who made the deepest impression. They were straight-forward and honest in a way that inspired instant trust. In particular it was a young man called Chris Canning who helped me so much at the beginning, and who became a real friend. He was in charge of a garden that was be-ing carved out of the jungle at the back of the ashram grounds. It was a delight to work with him. It was Chris who first taught me astrology. Every day we would sit in the chai shop for an hour after lunch while he showed me how to construct a natal chart using logarithms, an ephemeris and a table of houses. Using the charts of our friends as examples he taught me the basic symbols and language of western astrology.

Swami Muktananda was the focus of everything: he would lead the chants, give inspiring talks, and stride around the ashram with great speed and power. He always carried a stick, and would use it generously on residents he found disregarding the ashram dharma. One evening I was startled during the recitation of the Shiva Mahimna Stotram by the sound of a stick on flesh in the temple –a Swedish woman had been sleeping during the chant. How Baba had entered the temple without being seen I never knew. He led the offending girl, weeping, out of the temple. Whenever anyone would get hit by Baba, it carried a hint of blessing and status with it. We were sincere, but suffered from a western psychological condition I now call spiritual masochism: the belief that somehow suffering and self-denial were necessary on the spiritual path. This was encouraged by constant talk about "getting rid of the ego" or "dissolving the ego." There was a sign by the front gate that read: "Leave your ego with your shoes."

I was talking with my friend Swami Devananda one day and asked him about this. He replied:

"All this talk about getting rid of the ego….what humbug! I am not going to give up my ego…. it is all I have left!"

Peter said goodbye after a month or two: it was not his trip. I stayed, and soon became one of the cheerful gang of foreigners who worked in the upper garden and hung out in Senna's filthy chai shop, our only source of refreshment. The chai was so bad that from time to time we would complain to Senna, the sour-faced man who owned the place. But he clearly had a monopoly, and nothing ever changed. Greasy deep-fried snacks or perhaps a small package of glucose biscuits where all that was available to eat. At times I would walk two miles to the village of Ganeshpuri just to have a snack there. I found a small chai shop and rooming house called Madhu Nivas, which was owned and managed by an old man who, like Baba, had been a devotee of Swami Nityananda, and who had that wonderful quality called prem, or loving kindness.

The village of Ganeshpuri came into being because that was were Swami Nityananda had spent his final years. He had passed on there in 1961, and his body had been enshrined in a temple that became a pilgrimage place for thousands of devotees. Swami Nityananda had clearly been a genuine saint, immersed in god consciousness and living a simple, open life with no secrets.

In time it became my habit to rise at 3 a.m. and walk to Ganeshpuri through the perfumed darkness. There were very few lights along the country road, and only a few village huts made of reeds and mud. There was jungle on one side and rice paddies on the other. The road passed through the village and then ended at the samadhi temple beside the river. Across the river were a few more huts, fields, and then the jungle and hills. I would take my bath in the hot springs just in front of the temple. They were the same ancient tanks of stone where Nityananda had bathed. It was a holy place.

At four a.m. the temple would open, and I would sit there until the first bells for arati sounded at four-twenty. Then I would go to Madhu Nivas for a chai, and a plate of upma poha. I arrived back at the ashram in time for the Guru Gita chant from six-thirty to eight. At nine, morning seva began in the garden.

The ashram was alive with the power of Swami Muktananda. In India, the special energy that saints and yogis have is called shakti, and the more shakti they have, the greater their status. I had yet to learn that power is an amoral force that tends to consume those that have it, rather than serve them. With one glance or one touch Muktananda could put someone into a state of bliss, and we all fondly believed that by surrendering to him, this state would one day become permanent. There was no system taught there beyond faith in the guru, but as moments of grace were so rare most of us practiced meditation to help our progress along. We wanted to make sure we were doing it right, and often asked Baba for instruction, but instead of making it clear he kept us in a state of confusion. He often said that "So'Ham japa" was the highest form of meditation, and one day we all gathered in the courtyard to hear him finally explain just how this was to be done. He said that it was in fact "Ham Sa," with the syllable "Ham" being the natural sound of the breath coming in, and "Sa" when going out. For about twenty minutes he sang the praises of "Ham Sa" meditation, and we were happy this mystery had finally been cleared up. Then, in closing, he insisted that we should all do "So Ham," and so our confusion was restored.

His favorite way of avoiding a difficult subject was to declare: "This question does not arise!" and so leave the questioner feeling stupid for asking. I never once heard him say "I don't know". He spoke with authority, and, occasionally, with real insight. One day a visitor asked why there was so much wickedness in the world, and Baba replied:

"The problem is not the wicked people: the tragedy of this world is that the good people lack the courage and energy to make their goodness prevail."

There were two moments that showed clearly what he wanted for me. One day I was coming down a flight of stairs in a rare mood of relaxed joy and simplicity: my head was empty and my heart was full. At that moment Baba happened to pass by and he looked at me with his eyes sparkling and said "Bahut Accha!" (Very good.)

The second moment came when I was working in the temple helping with a long line of devotees. Hour after hour the people came into the temple, waited their turn, and went up to see their guru, make an offering, or ask a question. At last everyone had left –except me in my place near the entrance, Baba on his cushion inside, and the priest waiting beside the statue of Swami Nityananda. My turn had come, and a wave of energy carried me over to share a rare moment with the Guru. Again there was no thought, no self-consciousness or formality: just simplicity and happiness in action. Baba had seen thousands of devotees that day, and was delighted when I just showed up, wanting nothing. In my opinion this is the real spirit of yoga.

I had been there a year when Swami Muktananda announced that he was leaving on a world tour, and would be gone a long time. A few special people were invited to go with him and there was much tension in the ashram. What would we do without our guru?

I myself had no intention of following him, and no intention of staying on after he left. I longed to return to the solitude of the Himalayas where my cottage was waiting for me. Then one day while I was crossing the courtyard, Muktananda called me over. He asked me what my plans were, speaking through his translator, a man we called Professor Jain. Like a fool, I said lamely: "I don't know."

"Stay here until I get back. It will be good for you and good for my work."

I bowed my head to the ground and thanked him. Although I did not have much real devotion to Baba, I believed him to be somehow the master of the kundalini energy that had been awakened in me, and I imagined some special destiny or attainment would result from doing what he had asked.

A fourteen-day celebration was planned leading up to Baba's departure. We kept the chant of "Hare Rama, Hare

Krishna" going without pause for fourteen days and nights. Thousands of devotees came to say goodbye. I worked most of the day, and chanted most of the night. The finale and the feast that followed were without precedent. And then the blue Mercedes drove away, and we collapsed on our mats in the dormitory, exhausted. The order came that all the men were to report to the kitchen to scrub the dining hall floor. No-one moved. It was a mutiny that went overlooked, as the ashram manager, Gopal Desai, perhaps realized he had finally gone too far.

I became ill from exhaustion. Two weeks later, when I was up and about again, very few people remained. Within two months the only foreign men there were my self, "Garden Mark", David Durrell, and Alan Bishop. We all had two things in common: we had been born in England, and under the sign of Cancer. Perhaps we just did not know how to let go, or when to quit.

The food went from bad to worse. Cabbage was the only vegetable served for months. A foul dish was made from the puris that were left over from the Sunday feeding of the poor. They were curried, as if they had been some kind of desperate vegetable. It was so disgusting even the smell of it made me feel sick. Many of the people left in charge of the place had a sinister, haunted air about them, as if they were guarding some dark secret.

I spent more and more time outside the ashram, wandering in the hills and jungles. The chants in the ashram had a lethargic, compulsory feel to them, and were devoid of devotion and joy. I found inspiration with the poor folk in the village. I soon came to doubt Baba, the ashram, and most of the people there, but I never doubted Swami Nityananda.

About this time I was introduced to two old men who had a powerful influence on my life. The first was called

Maurice Friedman. He was an Austrian who had arrived in India in the forties, seeking wisdom, and had known both Ramana Maharishi and Mahatma Gandhi. He had married a Parsi lady and they lived in a suburb of Bombay. He took me to meet a friend of his, Nisargadatta Maharaj. The Maharaj, as he was called, lived in a very poor section of Bombay near the infamous red-light district known as "the cages." This was the lowest level of prostitution in a city where anything and everything was available. The women were displayed in tiny rooms protected by vertical iron bars that made them look like cages for animals in a cheap circus. There were no young or attractive women working there.

Whenever I made the four-hour trip into Bombay, I would stay with Maurice, and go for satsang with Nisargadatta. Sometimes I would be the only person there. He lived at Keth Wadi no.10 lane above a little stall where they sold beedies, the hand made village cigarettes that poor people smoked. He was a family man, and had a wife, a son and three daughters. His apartment consisted of two small rooms downstairs, where the women lived and cooked, and two rooms upstairs, where the Maharaj held court. The front room was about fifteen feet square, and had a small window onto the street. He would sit on a deerskin, with one knee above the other and his heels beside his hips. He was always dressed in the simple home-spun way of maratha men: the white Nehru hat, the white dhoti and long shirt. His eyes would shine and his gaze was both piercing and kind. From time to time he would smoke a beedie. I secretly hoped he would offer me one, and that we would smoke together, but this never happened. Instead, whenever I opened my mouth, he would tear my ideas and opinions to shreds.

After a few visits one afternoon I found myself alone in the satsang. There was no translator, and I had nothing to say, so I just sat there. I made no attempt to meditate, because that kind of self-important effort could attract scorn from Nisargadatta.

"Who is meditating?" he would demand: "What do you wish to gain?"

"Enlightenment, Maharaj!"

"Enlightenment….for whom?"

In this manner he left no ground for self, let alone self importance, so I just sat there, and after about an hour, he got up and went into the other room. I followed. He began a lengthy puja in front of an altar that included photos of his Guru, Sri Siddharameshwar Maharaj, Ganesh, and the goddess. Since the death of his guru Nisargadatta had been the leader of the ancient and mysterious Navanath tradition. He sang songs, recited prayers, and at one point gave me a bell to ring while he waived a flame before the photos. I was very happy to witness this devotional side of a man whom I admired but was unable to understand. He impressed me, but his words somehow left me feeling empty. I understood that he was a true Marathi, and his inside was soft and full of love, even though he could appear so rough and hard on the outside. His book, *I Am That* became very popular in the west, and after a few years many earnest seekers would find their way to his satsangs –but I doubt many of them knew that their 'man of knowledge' was at heart a humble devotee. His teachings were perhaps best and most simply put in his statement:

"Wisdom tells us we are nothing –the heart tells us we are everything: between these two our life flows."

Maurice also sent me to hear the famous Jiddu Krishnamurthi. They were friends from years gone by. Once again I was impressed by the powerful, penetrating presence of the man, but not by the words that he spoke. Arriving late at the J.J. College of Art where the talks were held I could find no empty chairs so I went up and sat right in front of the raised platform where Krishnamurti was to sit. When he came out and sat down, he looked right at me for a moment. I felt like a small, helpless rodent confronting a dangerous snake. A huge soul seemed to fill the man's small, shaking body. At times he seemed angry and disgusted with us all. He accused us of leading "shoddy lives" and of wasting time with the "utter nonsense of gurus."

"I have been teaching for forty years," he announced in a very educated, upper class English accent that I knew only too well: "It has been a total waste of time!"

It was wasted on me also. After the talk I found my way to the heart of old Bombay, to Mumbai Devi temple, and there I prostrated before the goddess. Devotion was its own reward.

But Maurice was not through with me. The next day, at tea, he grilled me about my life and my plans. I told him of my dream of returning to the Himalayas, and living as a sadhu.

"A sadhu indeed! Do you know what you are?" he asked.

"Not really," was my feeble reply.

"You are a remittance man. You are nothing more than a remittance man."

It was a shock to hear this, and I was able to convince myself that it was not true because I was not getting any remittances from anyone. But Maurice, like the Maharaj, had a heart of gold. Before I left, he gave me the very first copy of *I Am That*. It was full of his pencil notes and corrections. I asked him to sign the book, and then took it to the Maharaj, who also signed it.

One evening I was walking back to Maurice's place after satsang with Maharaj when I was stopped on the road by one of Bombay's many touts –the homeless men who survive by finding customers for the cities many vices.

"You want hashish mister?"

The persistent voice followed me like a phantom in the dark.

"You want cocaine, l.s.d., ganga... mister?"

"No thanks."

"You want girl, young clean girl?"

"No thanks."

"You want boy....all night boy? Air condition room?"

"No thanks."

You want foreign liquor? Best whiskey... vodka... rum?"

"No thanks."

We both stopped at the same time and, with a look of wonder, he said: "You no want girl, boy, drugs or drink: what are you doing in Bombay?"

It was a hilarious moment, and we both laughed. I did my best to tell him I was looking for god.

On another occasion when I was not in such a good mood a similar man came up and began the same routine, and I finally lost patience and said: "fuck off!"

He came very close to me, his skin and rags filthy with the dust of the city, and his eyes flashing with fury: "You one man tell me one man fuck off? You fuck off! One thousand times you fuck off!"

The street filled up with shadowy figures that had heard his voice and drifted out of the alleys to help. They surrounded me, these street people of Bombay, and I knew I had made a mistake. I had forgotten the only thing that is really expected of a visitor to India when confronted with suffering: respect. I kept walking, and they let me go. Years later, in the depth of my own suffering, this incident came back to haunt me.

I remained at the ashram for six months after Baba left. There was no talk of his return. It was a simple incident that finally pushed me away. I was working in the temple, cleaning out the little room where the offerings of sweets and fruit were stored. Behind a drawer I found an old photo of Swami Nityananda on his death bed, surrounded by devotees. Everyone looked lost and bereaved except Swami Muktananda, who stood there with one finger pointing in a composed and masterful way. I kept this photo with me and studied it. Something did not seem right, and one day I examined it very closely and discovered faint pencil lines converging on Baba's upraised finger. With an eraser I was able to remove these lines, and also the finger itself, which had been very skillfully drawn in. Without this one decisive feature, Baba looked as lost and hopeless as the others. It was a clever deception. I examined every photo of Nityananda and Muktanada together that I could find. Most of them turned out to be fakes.

I then made the journey to Khar Road and visited the shop where Nityananda's photographer still lived. His name was M. D. Suvarna. He was a devotee of Nityananda, and the only person who had been allowed to take his photograph. He showed me every photo of the two together that he had. They told a different story, one that I could believe. Muktananda had been as much in awe of his Guru as everyone else, and looked quite lost and incomplete when he was gone.

In India great importance is given to lineage, and it is believed that the power and wisdom of a saint can be passed on like an inheritance. Muktananda and the power brokers who surrounded him had managed to create the illusion that he was the successor to Nityananda, and although many had believed them, I did not.

I longed to return to a secluded and simple life in the Himalayas and within a few days was on my way back to Tung. The rhythmic clicking of the railways, the cries of vendors on the platforms, the vast nights of India all reflected the longing in my heart. Before I left, most of my friends at the ashram had told me I was making a big mistake.

At last I stepped down from the bus and walked over the grass to Harish's cottage. He was lying on the porch in the sun, smoking a cigarette and listening to the radio. I noticed he was wearing ordinary clothes, and had given up the orange clothes of a sadhu. He rose to greet me, but there was a heavy feeling of sadness around him, and his eyes held some secret tragedy. His long black hair and beard were gone, and what was left was turning grey.

After a few days, Harish confided in me: "You know," he began: "I tried to get married while you were away."

I could think of nothing to say. At that time, I considered marriage to be spiritual suicide.

"The girl next door," he continued, "Jasmine...I have been in love with her for years."

Feeling his sorrow and loneliness, I silently vowed never to end up like him. How little I knew of life at twenty-six.

"What happened?" I asked.

"It was a matter of caste. They are a Brahmin family, and I am Kshatriya. Even though they are very poor and I did not ask for any dowry, this barrier could not be overcome. I have given up hope. She is to be married to a Brahmin boy next year."

"I am sorry." What else could I say? I had seen Jasmine and her younger sister, Kermine, almost every day. They were quite beautiful, and seemed to enjoy teasing us on our daily walk to the village well. I would see them waiting behind the gate to their house, and when they saw us coming, they would walk just ahead with their skirts swishing, one hand steadying the clay pot that balanced on their head while the other rested on a shapely hip. The sidelong glance of a young woman like that can be enough to distract anyone!

Harish never recovered. In India, you must make a choice: either get married and have a family or else renounce the world and become a sadhu: there is nothing in-between, and those who fail at either end up as outcastes from both worlds. For me the peace of the place had been destroyed and it was clear that I would not be happy living in the room we had worked so hard to build. But I remembered the mysterious community of Tibetans on the mountain above Dharmshala, and after a week with Harish, I moved on to McCleod Ganj.

Batterbury family 1949: Left to right: George,
Mark, Adrian, Susan, Edward and Leonie.

Tung. Harish, and my cottage under construction.

The village of Tung.

Author, India, 1974.

The Chai shop, Shree Gurudev Ashram 1973.
Left to right: Chris Canning, Mark Mordin,
Robbie Rabbin, Author and Joe Malinos

The houseboat scene on the Ganges, Varanasi 1974.

A Chai shop, McCleod Ganj.
Author having tea with the locals.

"Thank You" from mother India.

Chapter 9: *McCleod Ganj*

Cold woke me at dawn, and I waited for the familiar calls of birds, but everything was silent. Then the low cadence of throat chanting and the roar of horns reminded me I was now in a Tibetan community. Silence and chanting came and went with the rhythm of the wind.

It was October of 1973, and the hilltop community of Tibetan refugees at McCleod Ganj had not been discovered. I found a room just above the town, in the backyard of a retired Gurkha, Brigadier Thappa. It was a secluded place and only a few minutes walk from the bazaar. There were about a dozen grand old mansions hidden in the pine forests around the town. This had been a less fashionable hill station during the British time, and had attracted people looking for real privacy. The largest and most central of these houses was known as the "old palace," because the Dalai Lama had stayed there for a few years before his new residence was built on the hill overlooking lower Dharmshala.

The town was a rectangle of shops around a small stupa and the prayer wheel near the bus-stand. To the west a road along the edge of the mountain led to the Dalai Lama's residence and the main Tibetan temple. To the east another road went on up the mountain. The oldest shop in town was Nowrojees. It seemed to have ignored the passage of time, and huge glass jars of sweets suggested that Mrs. Nowrojee was still expecting English children to come in and spend their allowance. She stocked luxury items such as hot chocolate, canned fruit, marmalade and oatmeal. She also sold tea from the Sidhbari estate nearby. It was the best tea I had ever tasted. Her most regular customers were the Dalai Lama and his staff. The Nowrojees made and bottled their own brand of soda. Later I recognized this store as being a feature of the novel *A Fine Balance*. The building was indeed anchored to the mountainside by a cable.

I continued my routine of rising early and taking a bath before dawn, the difference being that instead of the hot springs of Ganeshpuri, here it was the cold water of Bhagsunath temple. This was the original Shiva temple of the hill tribes who had been there before the English and Tibetans came. They were a quiet people, used to being treated as strangers in their own land. There was a waterfall and a bathing tank in the grounds of the temple, and there I took my bath before morning meditation and prayers. I was on my own, and had to keep up these practices without any external structure.

There was an atmosphere of excitement and freedom on the mountain and in the little town. Here and there in the pine forest the houses left behind by the English had been rented out to foreign visitors and dharma students who lived there, sometimes for years. About halfway up the hill between upper and lower Dharmshala, the Tibetans had built a library where courses in the Tibetan language and religion were taught. A community of dharma students had formed, and this library was their meeting place. Some of these students had ordained and become lamas themselves. I would see them walking around town or sitting in tea shops in their maroon robes. They always seemed to be talking about the dharma. In the courtyard in front of the temple and monastery at the Dalai Lama's residence, these discussions took on a ritual form, and the monks would dance and clap their hands as they debated the teachings. I became interested in Buddhism, and asked questions when I got the chance.

After my recent disappointment with Muktananda, it was interesting to hear about a path that offered enlightenment through ones own efforts. The focus of this personal effort was meditation, and I decided to learn how they did it, and what the basic teachings of the Buddha were.

There was a house on the far side of the hill owned by a German woman called Leah. She was a student of a meditation teacher from Burma called Goenka, and their form of meditation was known as Vipassana. I was so eager to learn that I asked Leah to teach me. This she was kind enough to do one evening while washing dishes:

"Oh no," she said, catching herself cheerfully: "I have taught you anna panna over the kitchen sink!"

This was mindfulness of the breath, the first step of Vipassana meditation. We laughed at the contrast between our spontaneous simplicity and the ceremony and ritual that was all around us.

I decided to find Goenka and attend a meditation retreat with him to learn more. I was told there was a twenty day retreat being held at the Burmese Buddhist Vihara in Varanasi during December.

It was another long and lonely journey to an unknown destination. The trains in India always seem to leave during the night and to arrive at some desolate station in the early hours of dawn when it is impossible to find accommodation. I would sit and wait, with only my inner longing for freedom to keep up my spirits. I found my way from the station to the gate of the Vihara at about six a.m., and waited there. Eventually it was opened from the inside by an American who led me to a desk where I could register for the retreat. Being a new student, I was signed in for two ten day retreats, as the continuous twenty day retreat was reserved for experienced meditation students.

The Vihara was situated in an industrial area of Varanasi, near the railway station, and beside a yard where state transport buses were repaired. A sheet metal shop was nearby. I wondered how anyone could meditate in such noise and pollution, but the Vihara soon filled up with people from every part of the world. I was delighted when I recognized a friend from Ganeshpuri called Claude, who arrived with two young women from Australia.

We all gathered in the meditation hall that evening, and waited for Sri S.N. Goenka to arrive. Everyone seemed to know what they were doing, and sat there with closed eyes. I attempted to practice the mindfulness of breath that I had been taught by Leah. Then a deep, soothing voice began to speak. Goenka had come in quietly and sat on the raised seat prepared for him. He sang a brief chant in the Pali language, and then led us in taking refuge in the triple gem of Buddha, Dharma and Sangha. That evening I heard the teachings of the Buddha for the first time. It was the four noble truths that hit me the hardest. When I heard that suffering was a noble truth of life, and that there was a cause of suffering, and end of suffering, and a path leading to the end of suffering, I could not stop crying.

Surrounded by the noise of traffic and industry, in a crowded room where the windows were kept closed and the air became so stuffy I could hardly breathe, somehow I began to practice Vipassana. Every evening there was a dharma discourse. Every morning there were beautiful chants that would end with Goenka walking slowly out of the hall, still singing in his deep, powerful voice. My favorite was a song of gratitude to the motherly woman who had helped him when he himself had been a struggling student in Burma. Then the bell would ring for breakfast.

I suffered for ten days in the crowded, stuffy room, and then had a day of rest before the second retreat began. During the long hours of sitting the pain of loss had caught up with me. The illusion that I had found a friend in Harish and a home in the Himalayas had been shattered. My second illusion, that I had met a real guru in the form of Swami Muktananda who would guide my spiritual journey, had also been shaken. I wanted something to believe in.

Claude and I took a rickshaw to the banks of the Ganges, and went for a ride on a rowboat. I was surprised to find myself overflowing with joy. That evening the second retreat began, and another ten days of knee pain, back pain and suffocation in the black hole of meditation.

During the second retreat I requested a private interview with Goenka. I was shown into his rooms, where he sat on a comfortable chair, eating breakfast. In a rather disdainful way, he pointed to the floor in front of him. I sat down, and he asked what I wanted to know. I said I had just come from a very different path where surrender to the guru was considered everything, and was confused about which way was right.

"Muktanand?" he enquired.

"Yes. He taught us that liberation is only possible by the grace of the guru."

"I don't think so," he said simply: "On this path you must work out your own salvation."

I continued to meditate with a growing pain in my heart. It was physical as well as emotional. I was disappointed that the discourses were exactly the same as the first ten days. Apparently they were always the same. I was also disappointed to notice the elite circle of "old students" who sat at the front and were only too happy to remind new people of the many rules. I asked why the windows were kept closed, and was told that the draft would disturb our concentration. This did not make any sense, and the stuffy atmosphere continued to make meditation all but impossible.

On the final day, the pain in my heart finally broke open, and I finished the retreat on a happy note. I felt I had found a valuable path, but that this teacher and tradition were not right for me. Working out my own salvation was not going to be easy.

There had been a young English monk called Bhikkhu Kitty Subha sitting with us. He sat at the front with a few other men in the orange robes of Theravadin monks, and I hardly noticed him. There was talk about some retreats to be held at Goa, on the beach, conducted by this monk. Claude and his two lady friends wanted to go and do some more meditation and I decided to join them.

The four of us traveled south, hitching rides on trucks. It was a wonderful way to see the country. We perched on the roof of a highly decorated truck as it roared down the narrow highways, avoiding collisions by inches in what seemed like an endless series of miracles. We would stop for tea and meals at roadside hotels with stoves made of mud that all seemed the same. There would always be three or four huge pots, with vegetable curry, rice, dal and chappaties. As most truckers were Sikhs, it was the hearty food of the Punjab that was served. We were a curiosity, and I think there were

many jokes made at the expense of the girls that it was perhaps best we did not understand –but we were always treated well. For two days we were the guest of a retired driver
called Bhagwan Singh, who owned a truck stop restaurant
with about a dozen cots under an awning where tired drivers often spent the night. He kept us there until he found a
driver willing to take us to Khajuraho, our next destination.
As we were leaving, he pointed to the trucks and drivers
gathered at his restaurant, and then pointed to the open road
before us, and said: "Once I was king of all this."

As our truck pulled away, one of the girls called out:
"You're still the king, Bhagwan!"

Khajuraho had escaped the immense campaign of destruction carried out by centuries of Islamic occupation by
virtue of being lost in uninhabited jungle. It is a magical and
perfect setting for these jewels of Hindu architecture. The
temples are carved from reddish stone that seems to live and
breathe divinity. Every aspect of life is there, and it is all
pervaded with the beauty and power of god. I spent hours
among the temples, filled with a longing that I did not understand. Why did my heart ache so in that holy place?

Claude met the local Maharaja, and we were all invited
to stay in two spare rooms that he had in his simple palace.
We met the family priest, and old Brahmin who was dying
at peace in a cool room made of stone. The Maharaja was a
kind, quiet man with dark eyes that seemed to contain the
eternal mystery of India.

We also met a holy man who lived in a hut under a tree
near the town. He would spend his days sitting on a blanket
in the shade of his tree. I envied his simple life and the peace
he had attained, and imagined that he was free from the
many desires that tormented me.

The focus of my loneliness, together with strong sexual
feelings, was on one of the young women we were travel-

ing with. Filled with insecurity and devoid of confidence, I expressed my feelings, and was rejected without mercy. We carried on as if nothing had happened, but I was once again longing for solitude. I still imagined freedom to be a state where such desires and painful failures did not arise. During the retreat we had been told that the practice cultivated qualities of mind such as equanimity and dispassion, but in my case it seemed to be having the opposite effect. Perhaps the many sensuous, erotic carvings that decorated the temples were trying to tell me something.

I separated from my companions and returned for a short visit to the ashram at Ganeshpuri. Very few of my former friends remained. I bathed once again in the hot springs, visited the temple of the goddess at Vajreshwari, and the Samadhi of Swami Nityananda. In Bombay, I visited Nisargadatta once again. He asked me why I had come, but was not satisfied with my answer:

"Are you ready to die?" he asked me: "It is death to come here... do not return unless you are ready to die!"

I was tired of hearing about the death of the ego, and beginning to doubt the wisdom of the common belief among seekers that this was the way to freedom. I left, still wondering what Nisargadatta was trying to teach. It was a long journey back to Dharmshala.

I arrived at the beginning of March, and once again took a room in the Tourist Bungalow. It was so cold that I decided to delay returning to McCleod Ganj, 1500 feet higher up the mountain, until April. In Dharmshala, I found my first friend in a man called Puri Neelam, who kept a small coffee shop in the bazaar. He spoke good English, and was glad to pass the time talking and joking. His shop could seat six people, and was almost always empty. He made a few rupees a day. My second friend was the old Nepali stamp collector called Ranu, whom I had met two years before when I had first arrived in Dharmshala on my way to Tung. I met him again one day while buying fruit at the corner produce stall. He invited me to sit with him in the sun, and asked if I had any more foreign stamps. The stall keeper was his friend, and Ranu would spend an hour there every afternoon.

My third friend was called Kissan Sharma. He was a young music teacher with a wild nature that showed in his long, curly hair. I decided to learn sitar with him, and joined his lively group of musicians. They met every evening in a two-roomed cottage just below the town. One of the rooms was empty, and Kissan suggested that I rent it from him. The cottage had a small balcony that overlooked a stream. On the other side of the stream was a path that led up to the bazaar about ten minutes away. It was a beautiful place to live. I was alone all day, and in the evenings enjoyed the music. Kissan would give me a brief lesson on the sitar, and then the other young men would arrive and begin to play. There was a tabla player, a flute player, Kissan on Sitar, and various other local folk would drop in to play harmonium and tamboura, or just sit and enjoy the music.

When Kissan's birthday came, they decided to have a party. I was encouraged to ask young western women to attend. It was April by this time, and quite a few travelers were staying in the area. I invited the few I knew, and three of them showed up at the party. Kissan provided a huge jug of local liquor called Raaki. It was very strong. The music was wild, and soon the young Indian men began asking the good-natured girls to dance. I remember the flute player, Hari, who played very beautifully when he was not dancing. At one point someone fell down and crushed one of Kissans sitars, but he never missed a beat.

"All things must die," he commented, philosophically. I was very impressed by his lack of attachment.

Soon the young men were drunk, and a fight broke out over who would dance with the girls. I was not drinking: at that time I could meditate for hours, but did not know how to have fun. The girls became frightened, and left. Someone went outside and puked in the stream. The party was a great success.

About a month later I was stopped on the street by Hari, the flute player. He spoke with great sincerity:

"I want to thank you for that wonderful experience," he began: "I had never danced with a girl before that night. It was a very good experience for me."

His eyes carried some mystery and longing, perhaps caused by a separation of the genders that has been all but lost in the west. In his society, contact with women of his own age was almost unknown before marriage, and that drunken evening of music and dance had been an initiation for him.

"I had a mystical experience while dancing." He told me: "I am glad to have this chance to thank you for inviting those girls to the party. Now I return to Bombay."

Later I learned that his full name was Hariprasad Chaurasia. He went on to become the most famous flute player in India.

In May I began attending the Tibetan library as a student in a course called Lam Rim. It was an introduction to Tibetan Buddhism. The teacher was a monk called Lama Yeshe, who was visiting from Nepal. Every day I walked up the hill to the library for the teachings. After class I would have lunch at the little shop where cheerful Tibetan cooks prepared bread called Moo Moo and lentil soup. Our class had about twenty students who came from every part of the world. They seemed very serious about their studies, and had an attitude of respect verging on awe for the teacher. Whenever he arrived they would stand reverently with bowed heads as he walked slowly by. This was repeated when the lama left after class.

One teaching I remember well. From time to time students would tell Lama Yeshe their troubles, or ask him for help when their visas ran out and they had to leave India. One day he paused in the middle of his talk, and looked out at us in silence for a moment, and said: "Most of you have been coming here for the teachings for many months, some of you for a few years, and yet as soon as something goes wrong in your life, you act as if you had never heard a word of dharma."

Lama Yeshe taught in Tibetan, which was translated into English by two Tibetan monks. They were intelligent young men who were regarded by everyone as Dharma itself. They took turns translating, and their bright smiles and devoted attention to the teachings were an inspiration to us all. One day there was no translator, and so class had to be postponed. The two young monks were nowhere to be found. A few days later we heard a report from New Delhi where they had been seen, wearing blue jeans, and in the company of two blonde girls from America.

After three months of classes I graduated from Lam Rim with a basic understanding of the teachings of Tibetan Buddhism. What my intuition had told me had been confirmed: structured religions were just not for me. At the age of twelve I had rejected the Christian church, and I rejected Tibetan Buddhism for the same reasons: I wanted direct experience, not belief. I was looking for my own inner relationship with the creator, not an external relationship with the hierarchy of an organized religion.

When the warmer weather of summer arrived I moved up to McCleod Ganj. I found a room in the guardhouse behind the Old Palace for twenty rupees a month. It had a cool verandah where I sat and watched the monkeys playing in the rhododendron trees. Beyond the clearing around the guardhouse was the intersection of two paths, one that led around the mountain and the other up towards Dharamkot by way of a retreat center called Tushita. From time to time I saw a monk stop there to rest. He would walk slowly from the direction of Leah's house, and, after resting for a few minutes, continue up to the retreat house. He had an aura of calm and joy about him that attracted me, and one day I walked over and offered him a glass of cool water. He took it with a smile. This became a ritual whenever I saw him there. Neither of us said a word.

One day I decided to go on up to Tushita and see what was happening there. The door was open to the main room, and a group of students were sitting there, about to receive teachings from this mysterious lama. I went quietly in and sat on the floor behind him. He turned and smiled at me, as if so say, what are you doing here? I understood his meaning, and left –dharma class was not for me. A few days later I found my way to the little cottage were he lived. He was sitting quietly on the porch. I approached with folded hands, and gave him a ripe mango. He pointed to the cottage were a young monk lived who was his translator, and motioned for me to call him. I smiled and shook my head, bowed briefly, and left. This monk's name was Geshe Rapten, and by refusing any verbal communication with him, I unknowingly invited him to teach me in my dreams. In one of these dreams, he pointed me in the direction of the young English monk, Bhikkhu Kitty Subha, whom I had seen at the retreat in Varanasi. His suggestion was that I learn the dharma from him

Soon after this dream, my old friend Claude showed up, and invited me to help him cook for a retreat that was being planned in Manali with Bhikkhu Kitty Subha. He was very enthusiastic about the teacher and the direction his dharma practice was taking, and clearly believed that it would be good for me, too, but I was not ready to leave my routine of music lessons and personal practice. Claude said he would see me again in about a month when he got back from Manali.

It was a magical time to be young, healthy and living in India. As a Canadian, I did not need a visa. India had not yet advanced too far into the industrial revolution that forever changed the landscape and polluted the atmosphere in the 1980s. God was alive and well, and in particular I identified with the Hindu yogis and sadhus who had renounced the world to live in spirit. They were wild and free, and had more in common with the Respas of Tibet than with the well fed monks who lived around McCleod Ganj.

In the Himalayas, Hinduism and Buddhism have evolved together and the differences do not seem to be a problem. According to the teachings of yoga, one is free to believe in god or not, without it affecting the power of the practices. This seemed to me to be a very intelligent and practical approach. Although I met some Buddhists who were critical of Hinduism, I never met a Hindu who was intolerant of Buddhism, and it was universally accepted that the teachings of the Buddha were a part of the same Sanatan dharma that had given birth to so many great saints.

The debate between devotional people and those that valued knowledge was a part of Indian culture. Vedanta values knowledge, while Bhakti is the path of love. Buddhism was in some ways similar to Vedanta. It was language that caused the perception of differences. The existence of self was as obvious as the existence of a creator, and I had given up doubts about either.

As belief was not essential to the practice, and gave rise to endless speculation and argument, the Buddha wisely refrained from discussing these points. My quest was to experience what the words "God" and "Self" pointed to. To dismiss as Maya, or illusion, the obvious glory of creation was to me just plain stupid. I could not forget what had been shown to me in Mexico, and it was with a growing intensity that I continued my practice of self inquiry.

Summer came to the Himalayas with the glorious flowering of the rhododendron trees. On the mountain above the town, these trees became a forest of red where monkeys lived. Some of the flowering rhodos were as large as oak trees, and could feed a whole tribe of black faced langur monkeys. At higher elevations, there would be a few rhododendrons with white and even blue flowers.

I began to feel stuck in my own routine, and one day I decided to make some changes. I had been given a book called *Dice Therapy* written by Luke Rhineheart, and decided to put the simple technique into practice. I wrote down a list of six possible projects for the day, and then rolled the dice to see which one I would go for. The technique required that I have a non-negotiable determination to take action. It was suggested that at least two of the six suggestions be risky challenges that would take me towards my fears and avoidances. I had been avoiding women and sexuality. The first time I tried this experiment, after listing five fairly safe possibilities, I wrote:

"Make love to the girl who just moved in to room number three."

I rolled the dice and got a six. At this time it had been years since I had been in any kind of relationship. I had been very strict about celibacy and renunciation.

I knocked on the door of room number three and a cheerful girl with dark hair and brown eyes opened the door. She had just arrived in McCleod Ganj. I had seen her once before, and found her attractive.

"Hello", I began: "My name is Mark. I have come to make love to you."

I suppose I have used worse lines than this, both before and since, but the effect was interesting –her eyes widened with a rare mixture of shock and interest. Then she laughed in a truly wonderful way:

"Whoa! Slow down, Dude....would you like to go for a walk and talk a bit....so we can get to know each other?"

"Sure." This was fantastic! It was a lovely, warm evening. We sat on a hill and watched a flying squirrel walk out to the end of a pine branch to launch itself into the twilight and soar down the valley out of sight.

Her name was Gail. We both opened our hearts and talked about our lives and our travels. When I confessed my dice therapy experiment, she punched me on the shoulder. We kissed, but it was clear to both of us that we were meant to be friends, not lovers. This friendship lasted many years.

A few days later I again wrote six choices, rolled the dice, and got number four:

"Don't say no to anything today."

I sat on my porch, wondering what could happen. In the afternoon, a friend called John, who lived higher up the mountain, stopped by on his way down to the post office. I said nothing of my experiment. John liked to party while I liked to meditate. An hour later he stopped again on his way back up, and sat down on my porch to open a small parcel that had arrived from a friend in Thailand. John was delighted with the contents: "Far out! Thai sticks!"

"Would you like some?" he asked as a joke, lighting one up. I had not smoked pot in many years.

"Sure," I replied, much to his surprise.

I had never experienced a high like that. John continued on up the path to his cottage in Dharmkot, and I sat there in bliss. After so many years of yoga and self-discipline, the effects of the marijuana were profound. I was living in a truly magical land, in the prime of my life, with infinite possibilities all around me. The power of the place, the presence of the Tibetans, the awesome beauty and majesty of the Himalayas all came into focus. It was good to be alive.

The energy of McCleod Ganj would often accelerate the spiritual awakening of visitors in surprising ways. One young American called Neil had been inspired to embrace the Tibetan Dharma, and was spending much of his time in retreat. From time to time he would complain of the frequent letters he got from his parents that expressed their concern and implored him to return home and stop wasting his life. Finally Neil's mother wrote to inform him that she was on her way to rescue him. Neil dreaded the approaching arrival of his conservative parent, and continued his meditations. When the good woman finally showed up and began making inquiries about her son, Neil was away in retreat. In her explorations and search around town, she met a German man by the name of Dieter, who was charismatic and forceful in his quest for personal awakening, and always happy to share his ideas with others. By the time Neil came down from the mountain to meet his mother she was in retreat herself, and did not want to be disturbed.

It was during this summer that I met Mary. It was a mutual attraction and soon we were making love on a hill in the moonlight. Then she left with a guy from Switzerland. I was surprised to find the old feelings of jealousy and loss just did not arise. This was as close to free love as I ever got.

Chapter 10: *Upper Bagorta*

One day towards the end of summer I was sitting in my room meditating when Claude came in and gave me a hug. Over a cup of chai he told me the retreat in Manali had been great, and that they were planning to form a dharma community and hold more retreats near a hill station called Dalhousie. This time I was ready to join them. An advance party had gone ahead to Dalhousie to find accommodation, and had rented a house on a hill top called Upper Bagorta. I signed up for a retreat that was to begin at the end of June. I kept my room in the guard house, thinking I would return after the ten days of meditation.

Upper Bagorta was at an altitude of 9000 feet. On one side was a magnificent view of the Chamba river valley and the Himalayas beyond that rose to more than 20,000 feet. The hill top was circled by a quiet path called "ring road."

Here and there beside this road were houses that had been built by the British. Gita house was one of these, situated on the west side of the hill, and overlooking the town of Dalhousie. It was about a forty-five minute walk from the upper bazaar of Dalhousie to Gita house. Where the road up the mountain connected with ring road there was a chai shop. A man called "Muchloo" had built a shack beside the road, and put a table and some chairs at the edge of the cliff. Muchloo's was the only tea shop in Upper Bagorta, and became our hangout.

There were about twenty of us in the retreat, all quite young. At thirty-two the teacher, Bhikkhu Kitty Subha, was perhaps the oldest. I was now twenty-seven and had been in India for three years. We referred to our teacher as "Luong Pi," which is Thai for "young monk." The retreat began with great intensity and enthusiasm. Luong Pi was passionately dedicated to the dharma he had learned and practiced in Thailand. He gave two talks every day: in the morning he spoke in detail about the practice of insight meditation, and in the evening he spoke on life and the dharma in a broader context. A simple breakfast was served at eight a.m., a vegetarian lunch at noon, and tea and a piece of fruit at five. There was no evening meal. We alternated sitting and walking meditation, with the focus being on mindfulness of the sensations in the body, moment to moment. We did at least ten hours of meditation each day. At the end of the ten days I was feeling inspired and asked Luong Pi if I could join the group of students who were planning to stay on at Gita house to continue their practice, and he welcomed me.

When I returned to McCleod Ganj to collect my things, I felt that something was very wrong there. Rumors of conflict between India and China were circulating, and the Tibetans feared being forced to relocate. There was an army base near by, and the whole area was considered politically sensitive. One monk had committed suicide, another had been stung to death by bees, and my friend Puri Neelam had died suddenly. The dark mood of the place hit me in the gut when I got off the bus from Dalhousie.

I gave up my room at the Guard House and stayed with a friend who had a room near the town. Her name was Marjorie, and she was a doctor of psychology from Scotland who had been living in India for a long time. One night while we were talking she smoked a joint, and then ventured out to relieve herself in her usual spot among the bushes near the path. She came in from the darkness with her face drained of color, and said:

"Could you tell me what I have just seen?"

Her thick accent trembled when she spoke. Something had frightened her: "I mean, is anything really there? I'm quite stoned, you know, and could be imagining things…. but I don't think so."

She gave me her flashlight and told me where to look. I went slowly up the path from her door until a tiny flicker of light caught my eye. The flashlight revealed something like a miniature temple, or a toy house. It was made of colored yarn, pieces of wood and a paste of butter mixed with tsampa, the roasted barley flour that was a staple part of the Tibetan diet. A butter lamp burned before a perfect image of Marjorie that was standing like a doll at the centre of the construction.

"Yes, it's real." I assured her upon my return to the room. Neither of us knew what it was. The next day I saw another of these strange devices at the junction of two paths. Sticks of Tibetan incense burned in each corner, and the aroma of herbs drifted gently among the pines.

I later learned that they were called "demon catchers" and had been made by the monks in an effort to dispel the darkness that had invaded their town. Perhaps they had seen some negative energy around Marjorie, and were helping her as well. The intention was to attract the dark energy into the image and then neutralize it with prayers. Their efforts were successful, and when I returned five months later the mood of the town was once again happy, and Marjorie had left for Nepal.

Our sangha in Upper Bagorta was growing and the house next door to Gita House, Nirmal House, had been rented for people like myself who intended to stay on. In time, another cottage called Tupru House was rented for private retreats.

It was a golden time. The monsoon rains began, and our mountain retreat was bombarded with thunder storms and heavy rain. Then the sun would come out and the Himalayas shone with fresh snow in a sky washed clean of any pollution. Each month we held a ten-day retreat when about forty people would show up and we would have to sleep six or more to a room. Then, when the retreat ended, about twenty of us remained to continue our practice.

Luong Pi worked himself to exhaustion during these early months of his career as a dharma teacher. Those of us fortunate enough to be there got the benefit of his heart-felt, tireless dedication to the practice of mindfulness and the teachings of the Buddha. On the seventh day of each retreat, he would give a talk that we came to call "the U.T. talk", U.T. standing for "ultimate truth". We fondly believed that the state of awareness being described was, in fact, the ultimate truth. Emptyness...shunyata...no-self: this was the point of view championed by such teachers as Nagarjuna, Wei Wu Wei, and most who call themselves Buddhist. Could that pesky self, with its misery, fears and desires, be in fact just an illusion? I was determined to get to the bottom of this.

I increased my practice. Every full moon, I would sit all through the night. When my legs got cramped I would get up and take a slow walk in the moonlight. When dawn came I went to Muchloos for a cup of chai. Each ten-day retreat would end with a final talk about integrating the practice into daily life, and then we would sing dharma chants together, and have a festive meal. After ten days of silence, it was fun to meet the people I had been sitting with.

During these retreats, there would always be one girl I found attractive, and I would often sit and dream of her instead of meditating. There would also be one person I found very irritating, and upon them I would focus my negativity. I was not alone in this, and in time it became known as the "Vipassana Romance" and the "Vipassana Villain" syndrome.

After hearing Swami Muktananda talk about the power of celibacy so often, I was actually very one-pointed about keeping all my sexual energy within. From time to time sexual desire would arise and increase slowly, but I would continue to sit and breathe and not do anything to release it. Then the golden, creative life force would suddenly move up my spine and spread throughout my entire being in a most wonderful way, leaving me energized, full of joy, and without any desires at all.....for the time being.

During this time, Luong Pi was grooming one of his students to be his assistant. According to some of the people there, this young woman from Canada was "an enlightened being." Luong Pi certainly seemed to think so and soon Christina was giving talks and helping him teach. They began to receive special food, which bothered some of the people there. After all, we had nothing to do all day but practice mindfulness in very primitive conditions, and we had to find some distractions.

A few days into the second retreat, one of the women sitting with us became sick with hepatitis. Very quickly her condition deteriorated, and soon she was taken down to the hospital in Dalhousie. I saw her being carried out on a stretcher. Her face was yellow and drawn with pain. Two days later she died and Luong Pi gave a very powerful talk on impermanence and the value of our brief human life.

On another occasion, in the middle of a meditation, we heard a crash followed by shouting. Some people had been leaning on the railing outside which had collapsed, sending them over a twelve foot cliff.

"Watching the mind," said Luong Pi.

We kept sitting. When the hour came to an end, we went outside to find everyone o.k. The atmosphere in Gita House was cheerful, but very focused, and charged with the promise of freedom.

I volunteered to help cook for the next retreat. We were helped by the sweeper, Kirpoo, who came in every afternoon to make enough chappaties to feed about thirty hungry people. This was unheard of in Hindu society –the man who emptied the commodes also preparing food? Juttha.... pollution! When my time as a cook came to an end I was given the reward of a private retreat, with a room to myself in Tupru House about half a mile away. Meals would be brought to the door, and Luong Pi would visit once a day to discuss my practice. This was a golden opportunity.

My only book was the copy of *I Am That* by Nisargadatta that Maurice had given me. It was my practice in those days to stop reading when I came to a passage that I did not understand, or had not experienced for myself. Needless to say, I had not got very far.

Nisargadatta seemed to be always speaking with absolute certainty from a non-dual state of all-inclusive consciousness. To experience this was my intention and my goal. I began my retreat by spending an entire day doing nothing but standing meditation. I had an aversion to this form of practice that I wished to overcome. The next day, I began a more balanced routine of sitting, walking, yoga and chanting. I found a secluded rock where the morning sunshine warmed me as I sang the devotional songs I had learned in Swami Muktananda's ashram.

Meanwhile my rapport with Luong Pi was breaking down. While his insight into the dharma and his passion for the practice was unquestionable, I had trouble relating to him on any other subject, and I did not really feel at home in the practice and the dharma as he taught it, with the constant focus on emptiness. My meditation at this time was more in the way Nisargadatta and Maurice had shown me, a gut-level questioning of everything –including the teachings.

I had an unshakeable conviction that if anything could be known, it was not the final state, the real self-nature. I had been taught that the source of consciousness contained both the knower and the known. I was aware of my thoughts, my feelings, and the sensations in my body from moment to moment, and I just let go of them all. At this time I was enjoying very good health, abundant energy, and my body was light and flexible from years of yoga.

It occurred to me that the state of freedom must somehow be already attained, or it could not be my real self-nature. By the seventh day of my solitary retreat I was sitting with very little effort, supported by a deep sense of joy. One morning I felt in every cell a presence that had always been there. With great interest I watched thoughts, emotions, and states of mind with the awareness "not this, not this". This use of doubt to cut through appearances was called "neti, neti" in India. I rested on the faith that the self was already present, was already my very essence. But where, how was it hidden?

In a moment that was outside of time, the whole psychic force of "the seeker", of "me, looking," was suddenly known from a different level. The "I" became unreal, and could be seen as just a reflection of the known that arose within consciousness itself. The awareness that contained and knew all this was clearly the very ground of my being.

The first thought to arise in this clarity was the memory of the voice of the goddess in my vision:

"When the moment comes, look towards heaven."

When I raised my head in response to this memory, my heart exploded with love, and the clarity of consciousness was filled with ecstatic joy. The divine mother was there as a formless power that filled the space of consciousness. It was the very same unity of love that I had experienced in Mexico.

This wonderful moment was the culmination of seven years of intense effort. After sitting there for a long time, I got up slowly and walked to my rock on the hill. The sun shone on my tears that day as I sang my devotional songs with real gratitude and joy. Later that day as I walked around ring road on the way to Muchloos chai shop I passed Christina and Luong Pi, walking together and enjoying a rest from teaching. I smiled as they passed by….. there was nothing to say.

I relaxed in my room, and rested. One journey had ended, and a vision had been fulfilled, but I knew in my heart that this powerful awakening contained the beginning of an even more difficult vision, one that took far longer and demanded more suffering and sacrifice than I could imagine at that time.

Chapter 11: *Freedom?*

The next day, when Luong Pi arrived for my practice review, he knocked on the door and announced himself with a friendly: "Tat Tvam Asi," meaning "That thou art."

I greeted him and he took a seat, kindly waiting for my questions and a progress report. I just sat there with a big smile on my face, and said I was doing fine. What had happened was beyond description and I had a growing feeling that my new vision pointed in a direction that insight meditation and dharma teaching could not embrace. It was grace in a form that I call the Divine Mother that had carried me to the same experience as the mushrooms in Mexico. It was this same power that had now given me a new challenge: to overcome the obstacles that prevented that state of love and unity from remaining constant. In other words, to clear the clouds that floated in the sky of my consciousness and to free my heart from any conditioning that caused a feeling of separation from the creator.

I finished my ten days of solitary retreat without making any further efforts to meditate –there was no longer any point. Then I returned to the community in Gita house. It was a time of real happiness. The hours of sitting passed without effort: I just sat there, being still and enjoying the sounds that floated in. After a few days I joined my friend Mac in a bungalow called Agit House that he had rented for himself on the hillside above Muchloos shop. It had a magnificent view of the Himalayas to the North. My room had a fireplace with an old hand-knotted carpet in front of it and had been the living room in the time of the English. About a hundred feet below, on the same hillside, was a hut where the caretaker and his wife lived. They were old people who had been looking after the place for a long time. Mac had arranged for them to bring us breakfast and lunch.

I floated on a golden cloud. It was October and the rains had stopped, giving way to cool, clear weather. Across the valley the mountains gleamed with fresh snow. It was the season of cicadas, and their ecstatic singing came and went with the sun. Every morning I would sit from before dawn until breakfast arrived at about 7:30: two chappaties, a sweet dish called sera, and chai. After breakfast I would walk around the mountain, and then sit again in meditation. Before lunch, I would do an hour of yoga asanas, and then sit again until hearing the caretaker's call for lunch: "khanna.... khanna taiyar!" "Food.... food is ready!"

After lunch I would rest for an hour, and then again walk around the mountain. There was a canyon with a stream at the far end and a high, flat rock that overlooked the forest of oak and rhododendron trees. Flocks of finches would fly up and down the valley. They were all different colors: red, yellow, blue and green birds all flying together. Occasionally I encountered three Tibetan monks in the woods. The leader was huge, and had an aura of quiet power. They would pass by with wonderful, peaceful smiles.

One day at sunset I was sitting in my room just listening to the enchanting sound of wind in the pines. After about thirty minutes it occurred to me that there were no pine trees at that elevation. I went outside and found that there was no wind, either. The sound was coming from inside me. I sat on the narrow ledge of grass in front of my room and closed my eyes. A heavenly choir of voices was singing far away, like the sound of surf on some hidden shore of white sand. At times it sounded like a conch shell in a temple, at times like the sirens in Debussy's nocturne. It seemed to be the primal sound of OM arising within consciousness.

For about a week this inner sound was there day or night whenever I listened for it. I had never heard anything so beautiful, and for that week had no other desire than to let my soul be bathed in that music. Then it vanished as mysteriously as it had arrived.

During this time I would lie on my back at night and remain aware as dreams entered my consciousness. Periods of deep dreamless sleep were also known, and the awareness of my self as a separate individual would arise at dawn with the first sense impression. All this was in accordance to the dharma teachings I had heard about the nature of awareness. My definition of ego at that time was related to the "I" that arose in reflection of sense experience, as the subject that experienced. It was my belief that insight into this dependant arising had cut through and liberated me from the fetters of the mind. My understanding had been conditioned by the teaching of both Buddhism and Vedanta, and yet neither path remained under my feet. By my own efforts I had fulfilled the vision of the hongos, and yet my heart now contained the seed of an even deeper and more mysterious longing. A voice from the depths of my soul had asked to know the mystery of love...and love seemed to be unknowable.

One by one our sangha dispersed. The teachers were planning to visit a few places in north India and then conduct retreats in Bodh Gaya during the cool months of December and January. For a week I remained alone in Agit house. Winter was coming, and soon Dalhousie would be covered in snow. At the end of October I packed my few belongings and boarded the bus for Pathankot, and then the night train to Delhi.

I must confess that during this phase of my life no-one could tell me a thing, and I floated around India in a carefree but vulnerable condition. I had no belief system to follow, no teacher that I felt a real connection to, and no teaching that reflected my experience. For years I had worked to free myself from limiting concepts and the burden of accumulated knowledge, but I had nothing to fill the void that was all I had left. When I was in a state of bliss, this was not a problem, but the rest of the time, it was.

Although I still felt at home in India, where homeless people are forever wandering, it was impossible to remain in the noise and pollution of Delhi, and so I caught yet another overnight train, this time to Rishikesh.

In India, people have community. Regardless of a person's status or caste or religion, there are others to share life with, and solitude is all but unknown. Even the sadhus who had renounced family life in order to seek god usually belonged to some tradition or had allegiance to a guru, and that became their community. But I found myself quite alone. The one thing I had shared with my fellow seekers had been the search for freedom, the sense of suffering or lack that urged us on in our practice. Now this was gone, and I had no clear direction for my future.

A cold wind blew all the time in Rishikesh in November. Sand got in everywhere. It would soon be winter. The old sadhu trail began at Laxmanjoo Bridge and followed the Ganges up into the mountains as far as Kedarnath, Badrinath and Gangotri. The first rest stop on this pilgrimage route was Pulchetty Seva Ashram, and it was there that I stayed.

I was given a simple room made of stone. There was a porch overlooking the ashram gardens and the Ganges. Each day I spent two hours working in these gardens, and that was all that was asked from me. Each evening we gathered for Arati at the little Shiva temple before a meal of chappaties and dal was served. Few people stayed there since the road on the opposite side of the river had replaced the old pilgrimage trail. An energetic young sadhu called Shankar was the manager. He had left the comforts of home to practice yoga only two years before, and already his practice was so strong that he wore only a single cotton lungi around his waist, no matter how cold the weather.

The ashram was at the confluence of the Ganges and a smaller, warmer river where I took a bath every afternoon. A large Peepul tree stood on the bank, and I would sit there to meditate and recite my daily prayers. Every afternoon I would repeat the Vishnu Sahasranam, or the "Thousand names of Vishnu."

One day I went to visit Mastaram Baba. He spent his days sitting in a small cave under a boulder near the river. There was only room for two visitors at a time. I sat on the sand beside an Indian man who spoke English. Mastaram was an impressive sight, with his big, round body and long black hair. He had very gentle, bottomless eyes, and slowly tapped the side of his head against the rock as he spoke:

"Do you have any questions?'

"What can I do when the world appears as an illusion and I feel the self alone to be real?" I asked. The man translated, and Baba replied:

"If you feel this way, then you must find a guru and verify this for yourself."

"I have done that already." I replied, without humility.

Baba spoke again, and the translator looked at me with surprise, and said:

"This is a great achievement. What more do you want?"

I knew the answer to this question, but could not put it into words. After so many years of respect and awe for the gurus and yogis of the East, I was once again at the door of the unknown, but there was no-one to open it for me, no map to follow. The end of knowledge is not even the beginning of love.

With winter coming and the constant wind in Rishikesh getting colder and colder, I decided to join the retreats in Bodh Gaya. For the last time I watched Shankar going down to the Ganges for his bath, with his chest bare in the early morning cold. He was a true yogi, and I knew I would never be like him.

India seemed vast whenever I traveled by train. All day and then all night the Calcutta express roared eastward, finally reaching Gaya at dawn. From the station it was a thirty minute rickshaw ride to Bodh Gaya, a pilgrimage place of Buddhists.

The cycle rickshaw drivers were small, wiry men who had to put all their strength into even a slight uphill climb. Their average lifespan was about forty years. The only thing to do was pay them more than they asked, but it was a common sight in Bodh Gaya to see some visitor haggling over the meager fares they charged.

Bodh Gaya is a tiny village in a very poor area of Bihar. We passed Vulture Peak, a barren rock jutting out of a dry landscape. There were groups of simple, earth huts with thatched roofs and a few trees. The first building on the road into the town was the Burmese Bhuddist Vihara. Every

Buddhist sect had a temple or retreat here of some kind. The main temple near the Bodhi tree under which Guatama Siddartha is said to have found enlightenment rises eighty-four feet above the town, and has the warm, gentle richness of a Hindu temple. I paid my rickshaw wallah and found the nearest chai shop. Sitting there was my friend Marjorie, from McCleod Ganj. Over chai I learned that she had run out of money and was living in an empty tomb in the graveyard. She told me that people had already started gathering for the retreats. After tea I found my way to the tourist bungalow and checked in.

The manager had reserved half the bungalow for these retreats. I offered to help out and was stationed in the kitchen. There was a small dining area in a courtyard with a roof but no walls, and next to this was the room where food was prepared. The cook was a young Muslim man called Rashid. He had a staff of five boys helping him: the oldest was about 14, and the youngest just seven years old. On the first day of the retreat Rashid set about preparing breakfast for the thirty meditation students. He put about two cups of oatmeal in a wok and began to roast it. Somehow I managed to explain that we ate only twice a day, breakfast and lunch, and that a far bigger breakfast was needed. He was amazed at the quantity of oatmeal I suggested.

When breakfast time came and the starving, silent line of dharma students filed past our station with their bowls and cups, Rashid was surprised to see all the porridge gone. After that we got along very well.

On another occasion I was able to save face for him when a visitor from England who was learning Hindi began addressing him in the familiar "tum" that is reserved for servants and children. This was happening in front of his staff of boys, who were grinning at Rashid's discomfort.

I was glad to be able to take the visitor aside and explain the use of the more polite "aap", and Rashid gave me a look of gratitude when their conversation resumed. These little moments were about all I was able to contribute.

I spent many happy hours just sitting in the kitchen. I noticed that the smallest boy, Manju, had no parents and no home. He did his best to help out and avoid trouble from the older boys. Once, in the middle of lunch preparations, he suddenly ran and jumped onto my lap and curled up for a moment with his thumb in his mouth. Then he quickly got down, shook himself out, and carried on with his work. He had to behave like an adult to survive in the only refuge he had.

Sometimes Rashid's uncle would stop by in the evenings for a bite to eat. Once he was quite drunk. He spoke a little English, and explained to me:

"Yes I am Muslim, but I respect other religion. Especially I respect Buddha. He was a very brave and very gentle man."

He then staggered off into the darkness.

In the evenings I would walk to the Bodhi tree. Tibetan pilgrims placed thousands of butter lamps near the tree and around the temple. It was a beautiful sight. It was January, and the Dalai Lama was staying in the Tibetan gompa to give teachings. Buddhists from all over the world gathered there, but the Tibetans were by far the strongest presence in the little town.

The first retreat came to an end, and a second was planned. By this time it was known in the Thai monastary close by that a monk trained in Thailand was teaching Dharma, and Luong Pi was invited to hold a retreat in the temple complex. This was a boon, as there was a quiet area behind the Thai temple with a kitchen and access to a good meditation room. The men slept on straw mats in a space under the temple, and the women were given rooms in a separate building near the kitchen. In many ways it was an ideal place for retreats: we were close to the Bodhi tree, and inside a Buddhist monastery.

I attended the next retreat, and continued my meditation practice. After a few days Mary arrived, fresh from working with Mother Theresa in Calcutta. I first saw her during a walking meditation when she aimed a playful kick at me in passing. I had not seen her since she had left McCleod Ganj almost a year before, and broke rank to give her a kiss. As soon as the retreat came to an end, we walked together to a secluded place across the sandy river bed, and made love in the long grass.

I soon discovered that Mary had changed. We were walking home one day when she noticed a beggar woman sitting beside the road calling out for alms:

"Paisa de do baba, paisa de do! De do baba paisa amma paisa de do!" I had often passed this woman and heard this familiar cry: "Give me some pennies sir! Give me some pennies madam!"

But Mary could not pass by and I found myself carrying the poor woman back to our rooms, where her two friends from Calcutta, Josephine and Clara, helped give her a bath. I was given the task of washing her filthy sari –it was grey and heavy with dirt. There were little bundles tied in it where she had hidden small amounts of money and scraps of food. I untied all these bundles, washed the money and threw away the filthy, rotting pieces of chappati and little balls of rice. Then I noticed that the cloth seemed to be moving. I looked closer and discovered that it was not a grey sari, but a green one so full of lice that it looked grey. I made a fire and burned it, and then bought a new one at the cloth shop in the bazaar.

The bath finished, Mary, Josephine and Clara dressed the poor woman and I carried her back to her usual place beside the road near the main temple. She resumed her cry for alms, perhaps now at a disadvantage in her clean, new sari. Her body could not straighten after so much squatting, and she was unable to walk, but hopped along painfully in the dust.

We learned that a few years ago she had lived in the village with her husband and son, but they had both died and the resulting grief had been too much for her and she had lost her sanity along with her family and home. Out of the thousands of hungry, desperate faces I had seen throughout India, this one had come into focus and touched me in a very personal way, and I could never again pass a beggar by with indifference. Mother Theresa had indeed touched the heart of my dear friend Mary.

The retreats continued at the Thai Watt and Luong Pi and Christina where launched on careers of teaching Dharma. My own practice consisted of just sitting and being still. Inner silence, clarity and joy continued to be my usual state. I would often sit in the Japanese temple where Zen was practiced. The Roshi was a formidable figure, and no-one dared move when he was present. There was also a young monk in the role of Jikijitsu. He carried the traditional Kawatsu and would use it forcefully on anyone who was not making a real effort. The thwack of this broad piece of wood hitting someone's shoulder would awaken us all.

When New Years Eve came, we celebrated there by taking turns ringing a huge gong. It took two persons to swing the log that was used to strike this gong, and the sound could be heard a mile away. We formed two lines, and when I finally arrived on the platform, I found myself facing an elderly Japanese man with a long, white beard. He looked very distinguished and wise as we exchanged bows before pulling together on the ropes that swung the log. At our second strike, it was midnight, and the ceremony came to an end. We went inside for tea and cake. It was indeed a magical time.

Mary returned to Calcutta. She had noticed that an orphan girl in the town was being repeatedly raped. There was no-one to protect her, and no-one cared. One day Mary just took the girl with her to Calcutta, to Mother Theresa's orphanage. She risked being charged with kidnapping and doing time in an Indian jail. Mary was one of the very few real Christians I have known.

I had become increasingly restless with the smug western dharma students that had come to Bodh Gaya in January because the Dalai Lama was giving teachings. I was sitting at the tea shop one day, at a bench beside the road, when a scene unfolded before me that embodied my feelings. An American boy of about seven was running along ahead of his parents, perhaps on his way to the sweet shop, when he fell down and hurt himself. I had seen his parents before in McCleod Ganj, at the Library, and knew them to be serious students of Tibetan Buddhism. The boy was crying as his father picked him up, saying in a stern voice:

"There! You see what I told you? That is a perfect teaching of karma! You were fidgeting during rimpoche's teachings, and see what just happened to you? It is karma."

The boy shook with frustration and yelled through his tears:

"I just fell down! I just fell down!"

It was time to get out of dharma town. I packed my things, walked to the nearest main road, and stuck out my thumb.

All afternoon and into the night I rode on the roof of a truck until I heard the booming sound of metal under the wheels. We were crossing the bridge over the Ganges at Varanasi. I knocked on the roof to let the driver know I wanted to get down. I could see the lights of the city curving away into a night that lay sweet and heavy on the holy river. A shiver went over my skin. I was entering a great mystery and returning to something very familiar at the same time. I found a path under the bridge and walked towards the abode of Shiva.

It was about three in the morning when I reached the cremation grounds. There were seven pyres sending flames and sparks up into the darkness, and the air was sweet with the scent of burning human flesh. It was perhaps the only hour of the night when that ancient heart of Hinduism was quiet and deserted. I kept walking until I came to the second burning place at Harischandra Ghat. As Swami Muktananda had given me the name Harischandra, I felt drawn to the place where that famous king had suffered.

There were stone platforms standing above the river where Brahman priests set up shop during the day. I folded my blanket there and sat in meditation. That night was perfect –there was no struggle, no sense of effort in my mind or body. I heard bells ringing far away, and the sound of chanting and prayers as first worship began throughout the city. A mist covered everything and delayed the dawn. I was facing the East, waiting for the sun to appear beyond the cloud covered water and the empty sands across the river. Slowly the mist thinned and let sunlight through to warm me. Then the whole spirit of the place surged up from the ancient stones and filled my being. The river, the boats with their crowds of chanting pilgrims, the golden rays of the sun, the shouts of washer men as they beat clothes against the rocks: it was all the same song of life. All sense of separate self was gone once again, and only love remained with many forms and voices.

I saw a lone figure sitting on the roof of a houseboat just below me. It was my dear friend Mac, from Dalhousie. I went and sat beside him, and together we watched the mist vanish as the sun rose over the Ganges.

Chapter 12: *A Long Way Down*

Mac was living on a houseboat with his friend Patty, who had been with us at Dalhousie, and I moved in to the boat beside them. An old man called Kalu Baba looked after these boats. He had an altar to Shiva on his own boat, and there his friends would gather in the evenings to share a chillam and remember god. Mac and Patty were taking music lessons. They took me through the ancient alleys to the house of their teacher, and I continued learning tabla with him. There were free concerts just about every night in Varanasi. Quality musicians would perform in private rooms for small audiences, with no electrical equipment. The music was beautiful. Every Thursday there was music at Pandit Kisan Maharaj's house. He was the king of tabla and played with an intense, triumphant energy, but my favorite was Pandit Samta Pasad. He was an older man with big hands who had a wonderful feel for the music and expressed joy, humor and appreciation for the musicians he would accompany.

We would meditate each morning from four to six. Then we would row across the river in a small boat and take our bath on the other side where very few people ever went. A local belief had it that if you died on that side, your soul would not go to heaven. We could see the whole curve of the city from there, the old buildings made from rock glowing with soft, natural light. It must have looked the same a thousand years ago. No new buildings or advertising were visible. The same old sailing boats with their ghost like sails floated slowly across the water. Crowds of pilgrims made their way down to the river for their morning bath. The washer-men had laid long, brightly colored saris out to dry on the sand, right next to herds of buffalo.

After two weeks I was joined by Mary and her friends. They were on their way to Nepal. Mary and I shared my small houseboat, while Josephine and Clara shared a larger boat with a French Canadian called Jean. We seldom went far from the river. The alleys were cool and quiet, with tiny shops where we bought the few supplies we needed. It was possible to walk for miles through the city in these alleys and avoid the noise and pollution of the main roads. Always it was the Ganges that drew us home. To emerge from the shadows of the ancient buildings and see the turquoise blue sky reflected in those sacred waters that carried so much life and death was a joy that never grew old.

One morning as I lay on my back resting after meditation I was filled with an unfamiliar energy that held me in sleep paralysis. It flowed into me like a dark wind. I was used to experiencing bright currents of kundalini energy that I was convinced were evidence of my progress in yoga, but this was something very different. It was as if the opposite of my intentions was now taking place. My first thought was that perhaps it was a result of my renewed sexuality, now that I was living with Mary. I had heard so much teaching about the dangers of human sexuality, and how it was somehow contrary to spirit, that I was vulnerable to such fears.

Soon after this, Mary had to visit the local dentist. She had a bad toothache, and a tooth had to be extracted. Her friend, Josephine, went with her to the dentist. An hour later she returned and fell asleep in my arms, without saying a word. The next morning Josephine told me that the extraction had been extremely painful and that the dentist had not given the anesthetic time to work.

I thought no more about this experience at the time, but it went into my unconscious like a depth charge, waiting only for the right conditions to explode.

Shivaratri, the night sacred to Shiva, came at the beginning of March. All night we listened to music on the banks of the Ganges, and the last raga was playing even as the sun rose. It is said that this is the one night of the year when Shiva sleeps, so it was our duty to remain awake. This rest is needed because on the following day Shiva would leave for his summer residence on Mount Kailash. As the hot season comes swiftly to Varanasi after Shivaratri, we were soon on our way to Nepal.

A night train took us through country that was still ruled by bandits. There were about ten foreigners on the train, and we spent part of the journey in a special carriage with an armed guard. At dawn we came to the end of the line, and found the bus that would take us to the border at Raxaul. At some point on this journey one of my passports was stolen. I had two because by this time I had been in India long enough for my original passport to expire, and had got a new one from the consulate at New Delhi. Fortunately, the thief had taken only my old passport, but the alert guard at the border noticed that I had no entry stamp into India. My explanation did not satisfy him. Hours passed as people came and went through his dismal but all-powerful office. I noticed one sweating truck driver pass an envelope to the guard and then leave with a big smile and the comment: "Young officers are best."

He ordered tea. I advised my friends to proceed without me, but Mary insisted on staying, god bless her. Eventually the officer explained that he would have to send a man to Delhi to verify my story, and that this would entail great expense which he alone would have to bear etc. I finally caught on, and played along, expressing my gratitude for the trouble he was taking on my behalf, and quietly handing him a hundred rupees towards these expenses. He stamped my passport and allowed us to leave India.

We had missed the last bus to Kathmandu, and spent the night in Birganj. We found our friends waiting for us there, and the next morning we arrived together in the enchanted Hindu kingdom of Nepal.

It was 1974 and Kathmandu was magical. After the constant pressure and crowds of India it was relaxing just to be there. We found a room with five beds in an old hostel near Pudding Lane. In the evenings we took turns reading aloud from the Tolkien trilogy, and it was as if we had stepped through a looking glass and become part of the story.

There was beauty everywhere. In the distance, the mountains rolled upwards towards the snowy peaks, and promised endless adventure. All around us the richness of Nepalese life was illuminated by the wonderful quality of the light, warmer and softer than I had ever seen. Every doorway, building and courtyard was a work of art.

Something was making Mary restless, and one day she told me about a former lover who was living in Bodhnath, a place near Kathmandu that was sacred to Buddhists. He was an artist who had a room beside the great stupa. We went to visit him. Mary declared that she loved us both. He was French, and was studying Tibetan thanka painting by day and doing his own art by night. We just sat there on the floor of his room and meditated. We all had the longing to be clear and present for the adventure of life, as well as the willingness to work with the clouds that arose from our hearts and minds. After about an hour I got up to leave and Mary followed me out. We said nothing. I was glad she had made up her mind.

The whole place was charged with the power and grace of the Karmapa Lama. The sixteenth Karmapa, Rangjung Rigpe Dorje, was the spiritual leader of the Karma Kagyu lineage that was the form of Vajrayana Buddhism followed in many parts of Tibet, Bhutan and Sikkim. He was about fifty, and an awe-inspiring presence as he sat on his throne leading rituals in a Kagyu Gompa about two hundred yards from the stupa. He looked up and smiled at us when we walked in. We spent hours every day in the temple in the presence of this great man. Relaxed and friendly, and, at the same time, remote and ancient, he was a living Buddha, of this we had no doubt.

One day we attended the black hat ceremony. The huge horns roared, the gongs were struck and the attending monks knelt in awe and respect as the Karmapa placed the ancient hat of woven hair on his head four times. Josephine, who was standing beside us, gasped each time. She had never before seen Vajrayana in action, and I wondered what her innocent and naturally pure eyes were seeing. Afterwards we sat in a tea shop and she told us:

"The first time, he looked the same, only very calm. The second time he changed into someone else, a monk with a beard. The third time it was a different monk again. The last time, there was nothing there. He disappeared."

We had all felt the power of this ceremony. It was said that if you attended four black hat empowerments, you would become enlightened. There were many levels to the work and teachings of a man like the Karmapa Lama. He upheld religion and the orthodox teachings of the Karma Kagyu tradition and at the same time remained a real vajra guru to those capable of relating to him on that level.

Soon we were on our way to Pokhara. Mary had only two weeks left on her visa, and wanted to go trekking before returning to England. We found a room in a private home on the hill overlooking Phewa Tal. Across the lake we could see Machhu Puchari, the "fish tail" mountain, and we planned to take the path in that direction on our trek.

Jean and Josephine went out in a dug-out canoe and a storm blew up on the lake and they capsized and spent an hour in the water before being rescued. Mary and I were feeling separation coming on like night, but we did not talk about it. We were trying so hard to be "in the present" and to demonstrate that non-attached state of freedom I so desperately wanted to believe I had attained. After the amazing states of consciousness that had happened in India, I expected to find myself more liberated than I was.

It was in the lovely town of Birethani that I said goodbye to Mary. We sat on the warm, smooth rocks where two streams met and gazed up at the towering snow of Machhu Puchari. Mary was writing something in her dairy, and I looked over her shoulder and read:
"Being human means
blind, nameless desires sleep on your face
unknown love shines through your eyes."
Mary returned to England by way of India. Her money and time had run out. I stayed another day in the warmth of Birethani, and then went on alone to a hill-top village called Gorepani, or "horse and water." The ache in my heart grew and consumed my consciousness like a cancer. My mind once again spun out of control and became obsessed with suffering, in particular the suffering of women. This in turn

focused in on the tooth extraction that Mary had endured in Varanasi. It was as if that tooth was being pulled out of my very soul again and again, and yet there was no way for me to save Mary from the pain.

I walked alone along the ridge from Gorepani towards Gurung. It was almost dark by the time I reached the first rest house in the village. The long trek exhausted me and I fell asleep after a traditional supper of dal bhat. I dreamed that night of the Karmapa Lama. He was sitting as usual on a throne, and smiling at me. I became angry and ran towards him, but he calmly disappeared, leaving me with the message that I needed to go and see him.

I awoke to the usual mental anguish –the endless loop of tape about Mary's tooth together with a black despair. It seemed as if my spiritual quest in India was a failure, and the inner peace and joy had been shattered. I was determined to go and see the lama, but had no idea where he was. I inquired around the village of Gurung, and learned that there was a Tibetan settlement three days walk away. I set out the next day.

All along the beautiful path I was haunted by the memory of Mary and tormented by dark thoughts. Whenever I came to a large tree beside the path, I would sit to rest in the shade, and it seemed that the trees were offering kindness. By the third day, this feeling had become a conviction, and I sought out the big, old trees and rested my back against them. The gentle rustling and the scent of the leaves were comforting. How patient and giving they were. No doubt there was extraordinary beauty all around me on that solitary trek, but I was unable to enjoy it.

At one point I decided to take a bath in a stream that flowed under a stone bridge. I followed the stream up the hill in search of a private spot, and discovered a wonderful waterfall splashing down the sun-warmed rocks into a deep, green pool. There were bamboos and pine trees, grass and flowers, and a gentle wind. I plunged in, but the cold water did nothing to refresh my spirits, and I passed through that heavenly place like a ghost.

The Tibetan village was on the edge of the mountains at the head of a long valley. There was one simple hotel with only four rooms, and a small gompa. A carpet weaving business had been set up and refugee families had settled there. Everyone was busy preparing for some festival, and when I checked in at the hotel, I learned that the Karmapa Lama was expected in two days.

The excitement infected me, and when the day came I stood with about a hundred Tibetan people along the trail where the lama was expected to arrive. A cloud of dust was seen in the distance and from that very moment my consciousness changed. I felt as if I were suddenly in another dimension, where time hardly moved and ancient mysteries were alive and well. The cloud of dust slowly grew in size until we could see two specks approaching. They became jeeps, and pulled up at last in a field in front of the gompa. Two monks stepped out and held the door for the Karmapa. He seemed huge as his gaze traveled in a circle, taking in each one of the people present. Slowly he walked towards the temple. Even my mind became still.

We followed him inside with the six monks who had accompanied him, and he sat down on the throne I had seen in my dream. One by one we approached. When my turn finally came, he looked up as if recognizing me, and then put both his hands on my head. It was a powerful blessing.

I remained for three days, spending as much time as I could with the lamas. Three of them were staying in the same hotel as myself, and the manager took me to meet them one evening. They sat on small carpets and recited Tibetan texts that were piled before them on low, wooden desks. A senior lama sat in the middle, with a monk on each side. The manager whispered for me to approach the central lama, saying:

"Go….this is a very high lama."

He was a man of about forty, with dark, laughing eyes. He put a hand on my head and spoke to me in very good English.

"Where are you coming from? How do you know His Holiness?" Apparently he had noticed the familiar welcome I had been given. I replied that I was from Canada, and that I had met the Karmapa Lama in a dream. He smiled at this, without surprise or disbelief. We shared a moment of silence together, and then he resumed his deep chanting and the next person came forward for his blessing.

For three days the magic continued, and then once again we lined the road while little fires of pine sent up fragrant smoke to bid farewell to the lamas. The two jeeps were soon lost in a cloud of dust that blew away on the wind. People walked back to their homes and shops, and I returned to my room. Once again I was alone and without plans, but my inner peace had been restored.

I had no thought of going to Ganeshpuri for the return of Swami Muktananda. That phase of my pilgrimage seemed to be over. I heard later that he had returned triumphant from a very successful tour, of which about three years had been spent in America. I also heard that he had been unable to resist waiving a check for one million dollars in the face of a former rival –a disciple of Nityananda's called Kutiram Baba. Kutiram had remained unknown and poor, and later played an important role in my own journey. I decided to fly from Kathmandu to Thailand and meet up with my Vipassana friends.

There is a Chinese saying: "to take a wrong direction, and keep going, can definitely be called taking a wrong direction." Theravadin Buddhism and prolonged meditation was my wrong direction, but I kept going for several more years before realizing this. I continued to deny the existence of the unconscious, as if my suffering and my needs could just be dissolved in awareness itself. I did not want to plunge into the depths of my own psyche and find out what was there.

From the first day that I arrived in Thailand, I was welcomed and treated with respect as a student of the dharma. I did not pay for a single night's lodging, and very few meals. For two weeks I stayed in monasteries, and ate what was left over after the monks had finished. I met Bhikkhu Vajiro, an English monk who had been with us in Dalhousie, and joined him on the early morning begging round in Banghok. It was already very hot and humid, and I found it difficult to sit for meditation, but there was nothing else to do.

We traveled south together by bus and arrived at the monastery where Bhikkhu Kitty Subha, Christina and some of the others from India had gathered for yet another ten day retreat.

Vajiro took great pains on the journey to avoid allowing his robes to touch any women, not because he cared, but because local tradition forbade women from touching any part of a monk, and shame would have been on them no matter how it happened. This was nearly impossible on the crowded buses, and I had a hard time taking it seriously. I witnessed one hilarious scene at the monastery when Christina and Vajiro were caught by a sudden downpour of early monsoon rain while walking across the compound. Vajiro put up his umbrella, and Christina tried to share it with him, but this was forbidden, and so she got drenched.

On the day the retreat started the monsoon rains really set in, along with thunder and lightning, and the temperature dropped to a level that made meditation more comfortable. But try as I might, I did not feel at home in the monastery or the practice. There were monks and lay practitioners from many countries engaged in serious study of the dharma, and some who had been there for many years. One German monk had spent 25 years at a retreat in the jungle. Talking with him one day, I shared a thought about impermanence, and said: "I had seen that my death was now."

"There is no death," he said grandly.

"Well, perhaps for a Buddha there may be no death, but for me it seems real enough," I replied.

"Oh, you are not even trying to understand!" he retorted, while turning to walk away.

It was clear I did not belong in a monastery. I longed to be active, to have work to do, and to feel the cool wind of the West Coast on my face. Some of my friends were taking vows and becoming monks. There was a big ceremony after the retreat when six young men were given robes and had their heads shaved …right down to the eyebrows. Although I envied their sense of purpose I had no interest in doing the same, and decided to return to Canada.

Even my last night in that hospitable country was spent in a monastery. The rains were coming down hard, and the monks were settling in for the monsoon retreat. A monk's time in robes is measured by the number of rainy seasons he has sat through. After my time in Thailand, I was convinced that vipassana, or insight meditation, was by nature a monastic practice –a practice that was de-signed for the protected and insulated surroundings of a retreat. It was my personal experience that the "high" or calm, clear state of consciousness that resulted from the practice never survived for long after returning to the challenges of every day living. It was also clear that the enlightening moments that did, indeed, occur to brighten the long hours of sitting were not as valuable as I had once believed. I was gathering the strength to reject this con-stant denial of self and aversion to "ego" that I had heard from both Buddhist and Vedanta teachers alike. To me, at least, it was a path that had no heart.

After four years I left the east convinced that my journey there was far from over. I had no teacher, no path, and no feeling that I had anything of value to share with others. Although my trip had been in some ways wildly successful, a dark cloud followed me home.

Chapter 13: *The West Coast*

Finding work was a challenge when I arrived back in Victoria. Jobs were scarce, I had a B.A. degree, but my resumé and experience were hopeless. I saw an ad in the local paper: "Air Forestry now hiring." A company from Washington was salvaging cedar in the forests on the west coast of Vancouver Island, and needed cutters, so they hired me. I used my last four hundred dollars to buy a new Stihl 065 chainsaw with a thirty-six inch bar.

About this time my younger brother Edward showed up, also looking for work, and he agreed to come and work with me. He had experience in logging camps and I was glad for his help. Our long-suffering mother lent us her Volkswagon beetle and we headed to Jordan River for our first day of work.

We were shown some huge fallen cedar trees in the hills above the town, and I cut them into two foot lengths while my brother split them into bolts. It was brutally hard work, and it rained all day. We stopped at about four p.m. and went looking for a place to stay. There was only one hotel in Jordan River, and the rooms cost about twice what we had earned so far. We drove around hoping to find a cabin or an apartment, but there was nothing. We were headed back towards Sooke when, on a hunch, I turned up a gravel side road. It was dusk and we were discussing giving up when I saw a dog cross the road. I stopped to see where it was going, and noticed a little trailer parked in a clearing. Inside sat a young man, smoking a cigarette. I asked him if there was anything to rent around there: "Nope," he replied: "I don't know of any place around here...except maybe this old trailer. I don't need it...only come here for a smoke now and then."

"How much?" I asked.

"How about 50 dollars a month?"

"We'll take it." I called my brother over, and he agreed it was better than nothing. There were two bunks, and small kitchen and a sitting area. There was no water or bathroom, but we were tired, wet, cold and hungry.

I lived in the trailer for six months. Edward stayed with me for two weeks before leaving to find work in a logging camp. He was a frail looking, very secretive young man with glasses, but was deceptively tough and hard working. The loggers who hired him would always start him out pulling chokers, but when they saw him work they would promote him very quickly. He excelled at whatever he did. We had the same goal: to go back and live in India, with forty-thousand dollars in the bank.

I was working alone on a plateau half way up a mountain where some huge cedar trees had blown over. One morning I had just arrived and was squatting on a log to take a dump before starting up my saw. A bear came blundering through the bush directly towards me. I yelled and waved, but it just kept coming. I yelled louder, but still it kept walking towards me. This large, black bear seemed to be intent on rolling right over me. My pants were around my ankles, and it was with annoyance that I finally stood up and shouted as loud as I could, not knowing if the bear had seen me or not. It stopped suddenly, gave a little "woof," and ran away. I finished my business, feeling very Canadian.

Autumn came, bringing mist and rain, and the work ended. My last two paychecks bounced, and I never heard of Air Forestry again. I found a room in Victoria in a communal house and began a fruitless search for work. I applied for unemployment insurance benefits but it felt wrong to receive handouts, so I did volunteer work four days a week to justify my money. I went through a period of personal anxiety finding myself at the age of thirty without work, without a partner and without any real prospects. Meditation and yoga alone were just not enough.

One of my volunteer jobs was in a hospital for severely handicapped people, where I took patients out for walks and just spent time with them. After a few months they offered me a full time position. At first I enjoyed the work and took some pride in being employed. I had the enviable position of being a day-care nurse's aide, which meant being on the day shift Monday to Friday. When this ended I joined the regular employees and found myself having to adapt to evening and night shift work, as well as doing the regular grind of caring for the physical needs of people who were so mentally and physically challenged that even the simplest tasks were messy and difficult. My idealism soon gave way to hopelessness. In addition I found myself singled out for criticism from colleagues and superiors. Some of this was deserved, as I was slow and spent too much time trying to communicate with patients that could not be reached.

I had heard that there was a shortage of men in nursing, and that male nurses always had plenty of work. I was also told that bursaries were available to support me during training. Being miserable in my situation, I imagined that by going even further in a wrong direction I might find happiness, and applied to the local practical nurses training program.

The one passion that I had for life at this time was tai chi. I spent my days in school learning the basic skills and theory of nursing, and my evenings and weekends practicing tai chi. The bursary was enough to live on, but I became even more miserable. Nursing and hospitals were just totally wrong for me. I stuck out like a sore thumb and attracted no end of good natured teasing from the efficient, powerful women who dominated the hospital scene. They treated doctors with respect, and me with contempt. I pretended it did not bother me, and reminded myself that it was "right livelihood." I was quite lost, and even my dreams took on a dark quality.

I kept in touch with Mary and planned to join her in England once my training was finished. We shared a wish to join the dharma community in Totness that Luong Pi, now known as Christopher, and Christina had founded. Christopher was no longer a monk, having formally given up robes in Thailand, and he called his new approach to dharma "Engaged Buddhism."

One night I was having a nightmare and in the grip of dark forces when, from somewhere in my sleeping psyche, I called out the name "Baba" and found immediate relief. For years I had been trying to forget Muktananda and Siddha Yoga, as I had come to believe that dependence upon a guru was incompatible with dharma practice, but this unexpected experience made it clear that I was still connected to that path. I was desperate, and came up with a crazy plan: I would return to India, and ask Muktnanda to "let me go."

My attempt to fit in to western society and find meaningful work had been a total failure, and I was only too eager to get far away from nursing and hospitals. I called Mary to let here know I was coming, and was soon on a plane to England. I did not tell her about my idea of going back to India. I was confused and caught between a past that had not finished with me, and a future that had not yet come into focus.

Mary was staying in a flat in a nunnery with her two friends from India, Josephine and Clara. It was a beautiful place set in the English countryside of Oxfordshire, not far from where I had been born. It was good to see her again. Mary could sense that my mind was somewhere else. I explained how I had to visit India for a short time once more to clear up some unfinished business, and that I would return soon, but she was not fooled and clearly saw the confusion hidden behind my words. We spent our last night together with her friends, dancing to the music of Bob Marley. At Heathrow airport, when I reached my departure gate, I turned to say goodbye to her, but she was already gone. I never saw her again.

Chapter 14: *Return to Ganeshpuri*

I arrived at Bombay airport at two a.m. It was August and a heavy monsoon rain had turned the whole place into a vast, shallow lake of warm muddy water. I hired a rickshaw and paid extra to be taken to the little village square in front of the Samadhi temple of Swami Nityananda in Ganeshpuri. It was four a.m. when I left my bags with my shoes and lowered myself into the magic of the hot springs. Rain poured down on my head, while my weariness soaked away in the water that was heated by the hidden volcano in Mandakini Mountain. It was these healing waters that had first attracted Swami Nityananda to this place. He had lived near the temple under a lean-to made of leaves, and found relief from arthritis in the ancient bathing tanks that were part of the Shiva temple. Nearby was a small private hospital and rest house that had been built by a retired

Army Doctor, Major Kothawalla. The village of Ganesh-puri had been created by the devotees that came to visit and stay with their guru.

After my bath I put on clean clothes and went to sit in the Samadhi shrine and pray for guidance. The priests blew conches and performed the 'Kaka Arati', or awakening worship. Then I went to Madhu Nivas for chai and upma poha.

I walked the mile of muddy road back to the front gate of Shree Gurudev Ashram feeling as soggy and dark as the monsoon sky. They checked me in and gave me a locker and a bed in a dormitory with about twenty other western men. Wet clothes and towels were hung from ropes above rows of cots. Everyone had a little altar set up near their bunk or in their locker. There were photos of Baba everywhere.

As a newly returned disciple I was allowed to meet with Baba during the afternoon darshan. I waited in the courtyard for him to appear. A hush fell over the group and then there was a flash of orange as he took his seat on the marble porch. Everyone pushed closer. A man in orange known as Professor Jain was translating, and I stood near him until my moment came and he motioned me forward. Baba smiled when he saw me.

"So you have come again….and I am leaving again. This time you will stay until I return!" He laughed and banged me playfully on the head with his hand. My world collapsed.

"But last time I left. I have made so many mistakes."

"No mistake. Because you did that, this time you will surely stay. You have the grace of the siddhas."

I bowed and left. My elation lasted a couple of hours and then I went into shock. Stay? How long would he be gone this time? I had a return ticket and a few hundred dollars that would last only a few months.

I could not sleep or rest. At night I lay awake in the sticky heat, wondering what I had got myself into. Why had I returned? What about Mary and our life together in the dharma centre in England? What about my doubts and all the effort I had made to break all connection with this powerful yogi? My intention had been to ask him for permission to leave…to tell him I did not want to be his disciple. This was not happening. I had neither the ability nor the clarity of purpose to walk away.

After four days without sleep I walked back to the temple in Ganeshpuri. I was seeking some sign to help me accept this dramatic turn in my life. My meeting with Muktananda had convinced me that it had been a big mistake to leave the first time –after he had asked, and I had agreed, to stay until he returned. Now the same situation had come around again. Again I had been asked to stay, and again I had agreed. All my doubts, all my excuses had been trumped by the sheer force of Swami Muktananda's personality, the power of his shakti.

The hot springs did little to comfort me, and I sat on the marble floor of the temple with a heavy heart. I could hear the sound of devotional singing coming from an upstairs room in a building beside the temple. There was a flight of stairs leading up to a balcony. I was drawn to the happy music, and found a room full of Indian devotees sitting on the floor, singing. Feeling like an outcast I kneeled beside the window and looked inside. A swami with short grey hair was sitting on the bed with his back to me. It was Kutiram Baba, a man I knew to have been a direct disciple of Swami Nityananda. As I prayed silently for help, he turned around and gave me a frown, as if to say "get out of here."

I continued to sit there, looking at the back of his head and praying for a sign. Then he turned around and fixed me with his gaze. A current of liquid light flowed from his eyes into mine as tears spurted from my eyes and splashed the lenses of my glasses. He waved, and turned back to his devotees.

I returned to the ashram with my faith restored. Yes, there were doubts and questions around Muktananda, but about Nityananda I had no doubts. Years before, after meeting Baba, I had had a dream where Swami Nityananda had come to me, and said: "If you are Baba's devotee, I must look after you." Having got the sign I had been asking for, there was nothing to do but accept the challenge and make the most of it: this time I would stay until Swami Muktananda returned, come what may.

During the weeks leading up to Baba's departure the ashram became a beehive of activity. Those who were staying were given ever increasing duties while being prepared to take over positions left vacant by departing residents. I found myself working in the bookstore, and was soon responsible for the stock room, and for all books sent by post within India, or shipped overseas. The bookstore opened onto the street in front of the ashram, and during holidays it would be crowded with visiting devotees. I had to learn to communicate in Hindi, Marathi and Gujurati. I worked with a woman from England who had been the manager for some years, and was training a young woman from Canada, Sita, to take over her position. I was appointed to be Sita's assistant.

Thousands of devotees from all over India came to see Baba before he left. The darshan lines were endless, and the dining hall was filled again and again at each meal. Incense, flowers, music and the riot of devotion were everywhere. It was futile to resist –the only peace was in the eye of the storm. If I thought of myself and my preferences and comforts, I became miserable. But when I surrendered to the chaos, I found happiness.

About ten-thousand people gathered to watch Baba drive away in his blue Mercedes. Some were crying, some prostrated on the wet pavement, and some threw flowers. Once again, I was left in this strange place with an unknown journey ahead of me.

It did not take long for the ashram population to shrink down to a skeleton crew of diehards. With the one and only attraction away for an indefinite time, there was very little reason for anyone to visit, let alone stay on and work hard through the heat of summer. But for me it was a powerful time. My sense of spiritual purpose had been renewed, and I was sure that, having been given a second chance, I must make the most of it. I became very light and healthy, and had abundant energy. At about nine every night I would lie down on my thin mattress and fall asleep immediately. At 3 a.m. I would awaken, rested and happy from a velvet sleep, and get up at once to walk to Ganeshpuri for my hot bath. The days were full. I attended all the voluntary activities, starting with the morning arati at 4:30 a.m. Perhaps the hardest part of my routine was the 2:15 chant of the Vishnu Sahasranam, or one-thousand names of Vishnu. It was the hottest time of day, and while most people slept, I forced myself to sit straight and sing along with the little group in the temple. There was very little love in the ashram, and so I survived on faith and hope.

With much of the ashram empty, I enjoyed the luxury of having my own room on the roof of one of the residence buildings. I could see the whole Tejasi river valley and the mountains beyond. Whenever I found a few hours of free time, I would explore those hills and forests.

At the end of the day I would lie on my back and do my best to remain aware while passing into sleep. This was my favorite time, full of mystery and grace. Goddess kundalini would visit, sometimes gliding into consciousness on the vibration of a mantra. I would feel the rush of energy moving up my spine and filling my being with light. Sometimes I would ask questions, and get amazing replies:

"Why don't you give me someone to love?" I once asked, from a familiar place of loneliness.

The goddess put something on the pillow beside me –a pair of earphones. I was in sleep paralysis, and unable to move, although aware of my surroundings. With an increased level of intention and effort I was able to put those dream-phones over my ears.

"Hello there…." said a clear, friendly voice: "here is the answer to your question."

I next found myself in a dream, in a small sailing boat on the open sea. The weather was clear and a fair breeze chased the waves. I thought to myself, how wonderful it would be to have a companion on this journey. The next moment a beautiful young woman appeared. She sat on the seat opposite me, and smiled. Together we sailed the sunny ocean of my dreams. Slowly we moved closer, and I began to kiss her. Soon we were making love. I became blinded by passion, and forgot everything else. Finally I opened my eyes, and found that it was my self I was having sex with. I awoke, filled with self-loathing.

But I was still in the first dream, and the voice of the goddess was waiting for me: "The reason I do not send you someone to love is because every time I do, you end up hating yourself."

I immediately awoke, clear as a bell. This inner relationship with the goddess sustained me during my long years of practice in India. It was true that all my intimate relationships had ended with this feeling of disgust towards myself. It did not take long for me to feel that, whatever my personal problems, the ashram was where I needed to be, and I began to feel grateful that Baba had taken care of me.

The next challenge on my inner journey took a full year to resolve. The power of kundalini came again one night, this time riding the sound of a cricket that was singing somewhere just outside my room. In my normal state it was just the lonely song of an insect charming the night, but as I passed into the astral, the brilliant vibration became the vehicle for a powerful energy that took me back to the moment when contractions had first disturbed the peace and safety of my mother's womb. Crushing forces that I could not understand began to force me into a world I wanted nothing to do with. Terrified, I had resisted, and so started a pattern of not wanting to be here and experience life. Night after night this experience repeated, and again and again I resisted the suffocating contractions. When awake, I could understand what was happening and did my best to surrender and trust, but in the dimension where all this was taking place, I was still an infant without language or intellect, and blindly resisted the process. Little by little I trained my will to be with me there, and to have faith in the forces that were giving me birth, just as I was learning to trust the divine mother who was guiding my inner life. Finally the night came when the contractions met with no resistance, and I was able to be re-born with less resistance to the world.

After two years working in the bookstore and squabbling with Sita we finally had a real row and I was sent to the cowshed. I had just learned how to perform the worship of Ganesh, the remover of obstacles, and took this change as a good sign. I had been suffocating in the atmosphere of the bookstore and the front offices of the ashram, where the administrative busybodies hung around and gossiped. Status and fashion ruled there, and it was amusing to discover that, after my "downfall," most of my former co-workers would not give me the time of day.

I thrived in the cowshed. After my re-birth experience, it was a far more natural place for me to be. It is said in India:

"If you are seeking inner peace, go to the Himalayas. If you do not find peace there, go to the Ganges river. And if you still do not find peace, go to a cowshed. If you cannot find peace even in a cowshed, then you will not be able to find peace in this lifetime."

I found peace in the cowshed, and became healthy and happy there. My day began at 2:15 a.m. when I rose to help with the first milking. At about 3:30 I would take the milk to the kitchen, and hand it over to Swami Krishnananda, who was in charge there. He would make me a coffee while I waited, sitting on a sack on the floor of the cavernous place. Then I would walk to the village for my hot bath.

It was faith that kept me going. My money ran out, and I sent in the return portion of my ticket for a small refund. When this ran out, I was determined to stay on, even with no money, but then I remembered the little Tibetan carpet factory that had been started in McCleod Ganj. Perhaps I would be able to sell those carpets in Canada. I ordered a three-foot by six-foot rug and instructed them to mail it to my brother in Canada. He sold it for $400. He kept $100 for his share, leaving me with a profit of about $100, after all expenses. My next order was for two carpets, then four, then ten. They were a novelty, with snow lions, dragons and clouds woven in bright colors and simple designs. Compared to Persian carpets, they were coarse and of very low quality, but they were fashionable for a few years, and gave me the small income I needed. I had found a way to support myself without leaving the ashram.

During my happy year in the cowshed, I helped birth three calves, all female. The cowshed is one place in India where females are valued above males. Bacharri, as they are called, go on to produce milk and more cows, while the bacharra, or bulls, are only used for pulling carts and ploughs. I became good friends with the bull, and gave him the name "Big Business". The gentle, responsive nature of these animals reflected thousands of years of breeding that were more about intelligence than milk production. In India, it is the cow that is the family pet, while dogs and cats are left to fend for themselves.

After about a year in the cowshed, I had a quarrel with a man called Vankappa, who was the foreman of the ashram grounds. He was both feared and respected. I had been using a hose to clean down the floor of the cowshed, as I had hurt my back carrying buckets of water. He insisted this wasted water, which was not true, but he was the boss, and when I continued to use the hose, he busted me down to working in the garden. This was not so bad, as the fellow in charge of the garden, Mark, was a good friend of mine, and I enjoyed working with him. He gave me the rose garden to care for.

There were at least five-hundred hybrid-tea rose plants in the ashram gardens. The roses were used as decorations in the apartments of v.i.p's, and in the temples for worship. During April, May and June the mid-day sun was hot enough to burn the petals, and I had to cover the plants with baskets. I had my own small tool shed, where I set up a kerosene stove and made chai. This was a big attraction, as good chai was not available anywhere else, and these rose garden tea parties became a small source of pleasure in my simple life.

I was also given the task of growing asparagus. Swami Muktananda was fond of asparagus, and so a special plot was set aside to cultivate this luxury for his return.

I had been at the ashram for about three years when rumors began to circulate about when Baba would leave America and come back. His time in the west had been wildly successful, and had culminated in a sold out performance in Carnegie Hall. Thousands of new devotees, millions of dollars: they had even started something called the "Siddha Yoga correspondence course". Now it was possible to become a yogi in the comfort of your own home…for a price. All this made me feel quite sick. Any illusions I still had were destroyed when the "advance crew" of Americans began arriving to re-shape the ashram. They took over just about everything. An expensive cafeteria called Amrit was started, where western food and desserts were available. The few of us who had remained at the ashram could seldom afford these luxuries.

By the time Swami Muktananda returned in triumph, the ashram had been transformed. It was now called "Gurudev Siddha Peeth", meaning it was the "abode of a Siddha." Siddha was the word adopted by Baba to extend his megalomania to even more absurd heights. We now had "Siddha Yoga", or the yoga taught by the Siddhas. In Amrit they even sold something called "siddha coffee", which Garden Mark described perfectly as "regular coffee at twice the price."

The whole place filled up with a crazed new crop of devotees from every country that the tour had visited. By far the most numerous and dominant group were the Americans. The only way I could have a room of my own was to volunteer to be in charge of a place called the sadhu dormitory. This was a large upstairs room in a building that had been built in the upper garden for visiting swamis. Western men who wished to remain in the ashram for longer periods were allowed to stay there. I had a small room at one end, and did my best to keep the place quiet and sane.

The darkness and sorrow that had led me back to Baba Muktanada was totally gone. I was relaxed, confident, and performed my many duties with energy and joy. Although disgusted with the commercialism and hype that had taken over the place, I was still happy there. One difficult task had been fulfilled –I had remained until the guru's return. But a second task awaited me: I still had to finish breaking all connection with Siddha Yoga.

I had learned two practical skills during the three and a half years that Baba had been away: making malas, and rebinding old books. In the temple bazaar in Mumbai I had found a supply of large rudraksha beads, the kind known as "blood pressure" beads, because they were used to treat heart conditions. I had selected the thirty-six best beads and made a mala to present to Baba in gratitude for the years I had spent as his guest. Each bead had been cleaned with a small brush, soaked in cow's ghee, and then knotted on string that I had treated with bees wax. Perhaps I still hoped for some special reward, some little pat on the back for the hard time I had done. When I offered him the mala, he hardly gave it a glance, and with a small wave of his hand indicated the basket beside him. Subhash, his assistant, held the mala for a moment and looked at Baba with surprise, as if he, too, hoped he would show some appreciation, but there was nothing. Of course it was dismissed as "just ego" whenever we foolishly looked for any personal recognition from such a person.

The women fared even worse. A special darshan was arranged for the five western women who had stuck it out for the whole time the guru had been gone. They were gathered in the hallway outside Baba's room, dressed in their best saris. Muktananda appeared:

"What are these women doing here?" he demanded. Pointing to one shy black girl, he said in Hindi: "What is this black buffalo doing in my rooms?" and went back inside.

Such was the man I had once considered my guru, and had worked so hard to free myself from. It was not long before my doubts and questions were answered in a clear, powerful way.

Many devoted, deluded seekers were arriving from all over the world to be with the man they believed to be a "Sat Guru", or perfect master capable of guiding them to liberation. Some even believed that just a touch or a glance from this man could liberate them. One such devotee was sitting on guard duty in the hall between Muktanada's living quarters and the meditation room. A gust of wind suddenly blew open a door that connected the hallway with the women's rooms. There stood Muktananda with his lungi down. A female devotee was giving him a blow job.

It is to the credit of this young man that he told his friends what he had seen. His faith had been shattered. Soon, half the ashram had heard about, and believed, this event. The other half continued in blissful ignorance, convinced the guru remained celibate and was in fact divine grace itself. When a good friend of mine told me, I felt a great weight lift from my spirit. No longer did I have to feel that it was me who had the problem: it was, as I had suspected, the guru and his whole organization that was on the wrong track.

Celibacy was a foundation of Muktananda's teaching. He had told us men many times that not even a drop of semen should be wasted. It was believed that he was a life-long celibate, and had always lived the dharma of a sanyasin. I had taken this very seriously, and been celibate for seven years in the prime of my life.

Muktananda then put out a challenge, accusing people of spreading idle gossip and having weak minds. It was not the first time such rumors had circulated, and the damage control machine went into high gear. Lies, threats, intimidation: they used it all, as they had been doing for many years. I approached Muktananda as he sat on his throne one day, with massive body guards and a circle of loyal devotees around him.

"How can I trust you when you yourself do not follow your own teachings?" I asked. It is to his credit that Swami Muktananda responded with heart:

"You must now take refuge in god alone. Your work here is done."

"Are you sure?" I insisted: "Last time I left too soon!"

"Yes. You have done good work here. There is no mistake."

I thanked him, and walked away.

Slowly, I prepared to leave the ashram that had been home for more than five years. I visited all my favorite places: the goddess temple of Vejreshwari; the Hanuman temple; the hot springs along the river, and of course Madhu Nivas chai shop near the samadhi shrine in the village. My final days were spent working on the compost heap in the upper garden, chopping up banana plants and shoveling elephant shit. I had trained someone to take over the rose garden and the asparagus, and I wanted to finish up by doing the humblest work I could find.

Before leaving Bombay I went to say good-bye to Nisargadatta Maharaj. I found him lying on a bed, very ill with throat cancer, and attended by his wife and daughters. He looked up at me with eyes still clear and bright, and then waved me away. I offered a ten rupee note to his wife, who handed it to the Maharaj who then handed it back to me. I still have this note together with my copy of *I Am That*. Two weeks later Nisargadatta Maharaj was dead.

I had gone back to the ashram with the intention of asking Muktananda to let me go, and now I had earned my way out by becoming strong enough to just walk away.

A year later, in October of 1982 while living alone in a cabin in the woods on Salt Spring Island, I had a powerful dream. Baba came and fed me grapes with his own hands. Then he left, and Swami Nityananda came and gave me a huge, black stone. It looked like a gravestone, and was too heavy for me to carry, so I threw it into the ocean for safe keeping. I awoke feeling blessed. On my next trip into Victoria, I heard that Swami Muktananda had died that night. Such was my experience with this powerful, paradoxical man.

Chapter 15: *Wandering*

While working in the woods with my brother Edward we had shared the dream of saving forty thousand dollars so we could afford to live in India and continue our spiritual journeys. Soon after my return from India, he died in a plane crash while working for a forestry company, trying to earn that forty thousand. In fog and rain, somewhere along the remote west coast of British Columbia, the small sea-plane landed on the rocks instead of the water, and exploded. There were no survivors. Two weeks later I received a letter from the company telling me my brother had had an employee life insurance policy, and that I was the beneficiary. I was to receive forty thousand dollars. It was a terrible way to see that dream fulfilled.

My immediate need was for a place to live, so I decided to invest in a few acres of land with a cabin. At that time I was not planning on returning to India anytime soon, but wanted to continue with my meditation and yoga in Canada. My father helped me search for the right place and we drove around in his car until we found three acres with a one-room cabin on Saltspring Island. It had a stream running through and was the last place on a dead end dirt road going up the side of a mountain. It was 1981 and my new home cost just $22,000, so I had enough money left to live on.

There was plenty of work to do fixing the cabin and cleaning up the garbage that surrounded it. Once a week I walked five miles into Ganges to buy groceries. It was my routine to begin practice at midnight by doing a puja to Shiva, and then meditating until 1 a.m. I would sleep until five and then get up and meditate again. When my alarm would go off to awaken me to the next part of my program, my feet would always touch the floor before it stopped. After breakfast I would begin work, just as I had done in India. With no path or teacher to follow, I did my best to keep up a strong practice and remain focused on my inner journey.

One day while out walking I noticed a lot of cars parked near a farm house in a field. A crowd of people were sitting on the ground in the shade of a maple tree. I went over to see what was happening, and it was as if I had walked back into India. There sat a holy man in white on a cushion, surrounded by devotees. It was a happy, relaxed group and children were playing near the yogi while everyone laughed. This was Baba Hari Das on his annual visit to the Saltspring Yoga Center.

I became a regular visitor to the center. Every Sunday there was a public satsang with meditation and devotional music, followed by a vegetarian meal. I played tabla, just as I had done in India. Baba Hari Das was a humble and trustworthy man, and his wisdom was manifest in the community that had been founded in his name and based on his teachings. The members of the community lived creative and independent lives, and they had their own elementary school for the children. Most of the devotees were married.

Even with the friendship of this community I continued to feel like an outsider, and made very little effort to fit in. The lives and identity of the people around me were so much defined by their family and their work, and I had neither. Although I continued to have powerful experiences of kundalini energy, and felt sustained by the inner relationship with the goddess, I did not feel at home in the West. The strange, childish beliefs of so called "New Age" writers dominated spiritual thought, and I could not take it seriously. When I rented a collection of "channeled" recordings in an effort to understand what was happening, I thought the speakers must be joking and that the tapes were intended to be comedy, but I was wrong. One channel of "higher wisdom" even announced that the laws of karma had come to an end. Apparently this was what people wanted to believe. One young woman on the island even declared herself to be a "walk-in." She did not remember her former friends because she was no longer in her body, having been replaced by an alien intelligence –or so her followers explained. But it was observed that she had no trouble remembering where her favorite bakery was.

There was also a wave of interest in the goddess, but it was confused with feminism and political anger, and had very little in common with the worship of the divine mother that I had known in India. I made very little effort to make friends or meet people, and had no interest in having a relationship. It turned out to be impossible for me to keep up the feeling of being connected with spirit and being on a real journey of awakening while living in the West. There is an unspoken support for seekers in India, a feeling of being nurtured by thousands of years of spiritual tradition and nourished by the tolerant hospitality of the people. Without that feeling I was lost, and so when October came, and the days began to get short and wet, I made plans to return to India.

I rented my cabin to a man who wanted a quiet place to meditate. I now had about $15,000 in the bank and a small income from the rent. Just after Christmas I left with a one-way ticket, determined to make India my home for an indefinite period. I had been in Canada for only eight months.

Bombay airport, the friendly smiles of the customs men as they waved me through, the crowd of dark faces at the airport exit at 4 a.m....it was a familiar welcome. My rickshaw driver stopped in front of the ashram, expecting me to get down, and was surprised when I asked to go on to Ganeshpuri. From the end of the road I walked across the shallow river to a little island where sadhus stayed. It was dawn when I took my bath in 'gaukund', the name of the bathing tank there. A yogi was meditating under a tree nearby, and cowbells knocked gently in the distance as the rising sun found Mandakini Mountain. I was home.

Good fortune found me in the form of a man called Kailash Baba, who was the head of a small Hanuman temple on the far side of the river. I met him on his way back from his bath, and he invited me to the temple and gave me a room. This temple had been founded by a yogi called Hanuman Das who had lived there for many years. Behind the temple was an enclosure with about ten rooms opening onto a courtyard. The whole place was shaded by palm and peepul trees, and the nearest road was far away. No-one there spoke any English, and my Hindi was enough to get by on. The community was small, about ten people, and we were fortunate in having a young sadhu there who had been a cook in the army. He prepared two delicious meals a day: the simple vegetarian food of North India, always including whole wheat chappaties, dal and a vegetable curry. When my morning yoga and meditation was done, I would walk into the village and have breakfast in my favorite chai shop, Madhu Nivas. Often a cow would amble in from the street, pass just in front of my table on her way to be fed leftovers in the kitchen at the back, and then stroll out again.

It was part of my practice to find some work to do whenever I remained in the same place for more than three days. I noticed that no-one was cleaning the courtyard before the early morning arati, and so began to get up at three-thirty to sweep the flagstones. There would always be two or three scorpions among the pebbles and fallen leaves. I would put them into a jar and release them later on my way into the village. When the sweeping was done I would take my bath at the river and be back in time for worship. We would ring bells and light lamps and sing the Hanuman Chalisa, and so the day began.

Kailash Baba invited me to stay as long as I liked, and encouraged me to do my rainy season retreat there. It was a rare opportunity, but as I was feeling restless and did not have any sense of direction about my meditation practice at that time, I had to say no. After two weeks in the friendly Hanuman temple, I began my journey north.

I wanted to visit a man called Swami Prakashananda who lived near the railway station about five miles from Nasik city. Nasik is one of the four holy cities in India, where the Kumbha Melas are held, the others being Haridwar, Allahabad, and Ujain. Nasik and Ujain are not so well known, and their melas are smaller than the huge camps on the Ganges that can attract ten to twenty million visitors. These melas are the most important gatherings for Hindus in India. Sanyasa, the rites of initiation into the lifetime vows of a Hindu monk, are given at these melas. Seekers often find their guru at a mela, and sadhus who spend most of their time in solitude come out to meet old friends there.

During my years at the ashram in Ganeshpuri, Swami Prakashananda had been a source of inspiriation. Swami Muktnanada had given him sanyasa many years before, and from time to time he would visit the ashram and keep our spirits up by entertaining us with stories. When all around us Siddha Yoga was deteriorating into a marketing hype of spiritual illusions, Prakashananda reminded us that there was a very real dharma path to walk, with or without the ashram. His favorite topics of conversation were trains and rice-plates. He knew where the best meals could be found, and all the best trains that went to the many holy places of India. His favorite train was the Bhusuwal passenger. This was a slow train that left Bombay at 11 p.m. and arrived in Nasik Road at about 8 the next morning. It was the kindness, humor and humility with which he told these stories that made them special. There was no method or system of teaching –we would just hang out with this extraordinary being, and be nourished by the kindness and respect that surrounded him.

One of his best stories had begun: "A long time ago there was a good and wise king protecting the people of Nasik. A famous guru once visited the kingdom, proclaiming he knew the way to see god. Many people came to see this saint, who had one peculiar feature: his nose had been cut off. This was true of all his devotees. They had all had their noses cut off too. The guru and his devotees spent the whole day singing and dancing and praising god, and many people came to ask for initiation. One by one they would go into a small tent, and come out a few minutes later, singing and dancing, but without their noses. The king became suspicious and sent a minister to investigate. The minister hid inside the tent where the guru was performing initiations. He saw a man led into the tent, and heard the guru say that the way to see god was to have your nose cut off. The man agreed, and the guru took out a sharp knife and cut of his nose with one swipe. The man cried out: "Ow! That hurts. I do not see god...there is only pain!"

"Well," said the guru: "you cannot get your nose back, so you may as well join us! You must sing and dance and say you have seen god, and we will look after you. I myself lost my nose in an accident while cutting sugar cane."

"The man emerged from the tent singing and dancing and claiming to see God. The minister reported to the king what he had seen, and the king banished the guru and all his devotees from the kingdom."

In this story it seems Swami Prakashananda had been warning us about cults and what was happening around Muktananda. In a devotional mood, and out of respect for him, I took the Bhusuwal passenger as far as Igatpuri, where I planned to do a ten day meditation retreat. I was still practicing Vipassana, and wanted to deepen my meditation now that I had returned to India. A retreat was about to begin, led by one of Goenka's senior students. At registration I said it was my first retreat. I had a good reason for doing this: the one thing they had perfected there was the making of chai. Somehow their recipe was just irresistible –but alas it was the custom that old students were allowed only lemon water after 12 noon, while the first time meditators were given chai. It was beyond my limited capacity for equanimity to endure this, and so I broke the fundamental precept of truthfulness. I was busted when the person serving the chai recognized me from another treat.

I went for my scheduled interview with the teacher. He sat on a little platform, far too high, while I sat on the floor below him. He was very "serious," a word I heard often at the Vipassana Academy. The purpose of the interview was to clear up any doubts about my practice or the teachings, but as it was my observation that this sangha was beginning to resemble a cult, I had very little to say. After years of yoga it was easy for me to sit ten hours a day for ten days –in fact it was a holiday to be in a structured environment, with good food and a clean bed –but that was not sufficient reason to be there.

Ten days of meditation was a good way to empty my-self in preparation for wandering around India, and I arrived in Nasik road in high spirits. I was eager to see Swami Prakashananda again and in my hurry to find something to offer I bought some fried condiments in a dirty roadside chai shop. I arrived for the afternoon darshan, and was welcomed by the little group of devotees that sat around the Swami. At this time he stayed in a room at Dr. Rajan's hospital, while his closest western devotee, Harihar Chaitanya, looked after the temple at Kadam Mala near by.

He untied the string, opened the newspaper and ate some of my humble offering. Perhaps he liked such plain, greasy snacks, or perhaps he was giving me his blessing in this way, I don't know, but there were tears on my face all the same. Here was ancient Hindu Dharma in person, saying so little, yet giving so much. The dharma taught by the vipassana teachers was clear, simple, and perhaps true, but for me it was an unhappy path that left very little room for the mystery of love. I was on the journey from the head to the heart, and here I was face to face with ancient night itself.

I stayed with Harihar at Kadam Mala where we slept on the floor of the temple. He was kindness itself, overflowing with what is called "Prem" in India. His devotion to his guru, Swami Prakashananda, showed in the many services he did for visitors, including providing a noon meal. There were about six of us, and we sat in a row on the earth floor of the kitchen to eat. A retired postmaster lived in a shelter that he had built against the side of the temple cottage. On the roof lived several students who had no-where else to go. On the altar, beside the statue of

Saptah Shringi Devi, was the photo of a rather sad Indian woman. She had been the owner of the land and building where we stayed, but had been murdered by relatives who wished to gain possession of the property. She had willed it instead to the Swami, who was determined to see that their plan did not work and kept the photo there to keep her memory alive.

Years later, Harihar returned to England, and wrote a biography called *Agaram Bagaram Baba* about the life and teachings of this little known saint. I had no intention of staying on at Nasik Road and becoming a disciple of Swami Prakashananda, as I felt that my journey was leading me into the unknown, but I was still hoping to meet a teacher or guru who could give me back a sense of having finally found my way.

From Nasik I went to Shirdi for darshan of Shirdi Sai Baba. Shridi is a magical place and vibrated with the power and grace of the saint that is buried there. I spent my days meditating in the Masjid, and attended as many aratis as possible. This was rural Maharasthra: simple, poor, and honest for the most part.

A disciple of Shirdi Sai Baba's, Upasani Maharaj, had founded an ashram nearby in a place called Sakori. After Upasani Maharaj's death, the ashram had been left in the care of his disciple, Godavari Mata, and had attracted many female sadhus. While visiting there I was bitten badly by a dog. Back in Nasik I consulted with Dr. Rajan, who said it was very possible that the dog was rabid, and recommended the rabies vaccine. I was expecting a long series of painful shots in the stomach but instead the treatment was three injections in the arm of a new French vaccine. The doctor told me that a minister's son had recently been bitten, and the politician had used his influence to make this vaccine available for the whole state.

While getting my series of vaccinations I stayed a few

more days with Harihar. Swami Prakashanada said I must have been doing something wrong to be bitten by a dog in such a holy place. Perhaps it was wrong for me to visit a retreat meant for women, I don't know, but his comment somehow confirmed my feeling that it was time to move on. When the time came to say goodbye, I told the swami that I was thinking about taking sanyas, and spending the rest of my life as a monk. He became very serious, and told me, in a kind way, that it was not my dharma, not in my nature, to renounce the world. He gave me a little silver box full of the red powder that Hindu devotees put on their forehead.

I still had many unanswered questions about my meditation and kundalini yoga, and the only person I could think of who might be able to answer them was a reclusive and mysterious monk called Swami Pranavananda. He had lived with Swami Prakashananda at Saptah Shring for a few years before finding his own home about a hundred miles away in a secluded place called Pattana Devi. He spoke perfect English, and was considered by the few who knew him to be a saint similar in stature to Swami Prakashananda.

The train went as far as Chalisgoan and then a local bus took me another ten miles into the farmland beyond. The road became a cart track and the bus stopped to turn around in a dusty village. Beyond this there was nothing but jungle. It was dusk as I began walking the five miles to Pattana Devi. These were the times I lived for. My health was good, my spirits were high, and the awesome beauty and mystery of creation was all around me. Behind me, the sky turned red, and ahead of me the black shapes of cliffs stood against the stars. It was dark by the time I reached the dry river bed near the temple. There was a light on in a shed beside the path, and a man was cooking

chappaties. He called the chowkidor of the forest bungalow, and suggested I come back and have some food after
seeing to my room. This was India, where I always felt
safe and at home.

I awoke at four a.m. the next morning, bathed and
walked through the dark to the riverbed, where I built
a small fire and sat in meditation until dawn. Peacocks
began to yell, and when I saw smoke rising from the direction of the chai shop I went to inquire about Swami
Pranavananda. The chai-wallah told me that he had just
left for his annual retreat in the Himalayas. It was early
March, and would soon be hot. No-one knew where he
went for this retreat, and only one person, his disciple
Shivaji, went with him.

I spent three days in the solitude of Pattana Devi,
walking in the jungle and visiting the waterfalls and
abandoned temples. The goddess temple was in the care
of the forestry department, not Brahmin priests, which
was very unusual and meant that the Devi was available for darshan at all times. A priest from the village
came twice a day to perform puja, and a few pilgrims
came, but most of the time I was alone there. Next to
the temple was a tiny room of stone, about four feet by
six feet, where Swami Pranavanada had stayed for a year
when he first arrived. He was following the traditional
life of a Sanyasi, and had chosen this spot to end his
wandering. In time, the villagers had built him a hut
on an island in the river. After a few more years forestry officers had been impressed enough to give him a
plot of land where he built a small ashram. He only saw
people on Sundays and Thursdays, and later reduced this
to only Sundays. The ashram was surrounded by a hedge
of thorns, and was kept very clean, mostly by the tireless
efforts of Shivaji.

I decided to go to the Himalayas myself, and do my own retreat. March is a transition month for wanderers in India –the mountains are still freezing, while the plains are becoming too hot for comfort. The one place I knew that was perfect in March was Rishikesh. This "abode of the rishis" has, in fact, one of the worst climates in all India: cold in winter, very hot in summer, and infested with malaria during the monsoon. In October and November there is a constant wind that blows sand into everything. But in March, it is heaven. I had written to an ashram called Yoga Niketan, and arrived there after a two day train journey.

Yoga Niketan was the home of Swami Yogeshwarananda, one of the last true hatha yogis to live in Rishikesh. It was on a hill overlooking the Ganges. Visitors were given two simple meals and a room. The routine included two meditations and two yoga asana classes a day. On our admission form it was also stated that we were required to do two hours of seva, but no-one did anything. After two days I began picking up the garbage and litter that was everywhere, and burning it at the back of the ashram. I made myself a stick with a nail in the end so that I would not touch the trash and pollute myself as I thrust it into a sack. At first the residents were critical, and told me it was not necessary, but I persisted, and soon other visitors pitched in to help, and we kept the whole place clean. I also helped in the rose garden, a service for which I had prepared myself by bringing a pruning knife from Canada.

By the end of March the road to Gangotri was open, and we were given the opportunity to move up to the branch of the ashram there. Swami Yogeshwarananda was preparing to leave for Kashmir, where they held a summer yoga camp. I had decided to go to a place called Almora, in the Garwal Himalayas, a part of India I had never visited. In my own way I was following the tradition of the homeless pilgrim who is sustained by faith and hope while searching for an end to that longing of the heart that haunts us –that feeling that we are separated from god.

On the map Almora had looked like an ideal mountain retreat, but in reality I found it impossible. The whole area was a forest of pitch pines that were all tapped for resin. It was only about 1200 meters above sea level, and quite hot. The population was mostly Rajput, and it was the traditional dharma of the men to be warriors. In the absence of war, they sat in dirty shops drinking liquor and gambling, while the women worked.

Above the town was a long line of hills called "cranks ridge." It was here that eccentrics had lived during the British time, and this tradition continued. Lama Govinda and Li Gotama had lived there in a small gompa that was now managed by a Tibetan lama and his Bon-po wife. She was respected and feared locally after winning out in a battle of power with the priest of the nearby Kali temple. I searched the ridge for a room where I could spend the summer months, but found nothing. There was a place called Snow View where dope-smoking young tourists stayed, and a few rooms were available in the Kali temple, but the harsh, dry mood of the ridge did not feel right. I kept walking, and when it was time to turn back I found myself standing at a crossroads: behind me was cranks ridge and the way back to Almora; and ahead the road curled away around a mountain towards a village called Ayarpani. A third road went up the mountain, which was greener and higher than the other hills. I could just make out what looked like the roof of a village hut among the pines at the top. The place was called Binsar, and it had the right feel.

The following day I returned early and walked up the hill. The road went up in switch backs, and the forest became thicker. Near the top a sign on a gate read: "Khuli Estate." The word "khuli" means "empty." I followed the driveway past the hut I had seen from below, and found a single old, English style house standing in the shade of some trees. I knocked, and a kind woman called Didi took me to a small, round cottage behind the main house where I was introduced to Navnit Parek, the owner of the estate. Bidi was his wife. Navnit welcomed me, and sent for a tray of tea. He was interested in my long pilgrimage, and said he had been a devotee of Papa Ram Das, the founder of Anand Ashram in Kerala. I told him of my time with Muktananda, and he said:

"Yes, I met Muktananda once. I was not impressed."

"I became disillusioned," I replied: "now I am looking for a yogi called Swami Prananvananda. He speaks good English and can help me with my search."

"Swami Pranavananda?"

He paused, while a strange smile lit up his face: "Why, he is staying here, in the far cottage."

He took me to his balcony and pointed to the red tile roof of the cottage where the swami stayed. It was perched at the edge of the steep slope at the north side of the mountain. I asked if there was any room that I could rent, and Navnit said there was. Such magic happens sometimes when we leave everything in search of god.

My cottage was a single room with an earth floor and a roof of slate. There was a fireplace and windows without glass on three sides. The walls were made of adobe style mud and were about eighteen inches thick. The place had once been occupied by a farm family but had been empty since the new owners had given up agriculture. It was on top of the hill and surrounded by empty fields.

I did not dare disturb the Swami, and had been there about a week before there was a knock on my door. Shivaji motioned for me to follow him to where Swami Pranavananda was waiting on the path.

"How did you come?" he asked me, with a twinkle in his eye.

"I really don't know..." I confessed. There was no need to explain anything. He understood. Very few people knew where the elusive yogi went for his summer retreat.

"Well, it is good that you are here. How can I help?"

I had prepared my answer: "I would like to meet with you once a week. I have some questions."

"Very well...what day would you like to come?"

"Thursday," I replied. In the Hindu calendar Thursday was the day for honoring the guru.

"Come at three p.m. Thursday and have tea with me."

On Wednesday I walked the twelve miles into town and bought some sweets. On Thursday I bathed, put on my best clothes, and with my offering of sweets went and knocked on the swami's door. Shivaji let me in to a room with an orange bed at one end, and an altar with a large picture of goddess Kali at the other. The swami was sitting on a small balcony, and there was an empty chair beside him. We had a view of the valley and glimpses of snow on mountains beyond. Swami Pranavananda was in good spirits and seemed to enjoy having a visitor. I could hear the sound of a kerosene stove being pumped in the kitchen below us. After a few minutes Shivaji came up with chai.

Pranavananda was a devotee of the Divine Mother, and had a remarkable resemblance to Ganesh. He was round, a bit overweight, and quite short. His eyes were large and bright, with a quality of attention that made every moment with him special. He responded to my questions with real interest and enthusiasm. I told him of my experiences with the kundalini shakti, and the visions of the goddess.

He was surprised at the order: "Kundalini shakti is usually seen first as white, then red, then black, and the final vision is blue. For you the order has been different and you have seen black before red."

I had been concerned that the experience of the energy in dark form had meant something had gone wrong: "No, not at all," he replied: "You have done nothing wrong. It is simply the nature of the Divine Mother to contain all –all the opposites and aspects of creation, both seen and unseen. One day she will appear in blue form. It will be a wonderful experience. The sun and moon will unite here:" He touched my forehead between the eyes: "and you will be free."

When I told him of my meetings with the Karmapa, he was enthusiastic: "You could have asked him anything....he knows fully all manifestations of kundalini shakti."

I was surprised to hear that Vajrayana Buddhism and Hindu yoga could be so similar. It had not occurred to me that I could have asked the lamas about my experiences. I had nothing but the journey, always changing and yet always the same, and at times it seemed as if the only thing that was real was the wind on my face and the ground under my feet.

The hot summer months passed and the days were just not long enough. The pre-dawn hours from 4 to 6 a.m. were for meditation. During the days I explored the surrounding hills. Navnit and Didi sent over a meal at noon that was so large I was only able to eat half, and saved the other half for the evening. Occasionally people from Bombay would come up and spend a few days in the two other cottages that were there.

One night there was a concert in the Parek's home, with Anup Jalota singing his famous bajhans. His father, Purushottam Jalota, had once led us in singing beautiful devotional songs at Baba's ashram, and I was hoping Anup had the same feeling for the music. There were about twenty people sitting on the floor of the living room enjoying the concert. At one point the power went out, and I was amazed to find that Anup's voice was hardly audible without the microphone, even in such a small space. He was using technology to good effect, and would sometimes hold a note for what seemed like a long time, and get a round of applause. I was not impressed, and Swami Pravananda did not attend. The swami later commented:

"His father, Purushottam Jalota, was a great devotee as well as a great musician. We always enjoyed listening to him."

After the concert Navnit introduced me to Anup, with the comment: "He has surpassed his father."

In terms of fame and sales, this was true. It is to his credit that Anup responded with real humility: "Even after seven more incarnations I will not surpass my father."

At Khali estate, I was allowed access to the library. The books were all old, hard cover editions of classics. I opened *The Importance of being Ernest* by Oscar Wilde, and noticed a signature: "Jahawarlal Nehru." I asked Navnit about it, and learned that he had bought the estate from pundit Nehru's family, and many of the books were from his college days in England.

One day I met a couple walking up the driveway. The man was French and the woman Canadian. She asked me if I knew of any place where they could stay for two weeks, while they were on holiday from the heat of Calcutta. I suggested that they might move into my cottage, as I was just about to move over to Swami Pravananda's rooms for the rainy season. The swami had just gone back to Pattana Devi, and I did not trust the little mud hut in heavy rains. I moved that same day and the couple were happy to have a place to stay.

Later, Mr. Parek told me who they were. It was Dominique Lapierre and his wife, taking a break from writing *City of Joy*. Dominique had a fearless passion for the poor of India. His portrayal of Hasari Pal and his family is the most powerful and accurate portrayal of the struggle of India's urban poor that I know.

After they had left, I met the family of the priest of a Shiva temple on the grounds of a Maharaja's summer house higher up the mountain. With the passing of time, the revenue from the temple had dwindled to almost nothing, and the Maharaja's fortunes had been stripped by India's secular post independence government. Power and wealth were now in the hands of the politicians. The hereditary priest of the temple was reduced to keeping a little chai stall beside the empty road. He had six children and they all lived in a single room made of wattle and daub, with a roof of thatch. In winter there could be six feet of snow on their tiny village. The family land had been divided so many times by the passing generations that they had only a fraction of an acre where they grew marijuana. This crop was legal in that part of India, as the people used the seeds in their cooking. It helped them keep warm. Needless to say, the priest lost no opportunity to sell his produce to travelers. I helped by having chai at his stall every time I passed, and always paid him ten rupees instead of one.

But it was the Lapierres that they remembered. The priest's wife could not say enough about them: how generous they had been, how kind. As she showed me pots and blankets that they had been given, there were tears in her eyes. Very few rich and powerful Indians care much for their poor, except when it comes to election time, when they do whatever is necessary to get their votes. I had met greatness unawares.

There was a sad and empty feeling around the Shiva temple, and the old house where the Maharaja and his family had once spent their summers. My grandfather had been an Indigo planter in Bihar, and I had deep nostalgia for the faded glory of the Raj. The British had managed to get along quite well with most Indians, most of the time. The writings of Rudyard

Kipling and of M.M. Kaye are the only honest, kind accounts of this time that I have read. I heard that the Maharaja's estate had been for sale for years. Perhaps no one wanted to take on the added expense of maintaining the temple.

There were other empty houses on that mountain. They were beautiful places, built out of wood with high ceilings and wonderful tall windows that looked out over seemingly endless forests and hills towards distant snowy peaks. Part of me indulged in dreaming that I could have been at home in British India, and another part imagined that I could find comfort and meaning in the life of a monk. But I knew the question "who am I?" could not be answered by taking on a social identity, but only by deep searching within.

The rains began, and the roof of my new cottage leaked. I informed Mr. Parek, but he refused to believe me.

"No one has ever complained before." he insisted.

"Come. I will show you." It was raining hard, and the pots I had put to catch the leaks would be overflowing. But in true Indian fashion, he just did not want to know, and wanted even less to see for himself that anything was wrong. So often I had noticed that if you complain in India, it is you who are wrong. If you see garbage or pollution, it is you who are dirty. I learned to live with the leaks, and arranged my bed carefully along the one dry wall.

After a month, the rains let up a bit, and I decided to risk a short trek to Mirthola ashram, a place made famous by Sri Krishna Prem. The statue of Krishna in the temple there had shed tears one day in response to this English devotee's prayers. I read somewhere that there was a forest rest house in a village about five miles from the ashram, and planned to stay the night there after my trek, and then visit the ashram the following day. There was a trail around the hill below me that went in the right direction. I packed some blankets, my umbrella, and set off.

It began to rain. The path wound on endlessly through forests of pine. I walked for hours before seeing the first village, a dismal little group of mud huts that must have belonged to pitch collectors. There was not even a tea shop. I kept walking. The path became a dirt road, but there was no traffic, not even a cow. At one point I decided to take a short cut where the road made a wide bend up a mountain side. I passed a house where three girls giggled at me from a balcony. Soon I was lost in a thick jungle of vines and broad leafed trees. The rain was soaking me. A trickle of blood found its way into my mouth, and I pulled a leech from my forehead. I clambered up the steep side of the hill, and then suddenly and unexpectedly stepped onto a narrow road that wound along the very top of the ridge. A couple of miles further on I came to the town where the forest rest house was supposed to be, but no-one there had heard of it. Finally a man told me that it had closed years before.

Once again there was not even a tea stall to be found. There was no choice but to walk the five miles to Mirthola ashram, and seek hospitality there. The road to the ashram was very beautiful, and passed through a forest of pine trees that had not been tapped for resin. I arrived at dusk, and saw a western man working on the front gate. It was Madhav, who had been left running the place after Krishna Prem's death. I explained my difficulty, and asked if I could have a place, any place, to spend the night. I must have looked a sight, soaking wet and covered with blood from numerous leeches that had dropped onto me in the jungle. I was also exhausted, having walked at least thirty miles, some of it through dense bush.

"No, that will not be possible without a letter of introduction," this holy person replied.

"Then may I have darshan of Krishna?" I asked. That he could not refuse, and so led me to the little shrine where I made an offering and said a prayer. On the way I passed a western resident who looked at me with obvious distaste, and ignored my greeting.

"I can offer you a cup of tea," said Madhav.

"No thank you," I replied, and began to walk away, planning to reach Jogeshwar before nightfall.

"Not that way," he said crossly: "There, follow that trail. It is about five miles." Without looking back, I continued my soggy pilgrimage. At least it had stopped raining. I wish I could say that this experience was the most unpleasant encounter with "spiritual" types I have ever had, but alas, it would not be true.

It was quite dark by the time I reached the ancient Shiva temple of Jogeshwar. It was one of the twelve Jyoti Lingams of India. These are temples where Shiva has appeared in answer to the prayers of devotees. The road was dark and shadowed by huge pine trees. I could hear a stream. There was a village in the narrow valley behind the temple, and there I found a room for the night. My mattress was lumpy but dry. I could feel mosquitoes, fleas and bed bugs all biting me as I sank into an exhausted sleep. My last thought was: have your feast tonight, little friends…. I am too tired to care.

It was raining next morning. I was burning and itching all over and there was nothing to do but walk it off. I found a tea stall, and had some samosas for breakfast. The chai wallah directed me to a house higher up the hill where I could get a decent room. I moved up there, and requested a bucket of hot water so I could wash the dried blood from my face and body. By evening the itching had stopped and I was feeling better. In clean clothes I went for darshan of Shiva. Walking my chosen path, there was no place for self pity or regret.

I did not know it, but my carefree, seemingly endless stay in India was coming to an unexpected end. On October 31,

1984, Mrs. Indhira Gandhi was shot, and it was found that the shooter had entered India without a visa from a commonwealth country. A law was quickly passed that required all visitors to have a visa, and those of us who were already in India without visas were required to register at the nearest police station. A few days after returning from my walk in the rain, I found myself at the Almora police station, where I was given three months grace. I had no desire to go and stay in Nepal for three months in order to apply for a visa in Kathmandu and then return to India. This was a reality check. The dream was over, and it was time to say goodbye to my life as a wandering seeker in India.

In September I spent two miserable weeks in Rishikesh. It was hot, humid and infested with mosquitoes and malaria. Once again I found myself wondering how the sadhus managed to live there and meditate under such conditions. My next stop was McCleod Ganj, and there the magic was alive and well. The air was clear, washed by the rains, and the mountains where gleaming with fresh snow.

It had been my desire to sit and listen to the wind in the pines with my heart and mind as spacious and empty as the sky. For moments, even hours, this had happened, and that would have to do.

On the way to Bombay airport I got down at Chalisgoan to say goodbye to Swami Pravananda. He told me that mother India would not forget me, and advised me to keep living in a simple, natural way, and to keep going on my inner journey. He died of a heart attack two years later.

I had a few days left before my flight, and spent them at Ganeshpuri, at the Kothawalla's guest house. Soaking in the hot springs beside the river and gazing up at mount Mandakini I wondered what lay ahead now that I would finally have to face myself back home in Canada.

Chapter 16: *Being Human*

My cabin on Salt Spring Island was cold, wet, and isolated. I kept up my routine of solitary practice in a vain attempt to preserve the illusion that I could just transcend, or at the very least get around, the overwhelming challenge of becoming a grounded, balanced human being. My real need was for meaningful work, real relationships, and a community to belong to, but I was only just beginning to understand how very necessary these things were.

I began to practice yoga asanas more seriously. Of the eight limbs of yoga this was the only one that had caught on in the West, and offered the possibility of earning a living. I attended classes that were offered through the Yoga Center, where the style, called Ashtanga yoga, was quite different and more advanced than anything I had done before. The postures were taught in a series, and each position was entered into through movements called vinyasa, with the result that the whole practice became vigorous and aerobic. The teacher, Nancy, was very good, and the style was popular. I attended all the classes and asked Nancy where she had learned her yoga. She told me about her teacher, a man called Pattabhi Jois who taught in Mysore, South India.

When spring came, I made my first attempt to participate in community life by showing up for the Saturday morning market in Ganges. I put out a colorful cloth and arranged some little treasures from India, and sat there like a trader from the East, and sold a few things. I also met a musician called Tom, who played guitar and flute. He had been to India and was interested in having me accompany him on tabla. Soon we were practicing together twice a week. We held a sale at his place one weekend, where I had my Tibetan carpets on display, together with his collection of curios from the east. In the evening, we gave a free concert. He played flute and guitar, while I backed him up on tabla and his wife played the tamboura. I made new friends, sold most of my remaining carpets, and met a woman called Maya who had also been to India. We began a conversation that I invited her to finish at my place the next day over a cup of chai.

I remember a sinking feeling as I watched her walk down my driveway. She was really very attractive, with a sexual magnetism that, after so many years of celibacy, I was in no condition to resist. It was not long before we became lovers.

The memory of past disasters made me very careful, and I decided to take full responsibility for preventing conception, and always wore a condom. We had a short time of happiness together. We meditated, went for walks, and made love. Then we would sleep together, and I was amazed to discover that I slept better with her than without her, an experience I had never had before.

Then one day the condom broke, and I just knew we had conceived. The fall from carefree solitude into the sudden rapture of sexual love, down into the chaos and confusion of a relationship gone wrong was quick and painful. It was not long before I was convinced that renunciation and celibacy had been the right path after all. But of course it was not that easy. I kept up my daily practice of yoga, but I had no foundation, no sense of purpose or source of inner strength. I was right where Harish had been –in limbo –the very thing I had vowed would never happen to me. On my own, it was enough to be a yogi or a seeker and fill my days with solitary practice, but with a woman I felt the need to define myself by my work. I decided to become a yoga teacher.

For the next few months I was tortured with guilt and remorse. Maya kept delaying her decision to have an abortion, and I once again lost whatever little clarity and inner peace I had found. After the abortion, there was just emptiness, and instead of intimacy we shared anger and resentment. This continued until I could take it no more, and decided to return once again to the place where I had known peace.

I wanted to study yoga with Pattabhi Jois, and at the age of thirty-six, I was already quite old to be taking up this path. The moment I announced my decision to return to India, Maya changed dramatically, and did what she could to keep me from leaving. I was determined to go, but like a fool I promised to come back to her, while she promised to wait.

On the way to India I stopped in England and went to visit my friends at Gaia House in Devon. I stayed for a one month silent retreat that was guided by Christopher. There was a young man sitting with us who was clearly struggling with personal problems. Members of the staff took turns spending time with him. During the final week of the retreat he went for a walk beside the ocean with a staff member, and suddenly jumped off a cliff to die on the rocks below. His body was laid out in a coffin that was kept in the living room of the retreat house for a day. This was a custom from the monasteries of Thailand that gave dignity to the dead and also served to remind the monks of impermanence.

During the month of silent practice we had private interviews with the teacher every few days, and a schedule was posted outside the room where these meetings took place so we would all know when it was our turn. It was a chance to ask personal questions and clear up difficulties we may have been having with our meditation or our understanding of the teachings. I showed up on time for my first interview to find three other men still waiting in the hall outside Christopher's room. I checked the schedule, and noticed that their meetings should have been finished. From inside the room I could hear the murmur of Christopher's voice, followed by the voice of a woman. According to the list on the wall, the women had been scheduled for the morning, the men for the afternoon. It was two p.m. and I waited for thirty minutes, and then left, leaving the other three men still sitting patiently in the hall.

Four days later, I saw that I was again scheduled for an interview, and again showed up to find a dejected little group of men waiting in the hallway, while Christopher could be heard in deep conversation with a woman on the other side of the door. I walked away, mindfully noting a feeling of disgust, and never looked at the interview list again. Although it was a powerful retreat, it was clearly time for me to seek the dharma elsewhere.

During the days following the retreat I heard that an American called Andrew Cohen was visiting the area. I had known Andrew in India, where he had been a dharma bum like the rest of us. One evening some people from Gaia

House invited me to go with them to visit him, and I went, expecting a happy re-union. I did not know that Andrew had become a spiritual teacher.

I met about a dozen people there who had been my friends at one time or another. They were all sitting on the floor, waiting. When Andrew walked in, a hush fell as he sat in the arm chair reserved for him.

"I am only interested in one thing," he began: "liberation."

He had been to see a man called H.W. L. Poonja who gave satsang in Lucknow. After only a few days, this guru had declared Andrew "enlightened," and everyone there seemed to take it very seriously. I was surprised by all this, and had my doubts, but greeted him warmly as a friend, and asked how he was doing. I had not come there to join his satsang, and did not want anyone to try to raise my consciousness.

We exchanged a few words and I saw people looking at me as if I were crazy. There was a sick mixture of pity and contempt in their eyes. I was clearly missing some great opportunity.

When I said to Andrew: "I am just feeling very happy to be here among friends again," he replied:

"That is how you should feel in My Presence."

The capital letters were quite audible and floated grandly in the atmosphere of that room, while my heart sank. Was this the promise of the dharma, the promise of the bottomless wisdom and compassion that can be seen in the eyes of Ramana Maharishi, the saint they claimed to be connected with? Why did the relentless quest for self-realization turn so quickly and easily into a popularity contest or a power trip? I looked around the room and saw the awe my friends had for Andrew, who was now a member of that exclusive club, the "enlightened" who had "got it" and held satsang so others could bask in their presence. They were always surrounded by people who seemed totally lost, but acted as if they had found the answer just by being there. None of the people present remained my friends. Whatever was happening, there was no room for those who did not agree. I never did go to see Poonjaji.

Feeling heavy and dark, I went through the familiar routine of endless flights, endless waits in the impersonal gloom of airports, and the eventual arrival at Bombay at three a.m. I had totally lost the precious inner joy and clarity that had taken so many years and so much practice to cultivate. Perhaps I believed it was waiting for me in India….that I had just left it there, and would pick it up again once my feet touched that sacred land.

This time, even the warm, familiar waters of the hot springs of Ganeshpuri could not ease my pain. I returned to the Hanuman ashram where I had been made welcome before, but after one day, Kailash Baba suggested that I go and stay at Kothavalla's rest house. I heard what he was not saying: that I no longer had the dharma of a sadhu, and that the ashram was not the place for me. He could feel the change in my energy, and his words deepened my sense of loss.

For the first time, the "ananda" of India was not able to reach me. I went on to Nasik, and visited Swami Prakashananda, who had been such a source of comfort in the past. He was spending his final years in Dr. Rajan's private hospital at Nasik Road, where a few western devotees were staying with him. I spent the night with Harihar at Kadam Mala. It was good to be with people I knew, but I was haunted by a sense of failure, and believed I had fallen from grace. I did not feel strong enough to travel to Mysore in the South of India where I did not know anyone, and so gave up on my intention to study yoga there. Instead I moved into the heart of Nasik, to the old city beside the Godavari River where the Kumbha Mela is held every twelve years. I took a room in a little hotel where I had a view of the river and temples. Surely there I would heal, surrounded by the ancient culture of Hindu India.... but it did not happen.

My room was infested with bedbugs. I filled the place with Tick-Twenty, a local insecticide, sealed it up with towels and then slept beside the river. The next night I was again awakened by the bites of bedbugs. I stood my bed in four little pans of oil so the insects could not climb up from the floor, and again sprayed the whole room with Tick-Twenty. Again the bugs tormented me in the night. I turned on my flashlight and saw a line of brown, flat bugs, crawling along the ceiling, and then dropping onto my bed when they detected the heat of my body. They were coming in from other rooms. Again I slept down by the river on the ancient stones. It was peaceful there. Once I was awakened by a policeman shining his flashlight into my face. I made "namaskar," the respectful gesture of the hands, and he left the crazy foreigner to his dreams.

After sleeping on the river bank for about a week I found a lodge in the oldest part of town, near Sita Gupha, the caves where Sita was said to have taken refuge when separated from Ram in the forest. It was called Kaka lodge. The owner was an old man with a long white beard. He was a devotee of Shirdi Sai Baba, and held weekly satsangs in his room on the roof. He assured me there were no "katmals" in his lodge, but there were. I stayed there for three months, and avoided the bedbugs by sleeping on the roof. It was cool and quiet up there above the narrow streets of old Nasik.

I paid a visit to the only person I knew in Nasik, Srikant Goswami, a man I had met years before at a mela. He belonged to an old Brahmin family who lived in the temple bazaar near the river. I told him I was looking for three things: a tabla teacher; a yoga teacher; and home cooked meals. Srikant was a real friend, and very willing to help. First, he introduced me to a local music teacher, Bhanudas Pawar, who taught music to children. I joined his morning class, and sat with about a dozen boys who found it an endless source of amusement to have a foreigner in their midst. Bhanudas had learned in a very good gharana, or tradition of tabla playing, that had originated with Tirkwa Khan, and been carried on by Nizamuddin Khan and Mohre Maharaj, his own teacher. There was no conflict with what I had already learned, which was a pleasant surprise, as I had come to expect that every time I found a new teacher, the first thing they told me was that everything I had learned so far was wrong.

Next I made my way to the apartment of a man called Manilal Jethalal Desai, who taught yoga in his home in the afternoon. He had only one other student. He was about sixty years old, and had taken up yoga when his career as a gymnast came to an end.

But the best part of my stay in Nasik was the food. I was introduced to a married lady who cooked for a few extra people in order to supplement the family income. Her husband was a lawyer, and their house was in an ancient compound called "Vakil Wadi." Law had been the family occupation for generations. It was traditional Maratha vegetarian food, with lots of garlic, and the best food I had ever had.

I prepared a simple breakfast in my room, and then went for tabla practice. At noon, I had lunch at Vakil Wadi. In the late afternoon I walked through the crowded, filthy streets to my yoga class, and then returned to Vakil Wadi for supper. It was as good a life as I could expect to put together in an Indian city.

Every Thursday and Sunday afternoons I went for darshan of Swami Prakashananda. Every Thursday evening, I joined the satsang of Shirdi Sai Baba devotees on the roof of Kaka lodge, where we sang songs and sat for meditation. I wandered the streets of Nasik, doing my best to feel the spiritual energy of this ancient, holy city. But it was no good. I was lonely and lost. My yoga was without real direction or purpose, and I was making very little progress on tabla in spite of hours of practice.

It was the pollution that finally drove me away. In the mornings I would cross the river on a low bridge and most days I could hardly see the buildings on the other side through the red clouds of smoke. Nasik had abundant water, and so about 500 factories had been built in the area. It had once been a destination for health and spiritual retreat, surrounded by forests that provided a temperate climate, but the forests were gone and the river and air were polluted by industry. I had developed a chronic cough, and decided to leave for the mountains.

Before leaving I went for darshan of Shirdi Sai Baba. While sitting in the Chowdi, I had a sudden, intuitive awareness that Maya had got together with my best friend back on Salt Spring Island. Same tired old story. At the time I felt relieved: the powerful atmosphere of Shirdi had for a moment made me feel like a sadhu again.

That night I had a powerful dream. I was back on the beach where I had been as a child, playing in the sand. It was a sunny day, but suddenly turned dark, and I looked up. Far away to the southeast the line where the ocean touched the sky had become ragged and dangerous. The waves crashed higher and higher on the beach and I retreated up the path towards home. The waves followed me, foaming through the trees as the wind broke branches above my head. Then I saw an awesome figure coming down the trail towards me, tall and green, like Neptune, carrying a trident. I hid behind a tree as it walked past with silent power and purpose, down into the fury of the sea.

I returned to McCleod Ganj for a month, and the mountains gave some peace, but I was longing to see Maya again. Once I returned to my solitary cabin in the woods, the shock of my loss caught up with me. Along with my lover, I had lost my best friend on the Island, and what little face I had had. Everyone knew I had been shafted, and was now just another lonesome jerk. To make matters worse, my intense yoga practice had greatly increased my sexual energy. It is not for nothing that the ancient texts of India recommend marriage for people who take up yoga!

My path seemed to have abandoned me, and I was left picking up the pieces of a disintegrating life. In a last desperate attempt to recapture a more enlightened attitude to my difficulties, I decided to do another vipassana retreat –after all, it had worked in the past. There was a two week retreat being held in a place called Joshua tree in southern California, to be led by a Sayadaw from Burma. Many of the western teachers of insight meditation were going to be there as they looked to the Sayadaw for teaching themselves.

It was my last retreat. I put in my best effort at mindfulness practice, and in the evenings sat through the discourses of the Sayadaw. What nonsense he did speak! For the first five talks, each lasting over an hour, his only point was the importance of giving generous donations to support the dharma and monks like him. I participated in small interviews where we were given the chance to ask our questions of the great man. He just focused on the prettiest girl with a lecherous leer that robes could not hide. I was unable to find in him a single quality to be admired.

For years, daily vipassana sitting, weekly participation in group meditation, and at least one ten day retreat per year had been part of my life. After more than forty ten-day retreats I had to ask myself if this practice was helping, and for me at least the answer was a resounding no. There were some insight teachers who had impressed me with their natural wisdom and compassion, and I will always remember Ruth

Denizon and Jack Kornfield with respect and gratitude. Perhaps my favorite was a man from New York called Norman Rosenberg. He taught meditation and Reiki together, and used stories from his time in the army to teach dharma. His retreats were full of humor and a heart-felt dedication to healing and recovery that grounded the meditation in the reality of the suffering in our own communities.

I re-focused on my plan to become a yoga teacher, and began putting more time and energy into my practice. I returned to India with renewed determination to study ashtanga yoga with Pattabhi Jois. If I was ever to be a teacher of that style, I had to learn from the master himself. I was also eager to get away from the small community where everyone knew me and my troubles.

My plane landed in Madras. I had arranged to visit an old friend, Swami Devananda, a Canadian sanyasi who lived near Madras in a private temple called Sri Vaishanavi Devi Shrine. He had been in India continually for over twenty years, and had embraced the life of a sanyasin in an authentic way.

Ever since I had seen that yogi in the cave near Mysore, I had believed that renunciation led to a state of inner peace and joy. With rather linear thinking, I had concluded that Swamiji, having been a sanayasin for so long, must be in such a state –but this was not the case. Although he had become critical of just about everyone, including me, he remained tireless in the defense of Hindu dharma as it came under attack from both academic, secular Indians and foreign churches. He wrote with great insight to expose the hypocrisy of Christian evangelists who were dressing like sanyasins in their stealth attack on Hindu India. We had coffee and caught up with our gossip. He introduced me to a delightful lady called Vasanti Amma, whose father had founded the shrine. We sat together in the evenings and our conversation was filled with laughter.

On my way to Mysore, I stopped for three days in Tiruva-namallai, the place of Ramana Maharishi. As it was my first time there, I did not know any good places to stay, and ended up in a room in the center of town. It was one of the noisiest, dirtiest towns I had ever been in. I visited the main temple, and found my way to the little room of Ram Surat Kumar and sat with him, surrounded by accumulated piles of offerings and what looked like garbage. I wandered on Arunachala Mountain searching for grace, for a touch of Ramana, but the place had filled up with pretenders, mostly from the West. The town and the mountain had a strong Shiva, or masculine energy, similar to Almora. The softer, feminine heart of the place had been alive and well in Ramana Maharishi, and shows in his photos... in his eyes. But I felt no connection to that sacred place and soon left for Mysore.

Once again I searched for a quiet room in a crowded and noisy Indian city. Once again I wandered the streets alone, looking for some place to eat. The one thing I had was a purpose, and I soon started yoga classes with Pattabhi Jois at his house in a suburb.

One day while sitting in a restaurant eating my usual meal of white rice and thin curries I noticed a group of athletic young men having coffee at a nearby table. They all looked strong and healthy. Desperate, I approached them with a question:

"Please tell me what you guys eat! I can't believe you are able to live on this diet."

They were surprised and a bit embarrassed by my question. I introduced myself, and told them I was visiting from Canada to study yoga, but was having trouble finding the energy on white rice and watery rasams. After a brief consultation in Tamil, one of them told me:

"Well, we're shy to admit it, but we eat ragi."

"What is ragi?" I asked.

"It is a local seed. We did not want to tell you, because it is generally only eaten by farmers and laborers."

"That's just what I'm looking for. Is there a hotel that serves it?"

"No. It is only available in the villages. But we know of one place…."

Again they consulted. Then he continued: "Come, we will show you."

They led me to the older part of town where there was a big covered market. In a lane near the market, they stopped at a low door in a simple hut. A young woman appeared with a boy of about twelve who turned out to be her son. Yes, they would serve me ragi.

That evening I found my way back to the room, ducked inside and sat on a sack with two other men. The boy handed me a plate with a large, red dumpling of ragi in a soup of soy beans and greens –a tasty meal that cost only one rupee and twenty five paise, the equivalent of about ten cents. It was the most nourishing and satisfying food I found in south India, and for the four months of my training I went there every day for lunch and sometimes for dinner. Soon, other visiting yoga students joined me and the little shop became known as "The Ragi Club." The lady who cooked and served our meals was a single mother who supported herself and two children by serving these simple meals to the men who did manual labor in the market…and now to visiting yoga students desperate for a healthy alternative to white rice.

Six days every week for four months I worked hard at learning the first two series of Ashtanga Yoga positions. Sunday was a day of rest. Mysore was a cultural center, and there were free concerts just about every night. South Indian music is quite different from the music of the north, and I was unable to develop a taste for it, but when Pandit

Jasraj, perhaps the greatest living vocalist of North India, gave a concert I was in heaven.

One afternoon I was sitting in the lobby of a hotel, reading a newspaper, when I noticed a man looking intently at me from the chair opposite. He had graying hair and glasses, and was well dressed.

"Why are you wavering?" he demanded without warning.

"Am I "wavering"?" I responded, rather weakly.

"Yes, you are wavering!" he repeated with a serious nod of his head. I asked what he meant.

"You know what to do. Why are you not getting on with it?"

I had become used to people seeing me perhaps more clearly than I saw myself. "I am here to study yoga." I explained, hoping for mercy.

"Enough study…. stop wasting time and get on with it!" he insisted.

It was a message I had heard before, and just as abruptly, from Ruth Denizon. She had inquired of her insight meditation group one day how many had already sat two or more retreats. Most of us proudly put up our hands, as Vipassana retreats can be quite addictive. "I am ashamed of you," she admonished us: "why are you not out there, getting on with life?" It was a good teaching, but for the most part wasted on us.

On another occasion, while walking the streets, I was approached by a small, energetic man who introduced himself: "My name is Rajendra. I am a collector."

"And what do you collect?" I asked.

"Foreigners," he replied calmly.

He took me to his house and showed me his collection of foreigners. It was a book full of addresses, photos, and short testimonials as to the helpfulness of the "Collector." He served me coffee, and collected my name in his book. He was the manager of a government canteen nearby, and had plenty of spare time.

Meanwhile, the yoga room where I had my daily class had become too crowded for comfort, and I moved upstairs into a smaller room to practice with Pundit Jois's nephew. I would go down from time to time to learn new positions with Jois, and would always do the difficult back bends under his supervision. Every day my class became a few minutes longer as new postures were added until I was doing asanas for about three hours. At the end of four months I was able to do both first and second series, and felt ready to teach. Third series was far too advanced for the average person and was full of positions that could only be performed by yogis who had been training for many years. The fourth series was an advanced preparation for pranayama and meditation that was seldom taught.

Four months of yoga lifted my spirits, and in a happy mood I took the train north to spend the six weeks left on my visa at McCleod Ganj. I arrived at the end of March, and it was still very cold. The Dalai Lama was teaching, and every room in the town was full. After hours of searching, I found a small, windowless room with a wooden bed. Snow began to fall as I cleaned it up and made it as comfortable as possible. There was just enough room to practice my yoga, and this I did as the only way to get warm. I was amazed to find that during the four days of travel, during which I had not done any yoga, my body had relaxed and become more flexible.

I bought a small electric stove, and used it for cooking and heating. The snow gave way to rain, and the days began to get warmer. When the teachings were finished at the temple, many dharma students left, and I was able to move in to my old room just above the town, in the servant's quarters of Brigadier Thappa.

I continued music lessons with Desh Bhandhu Sharma in the lower Dharmshala bazaar. After the first class, I walked back to McCleod Ganj, about fifteen hundred feet higher up the mountain. This climb had always left me tired and out of breath, but I was amazed to find that I reached my room still feeling quite fresh. Intense yoga practice had increased my lung capacity by about twenty-five percent.

I taught my first yoga class on the lawn in front of my room. My students were all Spanish speaking: three from Mexico and two from Spain. I learned a lot from them. One afternoon, we were sitting in the "Last Chance" café having tea when Julio asked me a question about meditation. I did my best to answer. Then their friend Juliette asked another more difficult question –something about Samadhi, or a state of consciousness. Again I did my best to answer. Then Julio's wife, Claudia, asked a really difficult question about the ultimate nature of reality itself. After a long pause, I said:

"I don't know."

"That is better," she replied.

We all laughed. The joke was on me.

After a month, during which we all became friends, the Spanish couple, Raphael and Helena, had a baby. It was a long, hard labor followed by a difficult birth in the military hospital about twenty miles away. They had driven around all night, trying to find a doctor, and finally the helpful taxi driver took them to the army base. After attending to hours of difficult labor with no result, the doctor left the room to get what was needed to perform a caesarian. While he was gone a kind nurse urged Helena for just one more push, and a healthy baby girl was born. Helena was fine, if exhausted, and Raphael was full of joy and gratitude.

We had a party at my place. Everyone came, including five Tibetan guys. Raphael sang a song in Spanish, playing his guitar in a passionate and beautiful way. He turned and sang a verse in English, just for me:

"If you are not happy, you are not wise: you have nothing."

Chapter 17: *Suffering*

When the time came to leave the mountains and cross the hot plains of northern India on the way home I was ready to make a real effort to create a life for myself back in Canada. My younger brother had been fond of saying: "A splendid suffering is better than a mediocre happiness," but I did not agree with him. There is nothing splendid about unnecessary suffering, and nothing mediocre about happiness.

I decided to move from Saltspring Island to Victoria, where I found a room and worked on a framing crew for six months. When I left, the boss said I had progressed from "utterly hopeless to just passable." I decided to start a part time gardening business, and began driving around Victoria in an old Datsun pickup, mowing lawns, pruning trees, and hauling garbage. I was looking for a place to live and teach yoga, so, with my father's help, I made a down payment on an old house that needed a lot of repairs and renovation. Everything turned out to be more difficult than expected. For example, the wallpaper on the ceiling of the living room would not yield to any effort or product that I tried. I decided it must be solid enough to take a coat of paint, and in this way discovered the one thing that removes old wallpaper –fresh paint. It peeled off in sticky patches that stuck to the floor. After six months hard work I broke down and hired a man to finish the painting.

I got an unexpected gift from a plumber. While replacing a toilet, he noticed the extra space in the basement, and suggested we put a suite in there. In fact, he was willing to do much of the work himself, because he needed a place to live. It turned out his wife had just left him, taking everything in the house, including their three children. Taking the house took a little longer. Seems he was working too much and had not noticed their marriage falling apart.

It was not long before I was teaching small yoga classes in the living room, and hosting weekly meditation groups in what had once been a dining room. We had some wonderful evenings of devotional music with vegetarian meals provided by the good-natured Hare Krishna people, who enjoyed these events so much they forgot all about trying to persuade anyone to join their path. I had income from the suite as well as from the two bedrooms that I rented out. When it was good, I had a small community to come home to, and when it was bad, I dreaded coming home at all. After a few years of this, I found myself in a relationship, and before long Barbara moved in with me, and the meditation and yoga rooms became her space.

One day I saw a notice about a Rinzai Zen retreat, or sesshin, to be held in Victoria. This was something I had never tried, so I registered, in the hope that Zen might fill the void left when I gave up on vipassana. The sesshin was to be led by a monk from Japan called Shinzan Miyame Roshi.

On the day the retreat was to begin I arrived quite confident that all the practice I had done would somehow mean something and that Zen would be easy. I had sat Soto style Zazen in India, no problem, but this was Rinzai Zen, and on the first day I was given a koan that just totally stumped me. I had read somewhere that a student of Zen must strive to become so focused on their Koan that "it feels like a red hot cannon-ball stuck in the throat: it won't go up, it won't go down...what to do?" Again and again I would appear before the Roshi and try to get past my koan, try to impress him that I had "got it," but he would just whack me on the shoulder with his stick, and send me away. For three days and nights I wrestled with the thing... I stood on my head, I said all manner of nonsense, but nothing impressed this monk from Japan. He wore black and had huge, dark eyes and a long, flat wooden stick, and he was not joking. When the time came for the retreat to end I still had not passed, but he said in broken English:

"Some very close..... one more time try."

Again we sat in Meditation, and finally, like a bolt from the blue, I found myself on the other side of the koan. On my last meeting with the Roshi he knew I had passed this obstacle when all my thinking, experience and personal history had been wiped out and I had finally answered with simplicity, like a child.

A few days later an American Swami I had known in India visited Victoria with a group of Siddha Yoga people and I was able to offer them all chai without my usual negative thoughts and feelings. This state of freedom and simplicity lasted for days, and so Zen entered my life.

My connection with India was renewed one day by a letter from a woman I had known at Swami Muktananda's ashram who wrote to tell me about a saint from Kerala called Mata Amritananda, or simply Amma. Amma was visiting the west for the first time, and my friend urged me to go and meet her. I had heard of her once before, in a letter from my brother where he had told me about a girl in a fishing village near him who was going into ecstasy and giving darshan of Krishna. Seems the people at his ashram, who were on the non-dual path of knowledge, disapproved – but to me Amma sounded like a real saint.

A three day retreat with Amma was scheduled to take place on Orcas Island, not far from Victoria, and I decided to go. It was a wonderful experience. There were only eighty-five people at the wilderness recreational center for this retreat, one of the first given by Amma outside India. The programs took place in a rustic meeting hall where we sat on the floor to meditate, sing, and meet Amma in a happy chaos of Hindu devotion. I joined the line for darshan, and Amma took us each in her arms and flooded us with unconditional love. Here was the Divine Mother, in the form of a humble girl from a very poor village, come to renew our faith, just as she was renewing the faith of thousands of people in India.

On some level I had always believed that salvation could be found by surrendering to a real saint, a real guru who was worthy of our trust. By the end of the retreat I had no doubt that Amma was a real saint, and I felt a strong pull to just give up everything and follow her. I told many of my friends in Victoria about Amma, and the following year most of them went to meet her, and so the Victoria Amma Satsang was born. Once a week we met for devotional music, and once a year there was a three day retreat with Amma near Port Townsend in Washington.

Meanwhile the combination of physical work by day and yoga by night was not going well, and I had a series of injuries. I was able to recover three times, but the fourth injury finally forced me to stop teaching yoga asanas. While resting and waiting for my back to heal, I decided to give astrology another look.

For years I had followed the movement of the planets relative to my natal chart, and formed some idea of the meaning of the symbols and the archetypes they represented, but had abandoned the study because the most meaningful and powerful experiences on my journey of self discovery had not been accounted for. I had concluded that astrology was not deep enough to interest me. Then I read about the discovery of a new object called Chiron. Chiron was perhaps an asteroid, or a comet, or a very small planet, and orbited between Saturn and Uranus. I decided to locate Chiron in my chart, and then look back over the years and see what correlations were there, if any. To my amazement I found that all my powerful awakenings and initiations correlated exactly with the movement of this new object. Chiron turned out to be the missing link between the personal realm of experience and the trans-personal realm that I had been exploring. I began to study astrology more seriously.

At this time I was having trouble sleeping. At first I thought it was a digestive problem, perhaps caused by parasites I had picked up in India. A series of five stool tests showed nothing. I was referred to a doctor from India who was familiar with internal medicine, but he could find nothing. My sleep became more and more disturbed until I was frequently spending the entire night awake with a strong pulse pounding in my abdomen. I was referred to an internal specialist who scheduled a colonoscopy. Still nothing was found. By this time I was getting only about five hours of sleep in a week. As many as four nights in a row would pass without a wink. I spent long hours between midnight and four a.m. just sitting in meditation, trying to at least rest my mind. The doctors I saw could not help me.

Throughout this period of my life I was working several hours each day at my gardening business, studying astrology in the evenings, and I had my property on Salt Spring Island to maintain, as well as my house. My partner, Barbara, was a rock of kindness and support, and the yoga room had evolved into her dance studio.

After a year living with sleep deprivation, and with an ever increasing pulse in my abdomen that got worse at night, I had exhausted all options. Acupuncture, naturopathy, homeopathy, and allopathic medicine had all failed to come up with either a diagnosis or a treatment. I was convinced the problem was some kind of parasite.

I finally met a healer who was an expert in muscle testing. He confirmed that the problem was indeed parasites, although he could not identify the type. He told me that they had progressed from my lower intestine to my small intestine and from there to my liver, spleen, gall bladder, and were just beginning to infect my heart and lungs. He told me that the situation was critical and that if it went much further I would be dead. I returned to my doctor and insisted that she test for all possible parasites. After another month of sleeplessness the diagnosis came back: it was a bacterium called Clostridium difficile. I was prescribed antibiotics which cured the infection, but not the cause.

Apparently these bacteria occur naturally in small amounts in the large intestine, and the ileocecal valve is intended to stop their migration into the small intestine. But my valve was not working. I began treatment with an alternative healer who specialized in kinesiology and the body-mind connection. He went very deep very fast and finally reached something that he was not able to deal with, and he had the amazing humility to send me on to a healer called Seamus.

When I went in to see Seamus, my abdomen felt like a cannonball. He guided me quickly to the source of this condition: unexpressed anger. For the first time I engaged the incredible rage that had built up inside me during my childhood years. Pillows became my former classmates and I pounded them all to pieces. When we were done, my belly was soft, and my ileocecal valve was working again.

It had never occurred to me to use any form of medication except antibiotics when absolutely necessary. I somehow survived two years of severe insomnia, passing the nights by alternating between lying awake and sitting in front of my altar. At times I had to roll on the floor to relieve the pain in my abdomen. Perhaps two nights per week I got a few hours of sleep. It had taken two years to get my health back, and I was eager to get my life back on track.

By this time Barbara and I both knew that our time together was coming to an end. This separation was not easy, but as smooth and natural as possible, and we were able to remain friends.

I continued to study astrology and after a year of reading books and attending local classes, I began doing readings for free to gain some confidence. Then one day I felt ready to turn professional, and charged ten dollars. My rate climbed slowly to forty dollars per reading, and I became more at ease with the process of talking about a client's life in terms of the archetypes of astrology. But I was not satisfied with my own understanding, and began searching for a living teacher. I had always learned best in the oral tradition, and decided to follow the same path with astrology.

I listened to many tapes of talks given by many different astrologers and one voice stood out with real depth and power –a man called Jeffrey Wolf Green. I searched his name and found a small ad in the Mountain Astrologer: Jeffrey was to teach something called the "Pluto School" in Vancouver. Without hesitation I picked up the phone and registered.

We are given a few moments in life that contain doorways –the opportunity to pass through into a new perception of life. Meeting Jeffrey was one of these. When I walked into the room where the Pluto school was to take place, Jeffrey was curled up in his chair with a coffee and a cigarette. I already had a lot of respect for him based on his recorded talks, and walked over to shake his hand. He took it, but this was clearly not his way of doing things. He looked at me as if he recognized me, and was not too happy to see me again. His energy, the soul that showed through his eyes, was quite unlike anything I had seen before. He was remote, ancient, and at the same time very humble and present.

It took time for me to stop my own momentum and change directions, like an overloaded cargo ship with a broken rudder. I was overloaded with what I thought I knew about the spiritual dimension of life, and believed I was only there to learn astrology. I had been saturated with views from Advaita Vedanta and Buddhism that denied the very idea of "self," let alone a soul and a creator. When Jeffrey freely used these terms, I found myself secretly thinking that my own spiritual insight was more evolved than his. I had been impressed by so-called "jnanis" or "men of knowledge" who, if asked a question such as "what is the nature of enlightenment," would reply simply: "enlightenment for whom?" In their company it became impossible to use first person singular pronouns such as "I" and "me" without attracting criticism. Now here was Jeffrey speaking in such a natural and simple way about the human psyche as I had always experienced it. In his Pluto school, ordinary life once again became filled with sacred purpose, and I finally had support to just get down and be human. Instead of transcendence and renunciation, we were taught about individual healing and the opening of the heart to embrace a natural relatedness with the creator. Everything was referred to the natal chart, where both the universal archetypes and our individual journeys were reflected.

But at first I resisted –after all, I had just spent twenty years going in the opposite direction. The turning point came dramatically. The material was presented in three sections, each lasting five days, with several months between for home study. In the middle of the second section, during a private talk with Jeffrey, I expressed the views I held about the "non-existence" of self etc. He replied quietly:

"Mark, in the human form, consciousness evolves and finds liberation through the emotional body."

The timing was right, and the truth of his words went straight to my heart. This realization shook my fragile foundation and I found myself standing at the edge of an abyss of emotion that was deep and unknown. Yes, I was very real and very full of pain. Perhaps the concepts of transcendence and enlightenment were attractive because they seemed to offer an escape –a way to avoid the hard work of emotional healing that was my most basic need. I remembered the dream I had had just before leaving India, and understood it at last. I would have to go down through those waves, into the depths of my emotions –into the storm.

It took me a year to complete the Pluto school. I also attended a special seminar on the astrology of sexuality, taught by Jeffrey in Vancouver in September of 1995. While I was there two amazing things happened. I read in the papers of a miracle that had started in India and spread around the world: statues of the god Ganesh were drinking milk. Ganesh was dear to me as the image of the part human, part animal daemon archetype, as well as being the guardian of the doorway to the mystery of the goddess and the unfolding of kundalini shakti. I bought a quart of milk, found the nearest Hindu temple, and was on my way to see for myself. The two friends I was staying with went with me. We approached the small image of Ganesh and, with a spoon, offered milk to the mouth of the statue. The milk disappeared. I offered more, and it, too, vanished into the marble elephant mouth. Both my friends offered milk, and the same thing happened. Then I noticed that milk was dripping out of a Shiva lingam about ten feet away. Ganesh and the lingam were not connected in any way, but sat on the same wide altar. We looked under the cloth around the body and feet of Ganesh, but there was no milk there: it was still emerging from the middle of the lingam and running down the stone. This miracle continued for about three days all over the world and then stopped as mysteriously as it had begun. I was amazed and saddened that such an event could attract so little interest and so much doubt and scorn.

The second event shoved me right into the deep end of Jeffrey's teaching about reincarnation and how our evolution continues, life after life, to offer opportunities to learn and grow. He often said that we picked up where we left off and that most of our intimate and family relationships were with people we had known before. In meditation I had seen an event from a recent life in Persia, where I had fallen in love with the daughter of a powerful man, but later been betrayed by her and put to death. The image I had recalled was the moment I had first looked into her eyes—that moment when my pride and learning had been reduced to ashes by the power of her beauty and the fires of passion. During the seminar I had turned to see who was sitting beside me, and she had turned at the same time, and I found myself looking into those same eyes. We had a brief, insane affair that ended as suddenly as it began, but somehow we managed to keep respect and kindness going and so ended a cycle of mistrust and what might be called "bad karma" with each other. Jeffrey encouraged me to take a good, honest look at an even earlier lifetime when it had been me betraying her. I would not have understood the purpose of this encounter without Jeffrey's help. He often said that it was our human relationships that were the primary vehicle of the soul's evolution, and so my many years of longing for the solitary life of a hermit finally came to an end.

This part of my learning was easy compared to what followed. During my final private check-in with Jeffrey, towards the end of the school, I told him I had the opportunity to go to Taiwan and spend a week in intensive meditation in a bamboo forest, guided by a teacher from Vietnam called Suma Ching Hai.

"It is just going to lead to more knowledge," he said: "you have been accumulating this kind of experience for too many lifetimes already."

I was still clinging to the idea that through meditation I could break free.

"Your spiritual future is shamanism," Jeffrey told me, then added: "Well, you are going to do this anyway." He looked tired. Jeffrey suffered from chronic pain and illness going back to his time in Vietnam and exposure to the chemical called 'agent orange' –in addition to capture and injury in combat.

I also mentioned a woman I had just met called Sara. He told me this relationship had real potential, and gave me priceless advice: "Let her lead." But I did not know how to do that.

It was in Taiwan, in the bamboo forest, that I finally felt in my gut how the direction of intensive meditation had been exhausted for me. The teacher reminded me of Swami Muktananda: powerful and charismatic, yet arrogant and vain. Thousands of people, mostly Chinese, followed her in awe, and although it is perhaps a very good path for some, it was certainly not for me. I finally dropped the idea of cultivating special states of consciousness and was ready to just open up to the unknown that Jeffrey was pointing to.

I had no idea what Jeffrey meant by "Shamanism." I had also been stuck on the concept that somehow spirituality was located east of Istanbul and was centered in India. It was hard to accept a humble western man of my own age and background as a spiritual teacher. It took away that final excuse –the sad belief that no-one like us can have anything of real value to offer. We worship those who seem far away and exotic and find in the safety of distance the child-like comfort of not having to take responsibility for our own evolution.

I returned from Taiwan with a sense of relief. I had put a burden down –but what was shamanism? My only idea was that perhaps the native people of my own area could help me.

I had heard of a ritual called the sweat lodge, and decided that this was the place to begin. I made inquiries, and found three people in southern Vancouver Island who held sweats from time to time. I left messages at all three numbers, and two weeks later, I had a call from a man called Uncle Joe.

"What's this about?" asked the voice. I had no idea who it was.

"This is Joe. You left a message." He spoke with a slow, even tone. I explained my search for an introduction to the sweat lodge, and to native ways.

"Well, I will have to meet you. Come on Thursday evening." He gave me an address.

The time came and I arrived with a bundle of sage and a twist of tobacco. He took my hand in both of his, looked into my eyes and said: "Thank you. I really appreciate it." He was a big man, over 200 pounds, and looked very powerful. His hair was long and black, and his eyes shone.

We were joined in the living room by two native women who were also preparing for their first sweat. Uncle Joe spoke about the sweat lodge and his traditions, and let me handle his bow. It was made of yew and I could hardly draw it. He told me how he had killed a bear with it –the arrow had gone right through the bear. Two sweats were planned for the winter. Joe told me to bring towels and wear shorts and a t-shirt. He had a lodge in his back yard, by the water. His wife gave us all some herbal tea.

That was when my fear began. It was October of 1996 and there were two months to wait before the first sweat. I had finished the Pluto school, and Jeffrey wrote to congratulate me, adding: "You are the first to do this."

I did not understand the significance of his words, and had yet to experience the full power of his teaching. The forces of adversity were gathering to test me. These were energies that I did not understand and did not want to know about. To understand the evolution of the human soul as taught by Jeffrey, it was necessary to become aware of the dark side, the dimension of creation that might be called "evil". It was hard to let go of the concept of perfection, the child-like desire to feel protected by a perfect god. I had yet to learn how to protect myself.

September rains came and my old roof began to leak, so I called a roofer to have it replaced. My only request was that the job be finished before the end of October, when storm season began. It turned out to be a bigger task than expected and when the first south east gale hit in November there were still only tarps and bundles of shingles where the roof should have been.

That morning I had driven my girlfriend Sara out to a job interview that was only supposed to take ten minutes. I ended up waiting two hours while the storm clouds darkened and the rain came down. She was in a bad mood as I dropped her off and our relationship was just about dead. By the time I got home, the wind had taken the tarp off the roof and bundles of shingles were flying through the air –it was a real south east gale, and an omen of things to come.

I had fallen I love with Sara before finding the ground under my own feet, and was in no condition to survive the forces that were being awakened. A child within me wanted safety and the unconditional love only a mother could provide, while Sara needed a man who could be strong while she healed her own wounds. This could not turn out well.

The day for the first sweat with Uncle Joe came and I woke up with a sore throat and filled with irrational fears. I called Joe, and he told me that a sore throat was the kind of trouble that people came to leave on the floor of his lodge. But there was another sweat in a month and I decided to wait and go when I felt stronger. This was a terrible mistake.

A few days later Sara and I finally broke up.

"You are such a child...." she yelled with disgust: "I want you to leave!"

I left. When the door slammed something dark and angry hit me between the shoulders. I went back to a house in a storm with no roof.

I called the roofer and we did damage control to survive until the work could be finished. I decided to go away and stay a few days at the Yoga Center on Saltspring Island, just to get away. My cat, Shadow, warned me not to go –he clearly communicated, looking directly into my eyes and saying "don't go... don't go!" in his own way. Light snow was forecast.

It was snowing hard as I drove slowly up the long, bumpy drive to the old farm-house that had been converted into the yoga center. I settled in for the night, and by morning, three feet of snow covered everything. It was a record for the area, and I was stuck there with nothing to do but reflect on my life as I sank lower each day: I was not a part of anything; had no family; no community; no work; no partner; no children and, worst of all, my precious inner peace was gone. There was no comfort for me anywhere –just a vast expanse of snow inside and out. Everything was frozen. The members of the Yoga Center community were friendly and included me in their activities and meals, but I was a hungry ghost. Someone remarked that I appeared to be in shock. This was true. My face was pale and there was no life in my eyes. The kindness and little gifts that were offered just blew away like dead leaves.

After three days I hiked into Ganges and bought a set of chains for my truck. I was worried about my cat. With fingers numb from the cold it took me an hour to get the chains on. Back in Victoria, the snow was just as deep. I was able to park, but then more snow fell, and my truck was stuck even with chains. It was Christmas Eve and I fed Shadow, lit a fire and went to bed early. That was the last night I slept for a long time.

I also had my last dream: I was following a river, trying to find the source, and became too tired to go any farther. I decided to dive into the water and see what was on the bottom, but it was too deep, and I was unable to return to the surface. At the same time, another part of me decided to fly into the sky for a better view, but gravity let go and I was unable to come down. There was the feeling of drowning and at the same time the feeling of floating away into space. I had torn myself apart.

On Christmas day I was alone with the presents I had wrapped for Sara. It was the third time that I had been rejected just before Christmas. Too many emotional shocks, too much sorrow –that night the floor dissolved. There was nothing under my feet any more, it was impossible to sleep, and my mind spun out of control with grief. This continued all the next day and was followed by another sleepless night. I lost the ability to make decisions, and ran out of food. At times I thought I should check in to a mental hospital.

I began to call friends for help, but everyone I knew was away for the holidays. There was one couple who lived nearby, Richard and Arlene, who I knew to be supportive and I dialed their number again and again, but there was no answer. Another day and another sleepless night followed. Again and again I called my friends, and, as night fell, it was clear I was not going to survive on my own. I wrote down the number of EMI, the local psychiatric hospital, but could not bring myself to call. I thought of my old father, and the grief it would cause him. One more time I called my friends, and this time Arlene answered. She was a social worker who had been a psychiatric nurse, and she knew right away I was in serious trouble.

They took me in. I walked through the snow, and saw Arlene coming to meet me. Richard was working graveyard shift at a detox center where he was a nurse. I spent the night lying awake on a bed in their spare room. At least I was not alone.

This was the beginning of the darkest passage of my life. The medical professionals called it a major clinical depression. I was going through hell. Demons appeared at night to torment me. They would come up close to my face, mocking and leering, and then turn, raise their tails and squirt shit. I lay on my back, repeating a mantra, my chosen name of god. For eight hours each night I lay like that, just doing the only thing I could.

Each day I returned to my house to feed Shadow and light a fire to keep the place warm. Richard took me to their doctor who started me on Paxil. I was having acute attacks of fear that would get worse as the day wore on: fear of madness; fear of the visions of terror that were waiting for me every night. Each day I became more exhausted, but sleep was impossible. Sleep had been my greatest comfort during the long years of seeking –it had been so sweet, so comforting, so refreshing, but now it seemed I would never sleep again, that there would be no rest from suffering.

After a week, when I returned to the doctor, she suggested I start taking sleeping pills. That night I took Imovane for the first time, and it knocked me out for three hours.

When I awoke, I took another, and got three more hours of unconsciousness. That became my routine. When I awoke at one a.m. it would be such a relief to know I could take another pill. But when I awoke again at four, I had to face another eighteen hours of hell.

After another week, the doctor started me on Lorazopam, and increased the dosage of Paxil. I was now fully medicated. I tried to hold out as long as I could before taking the tranquilizer, but by three of four in the afternoon, my knuckles would be white and I was shaking with blind terror, and so I took a pill. I felt as if my whole life had been wasted and all my efforts had been for nothing. Here I was, reduced to a drug dependant wreck, while the voices in my head repeated endless messages of self loathing and despair. It is perhaps fortunate that in such a condition it is very hard to work out any effective plan for suicide. After several pathetic attempts to slash my wrists with an exacto knife, I stopped trying.

Arlene worked during the day and Richard worked during the night. I would hear him come home just after eight in the morning. He would put wood on the fire and then go and sleep until about five in the afternoon. Arlene would be gone all day.

I could not imagine being alone after 4 p.m. when it began to get dark. The attacks of terror, the sweating, and the rush of madness became too much. Even with the tranquilizers, I was a wreck. I could not endure the sound of music. Color had no effect. Food was tasteless and there was no sexual energy left in my body. It was impossible to get an erection, and it seemed to me as if any possibility for love had also been lost. And a voice in my head told me this was forever.

The day for the second of Uncle Joe's sweats came and went, and once again I believed I was in no condition to go. I did not know then that a sweat lodge is a safe and healing place of prayer. I thought it would be some kind of test that I would surely fail.

I began to see a therapist twice a week, but she was totally out of her depth, and could only maintain her own position in face of the obvious fact that she was unable to offer much help. I went because it was something positive to do…. while my money lasted.

After ten days it was clear that Arlene and Richard were burning out, and they advised me that I could stay there only four more days. This was healthy boundaries, and I knew it, even though the thought of being on my own was terrifying. Fortunately my old friend Peter showed up in time to take me in. He came over one evening, happy to be back in Victoria, and found me sobbing on the couch. I looked at him and asked:

"Please do not be afraid of my suffering."

I did not want to be alone. Peter looked after me for the next three weeks, until the medication began having some effect, and I was able to return to my own home. It was another month before I felt I could endure an evening alone. Every night I found someone willing to spend a few hours with me. I made a list of my support network, and made sure I did not call anyone too often. It was amazing how many friends I had during that dark time. It was sad how few of them were still there four years later when I was finally out of the woods.

I slept on the floor of the spare room in Peter's house for three weeks. He was a professional therapist with very good listening skills. In the evenings I would describe my inner life and listen to his comments. In twenty years of practice he had not seen a more severe breakdown, and he told me that if I was a client of his, he would only treat me if I agreed to see him every day. I slowly began to accept that on one level I had a medical condition that was treatable. My spiritual pride prolonged the suffering and caused me to resist using the medications to best effect. Arlene had called them "my chemical allies," but I saw them as proof of my failure.

During my stay with Peter I had a vision that I did not understand. One day we went up Mount Tolmie, a local view point where Peter got his daily exercise by jogging up and down the hill. I stood on the summit and looked out to the west. The sun was perhaps thirty degrees above the horizon. There was a westerly wind blowing and a few thin, winter clouds. I saw a hawk come out of the north, riding the wind and looking toward the west. It stopped directly between me and the sun and hovered there for about thirty seconds before gliding on to the south. The hawk turned back and began to ride the wind north. Again it stopped when directly between me and the sun and hovered for about thirty seconds. Then it silently rode the wind north again and was gone.

I was in no shape to understand this gift. Later when I asked a native elder what it could mean, he just smiled and said:

"Ahh....the opening of the heart!"

During these dark times the creator communicated with me, but it was only years later that I could appreciate this. Meanwhile, I had a long fight for survival ahead of me.

It had always been my habit to be active and keep fit, and I planned to make exercise part of my recovery program. I went to the local recreation center three times a week. Then one day I walked into a situation where I needed to say no, but in my state of depression I just had to pick up the end of that heavy table.

"Turn it on its side." said the young, strong man at the other end, wrenching it over as he spoke. My back went out. Now I was physically as well as mentally damaged.

I was also over medicated –my doctor had been increasing the Paxil in an attempt to reduce my symptoms. I was working my way through a psychiatric nightmare, trying to find the right medication and the right dose, and it was trial and error. We settled on twenty milligrams of Paxil per day, and I continued to use Imovane for sleep and Lorazipam for anxiety. I was told that this would provide a platform upon which to rebuild my life and create a new self, one that was not depressed. This sounded impossible: the only self I had known was the spiritual seeker with a sense of humor who traveled and lived alone in strange places, and that persona had been destroyed.

My doctor referred me to a psychiatrist called Dr. James McNulty. I went, but with attitude, expecting to hear more lectures on the value of medication. Dr. McNulty was a man in his seventies. He wrote with an old fountain pen that he filled from a bottle of ink on his desk beside a circle of seven clay figures holding hands. I did not know it, but I was in the presence of an elder of my own people. At first, just like when I met Jeffrey, I was unable to recognize the quality of the man. And, just like Jeffrey, he was patient and kind, but really meant business.

"I have no time for people who are not willing to work." he told me one day. "You must learn to fight for your life… but do you believe that your life is worth fighting for?"

The voices in my head kept telling me I was a total failure that had thrown away every opportunity. I made no effort to change this, and in fact indulged in self-destructive thoughts and actions.

He said very little about the medications I was on, except that I should stay on them until I had felt I no longer needed them for at least six months, and then reduce the dose very slowly. He referred me to something called cognitive behavioral therapy.

One day, as I sat down for my session, I said as a joke: "I just want some sympathy from you!"

He replied: "If I thought it would do you any good, I would give it to you." Every word he said was to the point and meant to make a difference, but for the most part I was not able to respond.

During this time I was sitting at home one day when I got an unexpected phone call from Jeffrey.

"What's happening?" he asked, sounding very concerned.

I tried to tell him, but could not stop the tears and my voice kept choking up. He listened, and then said:

"Promise me you will not suicide!"

He made me say the words, knowing I would not break a promise made to him. Then he told me I needed to go through recovery as a child. Not like a child –as a child, because all the adult therapy and recovery steps would not work until I had healed emotionally at the level of an infant.

Jeffrey finished by saying: "You can call me whenever you need to."

A friend had called Jeffrey to let him know I was in rough shape at a time when I had been too ashamed to call him for help myself. I still remember this friend with gratitude: she was an angel when I needed one. After talking with Jeffrey I knew I had someone powerful on my side, someone who really knew me and what I was going through.

The inner dialogue gave me no rest, and fixed on the fact that I had not gone to Uncle Joe's sweats. The fear that had stopped me from going had grown until it owned me. I believed that if I had only faced my fear by going, the medicine and power there would have opened the door to my spiritual future, and the whole depression could have been avoided. These thoughts repeated endlessly as I beat myself up from within.

After a few more months of this, I finally got up the courage to call Uncle Joe. He told me to come and see him right away. When he opened the door he seemed to be looking at something behind me, then he took me to a hammock between two fir trees is his back yard, near the sweat lodge, and told me to rest there.

"Don't move," he said: "close your eyes and imagine how you would like your life to be. You can be specific, and create a vision for your future while I make up some medicine."

I lay there, thinking that it was no use, nothing and nobody could help me, I had blown it and other useless self talk.... but I did take the time to dream my own future. I had always wanted to live beside a river, to have my health back and be free from depression, and to have a partner and work that I loved. After about twenty minutes Joe came back holding a steaming mug:

"This is your big medicine tea," he told me: "drink it all."

It had honey and herbs and all kinds of strange things in it. There were even some fragments of sea-shell on the bottom. When I had finished, Joe looked into the mug, and said:

"There are still some pieces of shell in there.... drink them too."

I used my fingers to get every last piece into my mouth. Then he told me he would arrange a special sweat to help me get rid of what was troubling me. It was to happen in two days.

"Don't do anything until then," he said in a very serious tone: "the forces of adversity, this bad medicine that is troubling you will only get stronger now that you have seen me. It will try again to stop you from coming, but don't you let it. Call me if anything unusual happens."

This was amazing: I was being given a second chance.

All that day the darkness got worse and by the next night, I was caught up in a storm of fear and madness. Some force without name or shape was pressing in on me. I called Joe in the evening and could not believe the words that came out of my mouth. Something had taken over my voice, and while I had intended to ask him for help and advice, instead I more or less told him to fuck off. Then I took some pills and fell asleep.

The terrible light of morning made me aware of what I had done. My heart contracted in my chest. I called Joe again and tried to apologize, but it was too late.

"I offered you a gift, but you were not able to receive it, and so the gift stays with me. There are no hard feelings. Seems you have made a choice and now you must find the help you need from your side."

Horror and hopelessness tightened their grip on my soul. I had been given a second chance, and blown it! The voices in my head got louder. I had convinced myself that failure to go to those sweats had been a crucial mistake. For months I had tortured myself with the thought that if only I had gone, everything would be fine. I had prayed for another chance, and been given it. Any hope of recovering my spiritual purpose and following the path shown by Jeffrey now went out. How could this have happened? How could I be so stupid? It was more than I could bear.

Then the noise began. I was sitting in the kitchen one day, unable to decide what to eat for breakfast, when I noticed a thin, high-frequency sound coming from inside my head. It was not tinnitus, and did not arise from the inner ear, but from the base of my skull. Day by day this noise became louder, and gave me no rest. At night I had to focus my attention on my mantra, or it would drive me crazy. I researched this condition, and the only reference I could find was in an old, Chinese medicine text, where it was called "black noise". It is a condition that is caused by the extreme compression of consciousness in the base-brain, and is a rare symptom of deep depression. This was the very opposite of the inner silence I had always longed for.

For months I just took pills and lay on my bed. I did not want to feel or do anything. My muscles began to atrophy and I abandoned hope. Then I had a vision: I saw myself as a demonic man, sadistic and violent, causing much suffering in future incarnations. I saw myself slowly drawn down into a dark hole in the earth as my consciousness kept changing into lower and lower forms of life and my choices became fewer and fewer until the freedom of choice was lost altogether. But my consciousness retained the memory of who I had been, and what had been lost. This was something far worse than death or madness: I had seen involution, the opposite of evolution, and it was real. This vision was dark and terrifying, but it was a turning point. That final fall into hopelessness had not yet happened. I still had choices and opportunities. Two things had been made clear: if I did not turn things around, I would suffer beyond imagination –and I would also cause suffering to other people. This was enough to shock me into action.

Jeffrey had spoken to me about humility. I assumed I knew what it was, and that I had it, but I now understood the difference between false humility and the real thing. I had mistaken my low self-worth and masochism for humility. Now I had to get right down in the mud and root-hog or die.

My psychiatrist had recommended a program offered by the local hospital called cognitive behavioral therapy, but I had refused to go. It was just too humiliating to sit every day in a mental hospital with people in pale green gowns and little slippers that smelt of detergent and learn something so very un-spiritual. But that is where I started recovery. It was good stuff: real skills were taught, along with an understanding of the causes and symptoms of depression. I got to know the other patients and their struggles.

After four hours of training we were offered a bowl of soup and some crackers. One day as I sat there sipping the hospital soup with the others, I felt real gratitude and said a simple prayer of thanks. Nothing special: just the feeling, and a few words of appreciation that I was not alone, and that I had food. No albatross fell from my neck, but things did start to turn around.

The program lasted six weeks, and then I joined a special depression group that met once a week for ongoing support. It was run by an older woman with a doctorate in psychology who had been through depression herself and knew the ropes. She taught me a valuable phrase:

"Don't take valium, take action."

Slowly I reduced my use of medications. Of all the skills they taught the most difficult was something called simply "thought stopping." I believed it to be impossible. I had read about the practice called "stopping the internal dialogue" that Don Juan had taught Carlos Castaneda –it seemed to me to be the same thing, only without the glamorous setting. I decided to take it on, and for six months I practiced stopping all useless, self-destructive thoughts. At first I had to substitute a mantra, as my mind was in the habit of being busy, but gradually I was able to just stop thinking at will. In time it became my habit to only think when there was some real need, some definite purpose for the mind to focus on.

Most meditation teachers I had known had said that this was not possible. They had taught that it is the nature of the mind to be active –hence the need to practice meditation and so give the mind something of value to do. They were wrong.

Thought stopping was simple, but very difficult. I was able to do it because I had to. The next step was even more difficult. I was still in the grip of chronic anxiety. I could feel it eating up my kidneys and adrenal glands. My mind had a real problem to solve, so I used it, and understood that anxiety is a form of fear. Although it was not clear how to work with anxiety, as soon as I called it fear, I knew what to do: *feel the fear and do it anyway!* Fear was simple to work with, once

I was willing to really feel it while doing the very thing that I was afraid of. And I was afraid of just about everything, so there were plenty of opportunities to work with.

Having understood the principle, I went for it. One grey, lonely morning I drove up to a place in Nanaimo called "The Bungee Zone." A friend of mine had once worked there, and invited me to go and jump with him, but I had chickened out, so that is where I began my journey to overcome fear. I did it all in slow motion, feeling fear at every step. It was awesome. I made it to the edge of the jump, and a young man strapped the cord to my ankles as I stood there in abject terror. Then I remembered the vision of involution, and dived. I could hardly believe myself, bouncing around on the end of that cord at the age of fifty.

Next, I called Uncle Joe. I said I just wanted to buy some herbal medicine from him. "O.K." he replied: "Come on over."

Minutes later I was knocking on his door. He asked me to sit down while he fetched the herbs. I paid him for them and then said: "I am not really here for the herbs."

"I know," he said, with a look of real understanding and compassion.

Quickly he set up an altar and put a large glass bowl of salt water on it. Then he began moving his hands near my body, up and down. Suddenly he grabbed something from between my shoulder blades. I saw the water bubble and hiss as he plunged his hands in. Then he took the bowl outside and emptied it into the earth. He showed me his hands when he came back, and they had deep red marks in the palms.

"How do you feel now?" he asked.

I felt better.

"Did you see that? You had a harpoon of black energy stuck in your back. I saw it last time you came. It has been stealing all your strength and courage."

I could say nothing.

"You would have had to be superhuman to overcome that without help….it is good you finally came to see me. My people have a way of describing this condition. They would say you have been in the jaws of a wolf, and those jaws have been shut tight for a long time. Remember that you are still in those jaws, and when there is nothing but darkness, it is your task to stay there until you see a gleam of light between the teeth….then go for that light."

I replied: "Sometimes I feel tempted to just let myself go down and pass right through the wolf…won't I eventually come out the other end?"

"If you do that, then you will really become a piece of shit, instead of just feeling like one."

There was a lot more work to do, still a long way to go, but this was a good start. Uncle Joe had shown me a gleam of light between the teeth of the wolf.

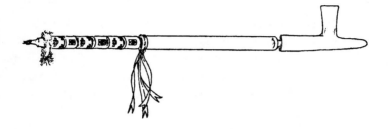

Chapter 18: *Sundance*

Spring came and I went back to my gardening work. I had to hire help as my back was not yet healed from lifting that table, but I wanted to keep my clients. Every week I went for some kind of treatment: massage; chiropractic; acupuncture; re-balancing...I tried it all. In the evenings I would go swimming at the recreation center. It helped to be in the bright light and noise, surrounded by happy people. I was beginning to understand that how I felt did not need to control what I did.

One day a parcel arrived from Jeffrey, and I put it on my dresser, intending to open it as soon as I felt a little better. I was still haunted by the conviction that I had let Jeffrey down. Days, weeks, and finally months passed, but that parcel remained unopened.

Meanwhile I met Solange. Uncle Joe had warned me about the adversity that faced me now that I was entering the good red road. He told me to look deep within myself and find a good reason for going through the hardships of medicine training. In Solange I found this good reason. I had noticed her sitting up very straight in our weekly satsangs, but had never spoken to her. I still considered myself unfit for relationship. One day we spent an afternoon together, just talking and hanging out, and I changed my mind.

Although Solange was only thirty-six years old, she had already been living for seven years with chronic pain. She had fibromyalgia, sjogrens's syndrome, arthritis, and endometriosis. At first she did not say anything about these medical conditions, but in the course of our relationship I learned her story. She had left home at age fifteen and learned how to survive on the streets. By eighteen she was through with drugs and parties, and was working evenings and weekends to finish high school. She went on to university with a scholarship, and finished her teaching degree with honors, working nights and weekends all the way through. Her goal was to teach art full time at the high school level. At twenty-six, just when she had been offered the position she wanted, the pain began.

Solange had become an advocate for women suffering with endometriosis, a disease about which very little was known until recently. She went to the U.S. to have surgery, but it was not a success, and after every procedure the pain just got worse.

I learned that she was the foster parent of a girl in India, and at times had gone without her own medication in order to be able to send the monthly support of thirty dollars to her foster family. I knew she deserved a better man than I was at that time, and so found the motivation to become stronger. It happened at a sweat with Uncle Joe. For three rounds I was lost in self pity and absorbed in my own struggle, but by the fourth round I was praying aloud to give up self-pity once and for all, and to find the strength I needed to be a real support to Solange. Joe heard, and said:

"You have spoken good words here today....may they always be true."

I have practiced keeping my word all my life. It was not long before Uncle Joe told me they were planning to hold a Sundance. I asked him what I could do to help, and he said he wanted me to dance in the East. This would mean going for four days without food or water, while spending a lot of time in a sweat lodge. I had heard about the dehydration.

It happened that I was in hospital in Vancouver the day before the Sundance camp was to begin. I had undergone a diagnostic procedure and was unable to move for hours. The doctor sent me home with medication and a hole in my groin where the scope had gone in. I did not take the medication they gave me. On the ferry to Vancouver Island I was puking my guts out. It was a decisive moment –self-pity…. or the unknown?

The next day I was at the camp. We were all given a cup of green medicine made from devil's club root, and then the fast began as we entered the sweat lodge for the first ceremony of purification. I had made it to the beginning –now I had to make it to the end. After the sweat I was thirsty, but nothing but smoke and prayers was to pass my lips for the next four days. By the end of the second day my tongue was swollen and my mouth was too dry to talk. There was nothing to say anyway.

This was not a Sundance for training warriors –it was for training medicine people. I had known a man from Africa who called the medicine men of his tribe "warriors of the moon." The warriors of the sun were young men who were fearless in the face of outer challenges, while the warriors of the moon were usually older people who were learning to face the darkness and pain within. They would perhaps return from their trials with gifts of healing and wisdom to share with others.

We fasted, sweated, and made tobacco ties for three days, and then prepared to dance. After a sweat on the third day, we put on clothes in the colors of our direction. I wore red, the color of the East. In the full light of the afternoon we walked in slow procession to the sacred circle around the tree that had been chosen as the center. A bower of willows had been put up, with gates in the East, South, West, and North. These willows had been hung with thousands of tobacco ties, or little bundles of tobacco tied up in red, yellow, blue or white cloth. I took my place in the East and began to dance. We remained in the same place, moving our feet, touching the ground with the ball of the foot, that part called the "bubbling spring" in Chinese medicine. The sun set and we kept dancing.... through the power of twilight we kept dancing, into the magic of the night.

No words can describe that night. A velvet healing darkness held us. There was no moon, but I could see by starlight how the tobacco ties glowed on the circle of willows that surrounded us.

Uncle Joe danced in the West, wearing a blue robe, and held that sacred space for us all. Early in the morning I needed to take a break, and Solange came to dance in my place. The moment she stepped into my spot, she passed out. I don't know how he did it, but Joe came around the circle in time to catch her as she fell to the ground. When I came back she was lying on the grass asleep.

"She is with the spirit doctors," said Joe, and went back to his place in the West.

I continued dancing in the East. During the darkest time of the night Joe asked me to dance on his spot for a while. It felt very familiar and natural. The central tree around which we danced became an open doorway to the spirit world, but I was not ready to pass through.

It was July and the night was short. All too soon the dawn came, and then the sun. It takes the rising sun a long time to warm the world. Finally we were dancing in the full light of day. About noon we stopped, and went once again into the sweat lodge for the final ceremony.

"In life, when we become sick, we pass through a dark time," said Uncle Joe: "during that dark time we go down and experience suffering, and find healing, and learn how to heal. Here you have done the same thing. You have danced from one day, through the darkness of night, into the full light of the next day. This represents the journey of sickness, healing and recovery."

After the fourth round, the dancers were each given a half cup of warm water. We drank slowly. Then cooled berries were passed around. How sweet they were!

I put on dry clothes and waited for the feast that celebrated the successful conclusion of the Sundance. I ate some watermelon and then enjoyed the food that the good people had prepared.

Later that day we sat in a circle around the fire. No-one was in a hurry to leave. Gifts were exchanged. Uncle Joe asked me if I had perceived anything, or had a vision during the dance. I had to say no. He asked me what I had learned. I had nothing to say.

"Next year, dance in the East again," he told me.

Slowly we all packed up and went home.

A week later Joe called to tell me a few people were getting together at the camp for a final sweat.

"Some of you are not finished yet," he added.

I had resigned myself to feeling good about making it to the end of the dance, even without any vision or special experience. The others had all had some kind of vision. There were only four of us in the lodge that day, three dancers and a native woman who had been there to help out around the camp. At the beginning of the third round, Joe said:

"A grandfather is here with us now. I am going to ask him to lead this round."

I was used to hearing simple statements that were full of meaning, and accepted these words without any thought. I was the door keeper, and when Joe gave me the nod, I brought down the blankets and we were sitting in the dark again. The rocks were so hot a dull red glow filled the inside of the lodge. Joe sprinkled medicine on the rocks and then lay down. I could see the others lying down also –it was cooler on the ground. I remained sitting up because it was my duty to look after the door and be ready to open it in case anyone said "all my relations… please open the door!"

An invisible ancestor picked up the brush of small cedar branches and began to splash water on the rocks. Joe was still lying down and there was no-one near the bucket of water beside him. The lodge filled with steam and I could no longer see anything. I closed my eyes and began to pray. The steam was gentle and strong and full of good medicine. There was a presence in the lodge like I had never felt before. The words that came to me as I quietly prayed were:

"Creator, even if it is not possible for me to find healing for myself, please let me make a difference for other people. Let my suffering teach me ways to help others."

As I prayed I could hear the eagle feather fan flying around inside the lodge. Then it began to fan my face. Just as I ended my prayer with the words "help others" it thumped me over the heart and came to rest in my hands. The steam continued to fill the lodge with a medicine that was so very gentle and filled with grace. Then it was over, and Joe asked me to open the door.

Afterwards I told him I thought it had been a great sweat, and thanked him for inviting me.

"It was awesome," he replied, holding my hands and looking into my eyes. He knew something good had happened. This experience was the completion of the Sundance for me, and pointed out in a clear, direct way the path leading on to recovery.

Chapter 19: *Recovery*

After the sundance I was able to be more present and supportive for Solange, who was in constant pain. Her periods were unbearable, and her doctor had prescribed medication for the worst days. The medical opinion was that a hysterectomy would bring relief, and with difficulty we came to accept that she could never have children. A date for the surgery was fixed.

I had reflected a lot on her suffering….it was too much for any one person to bear. She had found very little understanding and empathy for chronic pain in the medical system. Pain management was all about the needs of other people, and did little or nothing for the person actually in pain –they just learned to do things anyway, and not burden others with knowledge of their condition unless there was the realistic expectation of help. Doctors who prescribed narcotics were discriminated against by officials who seemed to be convinced that somehow the medical use of narcotics was in the same area as substance abuse and addiction.

It had been very hard for Solange to find a doctor even willing to accept her as a patient. Time and time again I would go with her to the office of a new doctor and see her go in, her blue eyes shining with hope, only to emerge a few minutes later in tears. Meanwhile, although I had made some progress, I was still tormented with feelings of guilt that I was damaged goods and not able to help as much as I should.

The idea of finding a safe and nurturing place where we could take the time to heal still attracted me, and I began to search. The cost of residential healing facilities in North America was way too high. Then I heard of an ayurvedic clinic in South India. I met a man who had been there, and he spoke very highly of it. I wrote a letter of inquiry to the place, which was called Keraleeya Ayurveda Samajam Hospital and Nursing Home. Within a month we had made our reservation at the clinic and were booking tickets to India.

Our trip to India was a dream come true for Solange. She longed to visit her Guru, Amma, at Amritapuram ashram in Kerala. For me, it was a return to the land that had given me so much. We were both in rough shape on the journey: Solange was in so much pain in Frankfurt we were not allowed to re-board our flight until cleared by a doctor. We were both very tired and only just managed to make our connecting flight with me pushing her along in a wheelchair.

Twelve hours later we got down at Trivandrum, and took a taxi to Kovalam beach, where we found a room and rested up for two days before catching the train to Amritapuram. I had been there before, in a vain attempt to become a disciple of Amma, whom I believed to be an embodiment of the divine mother. It had been a strange experience –I had waited in line for hours for Amma to give me a mantra, but when my turn finally came, she suddenly stood up, turned her back and walked away. The darshan was over. I had come to the conclusion that I was somehow not ready, not worthy to be accepted as a disciple, and now wanted to try again.

We caught a rickshaw from the station to a village on the water, then stepped onto a boat made of palm trees and were rowed across the shallow inland channel to the island. We could see the pink roof of the temple complex and the tops of the residential buildings rising above a swaying green mass of palm fronds. Sea eagles circled in the sky.

A very kind German man called Hans helped us with registration and we found our room in the ugly condo buildings that stood so tall above the reed huts of the fisher people that lived on the sand-bar island that was Amma's home. The time came for our darshan. Solange was in great pain, and it was hard for us to make our way towards Amma through the crowd of devotees that surrounded her. When we reached her at last there were tears and joy and that one prayer was answered.

Amma would give initiations only when in a divine mood called Devi Bhavana, and once again I waited for this special day to approach so I could ask for a mantra. When my turn came, Amma looked into my eyes, and said: "Are you one of mine?" It was done with such compassion and grace that I was able to realize with certain clarity that the answer was no. I still felt devotion for Amma, but I had been released from the nagging feeling that I could find freedom by becoming her disciple.

I had also planned to pay a visit to my brother's ashram near a town called Chengannur. I wanted to see the cottage he had built there, and meet the friends that had carried his ashes from Canada to rest in his spiritual home. I had observed the polite custom of writing in advance, and had also phoned to let them know when I was coming. One day during our stay at Amaritapuram I set off alone on this sad pilgrimage.

I was not feeling well, and the train journey of four hours was tiring. I caught a rickshaw from the station to Nangiaretu, the ashram founded by Sri P. Krishna Mennon, and now in the care of his son, Sri Adwayananda Gurunathan. They taught kevalya advaita Vedanta, which roughly means "nothing but absolute non-dual awareness." This was old, traditional Kerala at its best.... and worst. I inquired at the reception desk, where a disciple from America did his best to make me feel unwelcome. He asked where I had come from.

"From Amma's ashram, Amritapuram." I said.

He replied with contempt: "That woman?"

He acted suspicious, as if he feared I had come to claim my brother's cottage for myself. My brother's closest friend, a woman called Savitri, came and showed me around the complex of buildings, and then took me to Edward's cottage. It was a traditional Kerala style house, but in miniature, with tiled roof and wonderful natural wood finish inside. It must have cost a lot of money. I felt sad that he had died so young, and had to leave this beautiful place so soon. But I felt no such regret regarding the people he had known there. Lunch time came, and I was left to sit in the silence of the cottage for an hour, and then Savitri returned and showed me the river bank where Edward had worked to reclaim a set of old stone stairs that had become buried in the sand. It was so very like him, to find some work to do that would make a difference for the local people.

When it came time for me to leave, I said quietly:

"I have come half way around the world to visit the final resting place of my brother. Today I have traveled by bus and train for five hours with a fever, and have now been here for four hours, and no-one has offered me even a glass of water or the use of a restroom."

She looked surprised, and if it were not for the fact that she had been dear to my brother, I would have turned my back and walked away without another word. As it was, I drank the water, took a piss, and then left.

While standing beside the road in front of the place, a western man came up and stood beside me, also waiting for a taxi or rickshaw. I suggested that we might share a taxi into town, but he did not bother to reply.

My visit to Nangiaretu, the abode of "absolute non-dual knowledge," was the worst experience of spiritual pride and snobbery I have ever had. But my journey is not over, and who knows what else is waiting out there to test me?

We were with Amma for the New Year's Eve celebration of the new millennium. Amma went into samadhi while singing the names of the divine mother. Next day we caught the train north to the ayurvedic clinic.

It was a twelve hour ride and Solange' pain levels became unbearable. I had been confident that morphine would be available in India, but it turned out to be impossible to find. The whole country had taken a much harder stand on drug use of any kind. I prayed and held my hands over her body where the pain was worse, relying on my own version of Reiki. It worked, and within minutes Solange was pain free. But this did not last. When her medications ran out, cold turkey was the only choice we had. Fortunately, we were able to go through this in the healing atmosphere of the ayurvedic clinic.

Keraleeya Ayurvedic Samajam Hospital turned out to be a gem. The best of Indian medicine and hospitality were there. It was a traditional retreat with old buildings set among trees and gardens on the bank of a river. The town nearby was small –little more than a single street of shops. I arrived so filled with devotion that I confidently told Solange that the horns and whistles we heard were the sound of conches being blown in temples. In fact, they turned out to be the sound of trains coming in and out of the station nearby, and the joke was on me. There was a small temple of Ganesh in the clinic compound beside the river, and every treatment began with an offering there. Beside the Ganesh temple was a shrine to the deities of the nine planets that are part of vedic astrology.

Our rooms were also old and charming. We had a large bedroom with two single beds, a treatment room, a kitchen and a bathroom. The treatment room had a massage table made from a single slab of wood that had been soaking up oils for decades, and was fragrant with the promise of healing. I had found my way into the arms of the divine mother, and allowed myself to be looked after like a child.

The nurses all wore saris and ankle bracelets that jingled when they walked, so we always knew when they were coming with food or medicine. The food was part of the treatment, and each vegetarian meal contained the five flavors: sweet; salty; sour; bitter; and astringent. All the medicines were made there, using wood fires. We each had an Ayurvedic physician who did the diagnosis and prescribed the course of treatment. A team of technicians provided the warm oil massages and other physical procedures. Nurses brought oral medication, called kashayam, five times a day. Every day we had an hour of medicated oil massage from two technicians, one on each side. For my condition of noise in the head, I was given something called dhara, which meant a stream of cool oil was poured onto my forehead from a coconut for thirty minutes each day. It was wonderful.

Each afternoon I would sit under a huge pepul tree and meditate. One day, I noticed silence –the noise had stopped. For an hour I sat there in perfect peace and joy. That was the last time I experienced inner silence. The noise returned, grew louder, and has never since ceased. I have had to learn to accept it without aversion.

Women had only female doctors and technicians treating them, while the men had only male. All the doctors would consult together on the difficult cases. Solange had a very good doctor who diagnosed bladder problems, and wanted to treat accordingly. Unfortunately, Solange did not share my trust in Ayurveda, and insisted that her pain was being caused by endometriosis. Years later, the diagnosis of interstitial cystitis was confirmed by western medicine, and we finally understood the cause of that relentless pain.

We stayed at the clinic for three weeks. There was nothing to do but rest, stay out of the mid-day sun, and sit by the river to watch the sunset. When the time came for us to leave, we were each given about twenty pounds of medicine to take with us, and were advised to return at the same time for the next two years. I looked forward to doing just that.

We had to hire a porter to help us board our train. Our next stop was Bangalore, on the way to the village where our foster family lived. Solange finally met the little girl she had been sponsoring, and told me it had been the happiest day of her life.

We made our way north to Mumbai. I wanted to show Solange a few magical places in the old parts of that vast city: Bhuleshwar market; Mumbai Devi temple; the chor bazaar; the little alley near a Shiva temple where they made the best chai. Then we went on to Ganeshpuri, and by mistake arrived late one evening in the middle of a celebration called Shivratri, when the only room we could find was small and filthy. We slept while the chaos went on outside, and the next day, after the crowd of devotees had left, were able to move into Dr. Kothawallas rest house. The hot springs were wonderful again.

We relaxed for a few days and then hired a taxi to take us to Shirdi. After so many years of traveling by bus and train all over India, this was real luxury. We checked into a small hotel near the Samadhi of Shirdi Sai Baba. We could both feel the power and grace of this holy place. I longed to see the white stone image of Shirdi Sai Baba once again, and next day rose early to join the line of devotees. When my turn came, I bowed before the statue, and prayed for help to free myself from the dark forces that were still within me.

If I had not seen what happened, I would never have believed it. A shadowy shape leapt out of me like a huge frog, and disappeared above the statue. Some demon that had been hiding within my psychic structure was gone. I had always wondered what was meant in the bible when "casting out demons" was mentioned, and now I had some idea.

The hard evidence of this experience forced me to open my mind to yet another facet of creation that was hard to accept. My early training in science had perhaps led me to approach spirituality with the attitude that belief was not important –I wanted real experience, and did not settle for less. It was not my habit to form opinions and draw conclusions from my experience alone, but to listen to others and read what is written in scriptures. When all three agree, then perhaps it is so…but not always.

A few days after returning home I finally found the guts to open that parcel from Jeffrey. It contained a thick manuscript of his teaching material, and an invitation to help him teach evolutionary astrology. The letter was a year old. Jeffrey had written: "This is a way for you to crawl out of the darkness." Once again I had missed a golden opportunity.

My resistance to technology had delayed me from getting a computer for years, and had put me out of communication. Now that I was preparing to be a professional astrologer, I finally went on-line and was able to find Jeffrey's website and learn that he was teaching in Malibu the following week. I paid full price for my flight and showed up at the house of the student who was hosting the school. There were about twelve people in the class. Jeffrey looked tired and old. His body was wearing out. I burned with shame and could not understand what had made me delay opening his parcel for so long.

We had lunch together one day in a Mexican place beside the sea. He ate very little, and talked very little, but what he said was to the point. I asked about my stupid delay:

"It is the ongoing influence of evil in your life, Mark. You have got rid of some bad energy, but the essence of evil is still there in your soul. It will work to bring about the opposite of your intentions."

I asked him if he could help me, but he said his own energy was not strong enough at that time to rid me of this influence. Then he added: "What you need is an exorcism."

"Where can I find that?" I asked, hardly able to believe what I had just heard.

He looked towards the ceiling, and said: "The only place I can think of is the Catholic church. A competent priest can be empowered to perform exorcism, even today."

He had advised me to see Mother Meera in Germany on my way to India, and asked if I had done this. I had to say no… another mistake. He insisted that I go to Mother Meera.

The next day my spirits were very low. During lunch break I went for a walk on the beach and found myself alone on a point of rocks, praying for help from the creator. The waves rolled in and tears flowed down my face. Then I began to see dolphins. They came up near the rocks and began playing and splashing all around me….the water was full of them. For about twenty minutes I sat there watching the dolphins until it was time to return to class. After walking back over the rock for about fifty yards I turned for a final look, but the dolphins were gone. Later

I asked the man who was hosting the school if dolphins were a common sight around there, and he said they were very rare. This vision gave me hope, but I still felt like shit.

The next day I noticed that Jeffrey was in another world. He sat on the floor, leaning against an arm chair, and spoke as if on automatic pilot. At one point he said quietly: "I am in two places at once right now."

I was sitting next to my friend Walter. He was a black man about seventy years old. He was asleep and something was happening, so I just sat still. During coffee break Jeffrey continued to rest against the chair with his eyes closed, and Walter slept, leaning on my shoulder. Later, during lunch, I asked Walter what had happened.

With a look of wonder and delight he said: "Jeffrey was teaching me in my dream."

Walter went home early, and Jeffrey explained to us that he had known him before, in another life, and had been helping him prepare him for his next life. A few months later, Walter died peacefully. These warriors had met once again on an evolutionary journey of two souls that I did not need to understand. This was the nature of evolutionary astrology with Jeffrey Wolf Green –real wisdom, real power and real grace.

Six days of teaching came to an end. Every day Jeffrey had to stop earlier as his limited energy was used up. He had two assistants who then took over, using example charts to illustrate the days lesson. I could not help contrasting my own depressed mood with the high energy and obvious happiness of these people as they did what Jeffrey had given me the opportunity to do. Fortunately I was just getting tired of beating myself up, even when there was good reason to do so. I had enough on my plate without that, and knew how to just turn the useless mental chatter off.

Find an Exorcism? This was serious –but the Sundance

had given me strength, and Jeffrey had given me hope and I was able to believe it was possible. I returned home, and my only clue was a Benedictine monk whom I had seen many times over the years walking the streets of Victoria. He seemed to be a very pious man, and once, during the worst days of my depression, I had stopped him on the street and asked him about the fear that gripped me:

"Perfect love will drive out fear," had been his confident reply.

I visited the monastery where he lived, and asked to see him, but he was down town working in a soup kitchen. I found him in the basement of the Catholic Church, sweeping the floor. He wore the brown robes and hood of a monk, and seldom looked up from his work. I asked if I could speak with him:

"Certainly," he replied. We sat at the nearest table. Lunch had already been served and we were alone. I did my best to describe my situation, and my need for an exorcism. His face was serious as he listened with total attention.

"Are you a Catholic?" he asked when I was done.

"No." I replied. I did not go on to say that I was not even a Christian.

"The first step is to become a Catholic. I will help you. But to obtain permission for an exorcism we must approach the higher authority of the church. It is very seldom given."

I was silent, and he added: "You may visit me anytime, and I will help in any way I can."

It was as I had expected. I was now faced with a difficult decision: go forward once again into the unknown, alone with a very dangerous enemy, or take a step backward for the comfort and hope offered by an organized religion that I knew in my heart I could not accept. I thanked the monk, and went out onto the street.

I chose to go on alone, and trust that the creator would

show me a way. It was good that I had come to this desolation of spirit, for it led to deeper prayers.

Summer came and it was time for the second Sundance. I had been preparing myself, remembering my purpose and going to the sweat lodge at least once a month. This time it rained and there were some bad omens. Two people got sick and had to leave early. The night of the dance it rained hard. My helper asked me how long I could last before needing a break and I told him about two hours only. He then went to his tent and fell asleep for eighteen hours. I did not see him until the closing ceremony the next day. At about one a.m. I noticed that a fire down by the sweat lodge was sending a red spiral of sparks up into the night. At about three a.m. Uncle Joe sent us all down for a sweat. I was very cold. He gave us each half a glass of warm water, and then we rested until day break.

The time came for the final sweat to close the camp. The leader wanted to start before Solange was inside, and I protested.

"Get out!" he thundered.

I left the lodge, and missed the berry feast that breaks the four day fast. I went down to the stream to take a solitary bath. There was a blue heron standing in my bathing spot. The bird rose and flew away on huge, powerful wings. I went into the cool water. On the way back to camp I ate wild berries along the path.

That was the end of the road for me with Uncle Joe. I had learned a lot, and had many good experiences, and remember him with respect and gratitude. It was very clear by now that the creator was teaching me to stand on my own feet.

Before we parted, Joe had told me that he saw my journey coming to an end beside a river in India. He said I had to go full circle, and return to the starting place. At the time I did not know what he meant.

Soon we were on our way to India for our second series

of treatments at the Ayurvedic clinic. I made sure we had a stopover in Frankfurt, and made reservations to see Mother Meera. We checked into one of the hostels that catered for people like us who came for darshan. Jeffrey had told me that Mother Meera was the current avatar.

We went for evening darshan three times. We stood in lines – straight, German lines –and waited outside the old castle where Mother Meera stayed. Two hundred people each evening were ushered in to sit and wait for the appearance of the saint. She walked quietly in, wearing a simple sari, and with her head bowed. One by one we went up for darshan. She put her hands on our heads and looked into our eyes. I was praying silently for help getting rid of the darkness within me. I have no idea what happened, as Mother Meera is beyond my limited capacity to understand, but I did feel blessed, and took this blessing on with me to India.

We went to Varanasi. I believed this might be the place that Uncle Joe had seen in his vision, the place beside the river where I would come to the end of my search. It was December, and quite cold. I caught a fever, and kept finding excuses not to take the holy bath in the Ganges. Then one morning I told Solange I was going.

We hired a rowboat from Kalu Baba, the old boat man who is a devotee of Shiva. He remembered me, pointed to a small boat, and I rowed across the river to the empty sand bars on the far side, and there I took my bath. Solange watched as I walked into the river, ducked under four times, and then walked out.

"It was not the same man who came out of the river," she told me later: "you came out looking like a different person."

It was true. Something had left me there. When our time

in the clinic was over and we arrived home, the first thing I did was phone Jeffrey.

"It's gone," was all he said.

These were the most wonderful words I had ever heard.

Chapter 20: *Darshan*

November came and I returned to India for my third and final stay in the ayurvedic clinic. This time I went alone. As usual, my first stop was Mumbai, where I stayed at Whalley's hotel. My room was tiny, but it had a bathroom and a balcony with a glimpse of the sea. I was in the long process of reducing my medications, but still needed to take a pill if I wanted to get any sleep.

I traveled to Ganeshpuri, and stayed at Doctor Kotha-walla's rest house again. There I met a young man, Klaus, from Germany, who was filled with spiritual longing but had become stuck in Siddha Yoga. He had natural devotion and humility, and deserved something real.

My first step was to tell him about Shirdi, and he agreed to visit this holy place with me. Then I sat down and related my experiences with Swami Muktananda and Siddha Yoga. He went into shock, but said: "Why is it that I believe you?"

He cried for two days, and then we were on our way to Shirdi, where he experienced the grace of Shirdi Sai Baba. There is something so simple and honest about Shirdi. This time his tears were caused by joy as his anguish and sense of loss came to an end.

He was a Reiki teacher, and wanted to give me the master's degree by way of thanks for the small part I had played. I already had second degree Reiki, and trusted that healing method. We prepared ourselves for two days, and when the time came I found myself looking for some incense to sweeten the room. The place smelled of Lysol because there was cleaning going on outside. I did not find any incense, so we started anyway. I lit a candle on my altar, and noticed that the room suddenly filled with the scent of roses. For an hour we enjoyed the aroma of fresh roses while Klaus taught me the Reiki, and then it was gone. The nearest flowers were by the temple, about five hundred yards away. Afterwards, I could still smell Lysol in the empty hallway.

Klaus returned to Ganeshpuri, and I remained in Shirdi for another day. I found myself sitting in the Chowdi the next morning for meditation. The place was empty. From time to time a devotee would walk through, stop by the sacred fire to take some ash, and then leave in silence. At one point I opened my eyes and saw an old man walking slowly towards me. He was bent with age, but the deep lines in his face formed a wonderful smile. He wore the ragged white cotton clothes and cap of a poor Maratha farmer. His eyes were amazing.

It had become my habit while traveling in India to save money in any way I could. If I had planned to fly somewhere, I would end up taking a second class train, and give the difference to the poor. In Shirdi it was my habit to give ten rupees to anyone who asked, and to any poor pilgrim who looked like they might need a meal. The old man extended his brown, wrinkled hand, and I smiled and gave him a ten rupee note. He raised his right palm in the abheya mudra to give me his blessing. Then I closed my eyes for a moment.

Suddenly it dawned on me what had just happened. I opened my eyes to find myself alone. Hardly a second had passed, and there was no-one there.

I knew in my heart that I had been visited by god. The old man was the image of what I loved most about the Indian people. That humble old farmer was the form the creator took for me.

The rest of my stay in India was blessed. Everywhere I went, grace seemed to go with me. I visited Varanasi and swam in the Ganges every day. At night I attended free music concerts, and then slept in my room beside the river. The family I stayed with provided two meals a day. I wanted nothing, and Mother India gave me everything.

From Varanasi I made the long train journey south to visit our foster family once again. I saved five hundred dollars by taking trains instead of flying, and I gave that money to them in rupees, in a paper bag. Then I went to the ayurvedic clinic for my third and final stay, where I was finally able to stop using prescription medications. For two years I had used them to survive, and then it had taken another five years to slowly reduce and finally go off them altogether.

Back home I found a sweat lodge run by a native elder called Sammy Sam and his family, and went every week for four years, slowly learning the songs, how to build a lodge, and how to keep the fire. I had survived seven years of adversity, and whole sections of my former psychology were gone. The world became a bright and beautiful place once again, and the presence of the creator was everywhere. The feeling of being connected to the creator by way of my relationship to all things has not left me since. It is the feeling of an opening heart.

For forty years I have been a pilgrim on a journey without end. To be a devotee of god has been my great good fortune. I no longer seek states of higher consciousness, or cultivate emptiness, or wish for any special powers. Just being human and living in harmony with nature –that is where I have found freedom and happiness.

Yes, my heart was broken along the way, but in the end it broke open. The mystery of love contains me, and I do my best to participate without the need to understand. The word "enlightenment" holds no special meaning, and teachings about "salvation" seem to disrespect life. It is the sweat lodge as taught by Sammy Sam that has stayed with me. That is where I welcome whoever comes to walk beside me for a few steps. Mostly, what I express in there is gratitude.

The End.

Epilogue

I emerged from the storm of suffering like a blind turtle, but in time it became clear that I had been given new eyes, and was seeing life in a new way.

There are many different teachings that can help us to understand life –that attempt to explain the mystery of creation, and give us a way of communicating with the creator as we walk through the sands of time over the face of our mother, the earth. By far the most useful system that I have found is astrology. The lessons that we are here to learn, the unique gifts that we each have, and the challenges that we face are all reflected in our natal chart. This ancient, intuitive art was the gift I had received to help me find my way …. and help others to do the same.

In my work as an astrologer I have heard many stories of search and suffering, and have had time to reflect upon my own journey of self-discovery. The passing years bring it home again and again that it is the feeling of separation from the creator that is at the root of spiritual longing. No amount of knowledge, no passing state of consciousness will heal this pain of separation. It is only when I feel, in my heart, how close the mystery is, and how every day, in so many ways, spirit is communicating with me that this empty feeling goes away. In nature we can re-connect with our mother, the earth, through feelings, and in time these feelings ripen into the emotions of gratitude and joy. It is my prayer that we will learn to take good care of our mother...just as she has taken good care of us.

ISBN 142511201-3